Taylor's Guides to Gardening

Peter Schneider, Editor

Frances Tenenbaum, Series Editor

HOUGHTON MIFFLIN COMPANY
Boston • New York

Taylor's Guide to Roses

REVISED EDITION

Copyright © 1995 by Houghton Mifflin Company

For information about permission to reproduce selections from
this book, write to Permissions, Houghton Mifflin Company,
215 Park Avenue South, New York, New York 10003.

Taylor's Guide is a registered trademark of Houghton Mifflin Company.

Library of Congress Cataloging-in-Publication Data

Taylor's guide to roses. — Rev. ed.
    p.   cm. — (Taylor's guides to gardening)
  Includes index.
  ISBN 0-395-69459-0
  1. Rose culture.   2. Roses.   I. Title: Guide to roses.
II. Series
SB411.T33   1994   94-2023
635.9′33372 — dc20   CIP

Printed in Hong Kong

DNP 10 9 8 7 6 5 4 3

Contents

Preface to the Revised Edition

Since 1986, when it was first published, *Taylor's Guide to Roses* has fulfilled its original promise "to encourage the beginner, stimulate the experienced rose enthusiast, and to bring pleasure—through its magnificent color plates—to the armchair gardener." With more than 100,000 satisfied readers, one might ask why the need for a revision.

The answer is that in the past few years there have been major changes in the rose market—so major, indeed, that of the 392 roses pictured and described in this book, 102 are new to this edition. Foremost among these changes are

• The wide interest in and availability of the David Austin English roses, which combine the fragrance and form of old garden roses with the bushy habit and repeat bloom of modern roses.

• The explosion of interest in ground-cover roses, which exhibit low spreading growth and low-maintenance characteristics. Both David Austin and ground-cover roses are included in the category of shrubs, and we've enlarged that section by 40 roses.

• A more selective interest in growing miniature roses. When the original *Taylor's Guide to Roses* was published, miniatures were all the rage, and the guide contained 80 varieties of them. In this book, that number has been reduced to 28; we've kept only the best of the breed.

We've made other changes, too. Because of our commitment to reducing the use of pesticides and herbicides in gardens, we've replaced a number of the disease-prone varieties with newer, more disease-resistant ones. In addition, we've revised the section on pests and diseases to reflect our belief that natural controls are most desirable.

Contributors

Peter Schneider revised this guide. He is the coeditor and co-compiler, with Beverly Dobson, of the annual "Combined Rose List," which provides names, dates, and sources for all roses commercially grown and sold in the United States and many foreign countries. He is also the editor of "The Akron Rose Rambler" and the author of the forthcoming book *Peter Schneider on Roses,* in the Burpee Expert Gardening Series.

Beverly Dobson, the original author of the rose accounts, is a well-known figure in rose circles. She has served as a consulting rosarian and accredited judge for the American Rose Society and is the coeditor of the "Combined Rose List." She also publishes "Bev Dobson's Rose Letter," a periodical that brings rose enthusiasts up-to-date on the latest developments in breeding, registration, and awards.

Griffith J. Buck wrote the essays on classification and creating new cultivars. A specialist in rose breeding, he was professor of horticulture at Iowa State University for 37 years.

Holly Shimizu wrote the essay on the history of modern roses. A former curator of the National Herb Garden at the National Arboretum, she is currently assistant executive director of the U.S. Botanic Garden.

Illustrators

The drawing on the title page is by **Sarah Pletts. Mary Jane Spring** provided the anatomy drawings and the illustrations of rose pests and diseases. **Alan D. Springer** did the drawings in the essay "Getting Started."

Modern Roses: A History

Roses are the ultimate plants of legend, romance, and beauty. Throughout history, they have figured prominently in literature, art, and medicine as well as in horticulture. More than 2000 years have passed since the Greek poet Sappho christened the rose "queen of flowers"; the course of history clearly bears out this appellation, for their irresistible charm has not diminished over the centuries. Today roses entice the novice gardener with their promise of beauty and bring a special satisfaction to seasoned rosarians.

Ancient Evidence

Fossils found in Europe, Asia, and North America indicate that roses existed approximately 30 million years ago. Among the earliest representations of the flower were decorations on jewelry and ornaments from the early Minoan civilization, which flourished on the island of Crete from about 2800 to 2100 B.C. Approximately 1000 years later, roses began to appear in the paintings and carvings of the later inhabitants of this same island. The first literary reference to the rose is found in the *Iliad;* Homer tells us of the rose oil used by Aphrodite to anoint the fallen Hector.

It appears that the earliest cultivation of roses may have taken place in China; according to Confucius (551–479? B.C.), roses were grown in the imperial gardens of the Chou dynasty. The Greeks also grew roses — particularly around the time of Christ — but not to the extent that the Romans did. In the ancient world, the cultivation of roses reached its peak in the Roman Empire, in the 300 years following the birth of Christ.

The Romans were extravagant in their love of roses. Wealthy citizens used hundreds of thousands of rose petals to carpet their floors. Nets filled with petals were suspended from the ceiling; released during an evening's festivities, they sent a gentle cascade of color and fragrance onto the guests below. The

Romans made beds of rose petals and added the fragrant flowers to their bathwater to perfume and preserve their skin.

Supply and Demand

Eventually the clamor for roses became so great that even the huge shipments imported to Rome from Egypt were not sufficient to fill the need. In due course, the Romans began to grow their own roses. Displaying the same ingenuity that had led to the building of impressive networks of aqueducts and the sumptuous pleasure palaces at Pompeii, citizens of the empire built greenhouses, where piped-in hot water created the warmth necessary for cultivated plants to produce blossoms throughout the winter.

Long an emblem of festivity and luxury, the rose began to signify more than simple pleasure when Roman civic leaders endowed it with political import. A rose hanging from the ceiling during the course of a political meeting signaled confidentiality — those present must never reveal the secrets exchanged *sub rosa.*

Roses in Politics and Art

In more modern times the rose has also had its acolytes among kings and political leaders. The Wars of the Roses marked a lengthy period of civil strife in English history during which the houses of York (the White Rose) and Lancaster (the Red Rose) fought bitterly for the throne. At the conclusion of the hostilities, the red-and-white Tudor rose became a symbol of national unity.

The Empress Josephine, first wife of Napoleon Bonaparte, maintained grand rose gardens at her residence, Malmaison. Considered to be the first international rose collection, her gardens were unique because they were designed to show not only the beauty of the blossoms but also the beauty of the plants themselves. It is estimated that at Josephine's death in 1814, there were 250 varieties of roses being grown at Malmaison. Fortunately, many of these have been preserved for us in the paintings of the wonderful folio edition of *Les Roses,* by Pierre-Joseph Redouté and Claude Antoine Thory.

The elegance of the rose also inspired architects of the great Gothic churches of Europe; skilled craftsmen adapted the form of the blossom to create the beautiful rose windows that adorn many magnificent cathedrals, such as Chartres. Modern buildings, such as the National Cathedral in Washington, also show this influence.

Some varieties of old garden roses have long held a special place in history. The Provence Rose (*Rosa centifolia*), cultivated in the Middle Ages, found its way into art, appearing in many Dutch and Flemish still-lifes of the 17th and 18th centuries. The Damask Rose (*Rosa damascena*) has a similarly colorful history. The plants were first brought to Europe in about the 12th century, during the period of the Crusades, when tremendous breakthroughs in commerce between East and West were forged. But the first written allusion to the Damask Rose came from Virgil, who described them in 50 B.C.

Perfume of the Kings

The fragrant oil that roses produce, known as attar of roses, is said to have been discovered in the mountain kingdom of Kashmir, in what is now northern India. Legend has it that the wife of the ruler noticed an oily film on the surface of a stream that ran through her rose garden. Scooping up some of the petal-laden water, she put her hand to her face, becoming the first woman to inhale the exquisite fragrance of attar of roses.

Rose oil has been used by many civilizations as a perfume and to anoint the dead. In China, where the rose was a royal flower, only the ruling classes were permitted to use these precious oils. And in medieval France, commoners were allowed to enjoy this magnificent fragrance only on their wedding day. At various periods in history, this oil has commanded huge prices — up to six times its weight in gold.

Nutrition from Roses

Even before the earliest cultivation of field crops, roses were valued as a source of food in some primitive cultures. The Romans are thought to have been responsible for introducing the practice of flower-eating to Europe; many peasants living at the time are reported to have thought the practice wrong, because removing the flower prevented the formation of the fruit.

Fragrant Panacea

In the 18th century, more than one-third of all herbal remedies for various ailments called for the use of roses, and historically the flower has been significant in a wide range of medicinal applications. The healing properties ascribed to the rose were supposed to lie chiefly in the petals — particularly those of *Rosa gallica,* which is widely known as the Apothecary Rose. The petals, which must be thoroughly dried immediately after being picked, are said to be tonic and astringent in their effect.

A conserve made from rose petals was once widely used to strengthen the stomach and assist in digestion. Syrup of roses, made from the Damask Rose (*Rosa damascena*), was once commonly prescribed as a purgative. Rose vinegar, made by adding dried petals to a distilled vinegar, was given to relieve headaches. And even the fruit of the rose was employed in early medicine. The pulp was separated from the seeds; blended with sugar, it was sold as a curative for numerous ailments.

At present, roses are not so widely used in medicine; nonetheless, rose hips are employed in a large number of commercial products, notably tea and preserves. They are also one of the chief sources of vitamin C today. Some of the better edible hips come from *Rosa rugosa* and *R. canina*. Rose water is also used to make the confection known as Turkish Delight.

Wild Roses and Their Descendants

Most of today's cultivated rose varieties are descended from seven or eight species of wild roses, most of which are in the group that botanists term Gallicanae — *Rosa gallica* and its near relatives.

The wild species or natural varieties of the genus *Rosa* compose a group of extremely beautiful and interesting garden plants. Their potential has, unfortunately, never really been recognized, perhaps because these roses have been eclipsed by the more popular cultivars. For example, the Eglantine Rose (*Rosa eglanteria,* also known as Shakespeare's Rose) should be treasured for the sweet smell of pippin apples given off by the leaves. *Rosa virginiana* puts on a marvelous display of color all year long: the pink flowers of spring are followed by glorious dark red hips; in autumn the leaves turn various shades of red, yellow, orange, and green; and in winter, when the landscape is bare and gray, the arching red canes provide a welcome touch of color.

Notwithstanding the beauty of the wild roses, it is the cultivated varieties that have attracted the most attention and acclaim. The majority of garden roses grown today are derived from two or more of the following species: *Rosa chinensis, R. damascena, R. foetida, R. gallica, R. moschata, R. multiflora, R. odorata, R. rugosa,* and *R. wichuraiana.* All of these species are of Asiatic origin.

A Complex History

Despite this rather limited pool of ancestors, the evolution of our garden roses is complex. When the China Rose (*Rosa chinensis*) was introduced into Europe in 1789, a sort of rose revolution took place. Until that time, the only roses found in Europe were hardy shrubs that bloomed for a short period in late spring or summer. This and other exotic oriental species brought with them a capacity for repeat flowering. Some of them bore yellow flowers — also a novelty — and some had a climbing or trailing habit.

With the introduction of Asiatic discoveries, an increasing number of hybrids began to appear. Throughout the 19th century, which was a very active period in the development of cultivars, it was common practice to plant naturally pollinated seeds; for this reason, the antecedents of many well-known cultivars can be traced only through the maternal side. The hips of some cultivars were gathered at random; for these, the lineage is left to conjecture.

By the late 19th century, the roses of the East and West had been crossed and recrossed many times, creating a range of repeat-flowering roses in many colors and culminating in the creation of the hybrid tea class. Although other classes have come into being since that time, the hybrid teas are still considered to be the most popular of all roses.

Looking Ahead

There is still a great future for those interested in developing and hybridizing roses. Rosarians have become increasingly concerned with developing cultivars that are resistant to diseases and insect pests. David Austin's English Roses demonstrate a renewed appreciation for the form and fragrance found in old garden roses; ground-cover roses have opened up a whole new dimension for using roses in the landscape. And there are still many species that have never been used for hybridizing. Through our increasing knowledge of roses and our appreciation of them, we can all play a part in their exciting evolution.

Classification

Roses have the distinction of being among the oldest cultivated ornamental plants found in today's gardens. This distinction is in no small part due to the fact that roses grow wild around the globe, from the Arctic Circle to the equatorial zone.

To understand fully the way roses have developed and how new varieties are produced for our gardens, it is helpful to know how plants — especially roses — are classified.

Order, Family, Genus, and Species

Depending on their stem anatomy, all seed-producing plants are placed in one of two categories, monocots or dicots. Roses are dicots. Dicots are further subdivided into orders, based primarily on their floral traits and plant characteristics. Roses belong to the order Rosales. The orders are then divided into families; roses belong to the Rose family, which is called Rosaceae.

A family is made up of still more narrowly defined groups of related plants that share a certain level of similarity, and often a fairly recent common ancestor. Such a group is called a genus (plural, genera). The rose genus, *Rosa*, like other genera, may include one or more species.

A species is a wild population of plants that can reproduce themselves true to type from seed. Each species has a distinctive name, composed of two parts — the genus name, which is always capitalized, and the species name, which is not. Some examples of species are *Rosa damascena, Rosa multiflora,* and *Rosa gallica.* In addition, each species may have one or more common names, depending on its cultural history.

Naming and Registration of Cultivars

Rose cultivars, because they are not true species, do not have a two-part scientific name. A cultivar can be named to suit the breeder and will carry that name throughout its existence. The names given to rose cultivars are subject to the restrictions of the International Registration Authority for Roses. Most registered roses are also assigned a code name, which consists of three letters (usually based on the breeder's last name) plus two or more additional letters. This code name will stay with the rose, even though the cultivar name may be changed. Some roses, in fact, are known by different names in different countries, so the code name given a cultivar serves to standardize the name. Carefree Beauty (BUCbi), Paul Shirville (HARqueterwife), and Sun Flare (JACjem) are examples of cultivars and their code names.

Classes of Roses in This Book

A rose is assigned to a particular class on the basis of its ancestry and, in certain cases, how long it has been in cultivation. These classes are discussed fully in the main text of this book. Before you begin to use the book, it may be helpful to become familiar with the different classes and subclasses of roses included here:

Species roses
These are the naturally occurring roses found in the wild. Most have only five petals. There are about 200 species roses altogether; 24 are included here.

Climbing roses
These are cultivars that can be trained to grow up a trellis, arbor, or building. There are several classes: climbing hybrid tea, hybrid bracteata, large-flowered climbers, kordesii climbers, ramblers, and wichuraiana climbers.

Shrub roses
This is a catch-all class of cultivars that do not belong with either the old garden roses or any of the more modern classes. Subclasses included in this group are eglantine, English, ground-cover, hybrid musk, hybrid rugosa, hybrid spinosissima (in part), polyantha, and shrub roses.

Old garden roses
In cultivation since 1867, the old garden roses include the following classes: alba, Bourbon, centifolia, China, damask, gallica, hybrid perpetual, hybrid sempervirens, hybrid spinosissima (in part), moss, Noisette, Portland, and tea.

Floribundas
These are a modern group of roses, the result of crossing hybrid teas with polyanthas. They typically have many blooms per stem.

Grandifloras
Another modern group, the grandiflora class only came into being in the mid-1950s; it was established for the cultivar

Queen Elizabeth, which was seen as the first of a class of large-flowered, abundantly blooming roses.

Hybrid teas

This is the most popular class of roses of all. Many familiar long-stemmed varieties are included here, in a very wide range of colors.

Miniature roses

Another popular group, the miniatures look like their larger relatives in every way except for size. Many grow very well in containers; some also do well indoors.

Anatomy

Anatomy

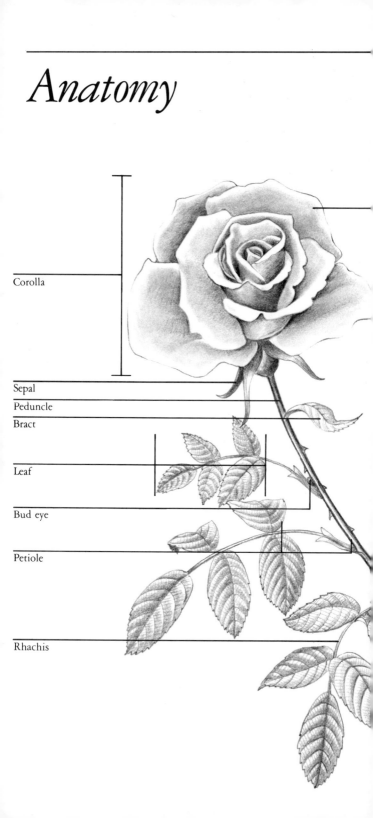

Corolla

Sepal

Peduncle

Bract

Leaf

Bud eye

Petiole

Rhachis

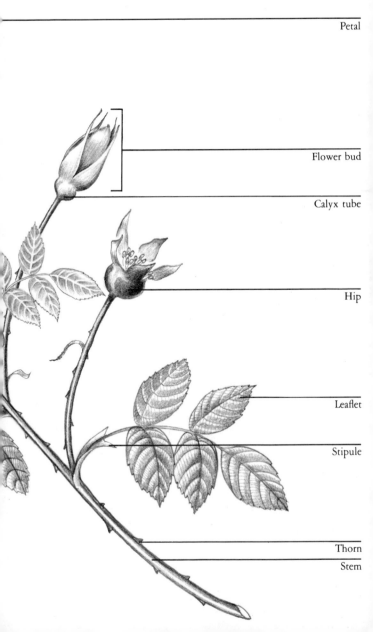

Petal

Flower bud

Calyx tube

Hip

Leaflet

Stipule

Thorn

Stem

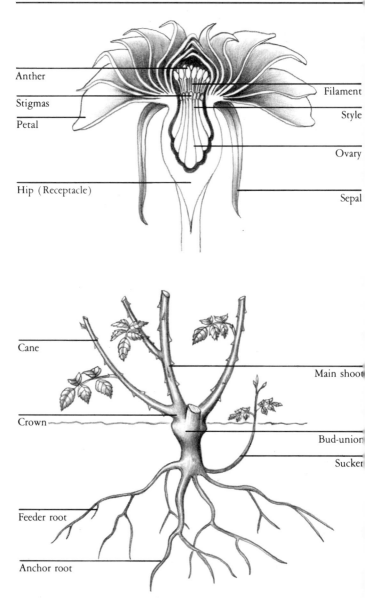

Anther

Filament

Stigmas

Style

Petal

Ovary

Hip (Receptacle)

Sepal

Cane

Main shoot

Crown

Bud-union

Sucker

Feeder root

Anchor root

In bloom the rose plant has 7 basic parts: blossom or corolla; leaflike sepals; buds; hips; leaflets; stems or laterals; and main shoots or canes. Blossom petals protect reproductive organs inside: Male organs, or stamens, consist of round anthers, containing pollen, and stemlike filaments; the female organs, or pistils, consist of the stigma, which catches pollen, and the style, in which tubes develop, carrying pollen to fertilize eggs in the ovary.

Getting Started

The first important consideration in growing beautiful roses — and one that is often overlooked by the beginner — is to start out with good plants. To be sure of obtaining good, healthy plants, it is a smart idea to purchase your roses either from a reputable mail-order company or from a local nursery or garden store.

Price vs. Value

Don't assume that the price of a rose determines its value. Numerous older hybrid teas, floribundas, and miniatures are less expensive and may also be superior to newer, patented varieties. Many older roses have stood the test of time; still popular with the public, they merit consideration for your garden. The price of a patented rose, however, includes the royalty paid to the hybridizer, and is therefore sometimes much higher than the price of older roses that were never patented or whose patent has expired.

Mail-order nurseries generally ship hybrid teas, grandifloras, floribundas, and climbers as dormant two-year-old field-grown plants. These are budded onto a particular rootstock that will provide you with a well-developed root system. Miniatures, as well as many old garden roses and some landscaping shrubs, are sold as potted, own-root plants. A rose variety that grows true from its own roots is more likely to rebound from severe winter dieback.

Grades of Rose Bushes

Rose bushes are graded (No. 1, 1½, or 2) in accordance with established standards, initiated in 1923 and revised when necessary. The American Association of Nurserymen Standards are a sound guide for the commercial rose grower as well as for the amateur. These standards apply to field-grown two-year-old roses, sold either bare-root or packaged. The commercial growers adhere to these standards to provide their customers with the best possible plants. Some nurseries note the grades of the bushes they sell in their catalogues. If they are out of No. 1 grade bushes, they will substitute No. 1½ grade bushes, if you wish, at a lower price.

Bushes in each grade must have a well-developed root system in a rounded, well-proportioned pattern so that when the bush is planted in the proper manner, it will grow properly. The canes should show no damage such as blackening or shriveling caused by drying. The bark should be green and the pith should be white or near white, with no sign of shriveling.

Greenhouse-grown own-root roses will not meet the standards established for field-grown plants. Sold in small pots, they may require a year in the South or two years in the North to reach the size of a field-grown No. 1 grade rose. Sale or distribution standards have not been established for miniature roses.

Planning the Garden

An important thing to remember as you prepare to plant your rose bushes is not to plant them too close to existing trees and shrubs. The roots of these other plants will compete with your roses for food and water. The larger the tree, the farther its roots will extend from the base. If a tree is not fully grown, attempt to visualize its size in five or ten years before you plant your roses.

Roses need at least six hours of sunlight each day. If there is a choice of morning or afternoon shade, it is better to choose the afternoon shade. Morning shade increases the possibility of mildew and black spot on the bush because it takes longer for the morning dew to dry. Afternoon shade protects the plants from too much summer heat, helping the plants grow and retarding the drying out of the soil. As the trees in your garden grow, they will also create more shade, so bear this in mind when you plant.

The next decision you will need to make is how many roses you would like to have in your garden. Beginners should not start on too large a scale. A dozen rose bushes will give you a chance to find out what is involved in growing roses and help you decide if you have the time to care for more.

Selecting Varieties

Choosing your rose varieties, or cultivars, can be difficult, but there are several ways to educate yourself before making a selection. Visit a public rose garden or the gardens of friends and rosarians in your area. Join a local rose society if there is one near you, and attend its rose shows. Obtain catalogues from leading nurseries and mail-order rose growers. And by all means consult this book. The varieties included here are grown extensively in the United States. Some, especially species and old garden roses, may be available commercially only from specialist growers.

Soil Analysis

After you have determined where to plant your bushes, take a sample of the soil to be analyzed. This analysis can be made by a private laboratory or by a state agricultural college. (Some areas of the country have a county agent, who can supply you with a container for your soil sample and may even send it to a college to be analyzed for you.) To take a soil sample, remove the top two inches of earth and then dig a hole about six inches deep. Take a slice of the soil, running from the top of the hole to the bottom; this gives a representative sample of the six inches of the soil beneath the top two inches, which is where most of a rose's feeder roots grow.

In the report you will find an analysis of the phosphorus and potassium content, two macronutrients very necessary for plant growth. Other elements reported on will be calcium and magnesium, and possibly iron, manganese, sulfur, and copper, proper amounts of which are also necessary for the growth of the plant.

The Importance of pH

Along with your analysis, there will be a report on your soil's pH — the acidity or alkalinity of the soil. A pH of 7 is neutral — the value for pure water. A higher number (8 or 9) indicates that the soil is alkaline, and a lower number (6 or 5) indicates that the soil is acid. When the pH changes from 7 to 6, the acidity increases tenfold, which means the soil is ten times as acid. Roses prefer a slightly acid soil with a pH of 6.5 to 6.8. They will grow, however, in slightly alkaline soil, with a pH of 7.5, or in more acid soil, with a pH of 6.

Changing the pH Level

Your local garden center can help you determine what type of soil you have — clay, sandy, or sandy loam — and can advise you on how to increase or decrease its pH level to that preferred by roses. To raise the pH level, you can add agricultural lime or dolomitic limestone; to decrease it, you can add sulfur.

Whether you are adding limestone or sulfur to a new bed, be sure to mix it well into the soil, preferably with a garden tiller. Later, when you have established your rose beds, you may find that the pH needs adjusting. Consult your garden center about what amount of limestone or sulfur to use, and try to distribute the material evenly over the beds, scratching it into the soil.

The Size of Your Rose Bed

A rose bed can be almost any size or shape you like — rectangular, square, circular, or curving. Rectangular beds are the most common and probably the easiest to prepare. They will fit into the landscape rather easily as well as into the physical surroundings. A rectangular bed may consist of a single row of bushes, a double row, or three rows. The distance between the bushes depends mostly on climate, and somewhat on each bush itself, but be sure you leave enough room to work. Crowding makes it easy for insects and fungus disease to thrive and spread.

In states such as Pennsylvania, Ohio, Illinois, and those farther west, rose bushes are usually planted two feet apart. Farther north this distance may be only 18 inches. In the North, the edges of the bed should be at least nine inches from the center of the bush, thus making the bed 18 inches wide.

In the South, where the longer growing season produces larger plants, rose bushes are usually planted at least three feet apart (measuring from the center of one bush to the center of the next). The beds should be at least two to three feet wide, according to the space available. Planting bushes at the distances suggested will avoid crowding and ensure free air circulation.

The distances given for planting are for hybrid teas and grandifloras. Floribundas can be planted a little closer if they are the smaller bush type: 18 inches apart in the North, and 30 inches in the South. Shrub roses, old garden roses, and climbers should be planted farther apart than hybrid teas — as much as four to ten feet apart, depending on the growth habit of the plants involved.

Staggering Your Bushes

Staggered planting gives a more solid mass effect, eliminating gaps between the bushes, and allows all the bushes in the bed to be seen from one side. In the North, the bushes should be two feet apart in both directions, in a bed at least 42 inches wide. In the South, plant the bushes three feet apart in a bed at least five feet wide. The distance from the bushes to the edge of the bed is again nine inches in the North, 12 inches in the South.

Preparing the Bed

With the site selected and the size of your rose garden determined, you are now ready to prepare the bed. The best time to do this is in the fall, so that the materials added to the soil can begin their work and be settled by spring.

There is no single procedure for preparing a bed, because soil conditions vary throughout the country; the soil may even vary in composition within a small area.

The most common soil is clay. Roses grow well in clay soil, but the clay soil needs to be loosened and kept loose to allow it to breathe and be penetrated by water.

If the soil is sandy, more humus — organic material — needs to be added. Well-rotted cow manure, compost, or peat moss will serve the purpose here. In very sandy soil, you may add humus up to 50 percent by volume, but do not exceed this amount.

If there is grass sod on the surface, remove this two-inch layer and use it where needed in your yard. Now loosen the soil with a spade to a depth of 18 to 20 inches. Some gardeners prefer a depth of 24 inches, but it is harder to loosen the soil at that depth without removing it. Next, work some compost or peat moss into the soil; well-rotted cow manure may also be used. Along with the organic material, add some gypsum. This mineral has the ability to change clay soil from a cohesive substance to a crumbly, easily workable soil. A rotary tiller can be used to turn the earth and churn up this mixture of gypsum, peat moss, and soil.

You should use about 15 to 20 pounds of gypsum per 100 square feet. Within these guidelines, the exact amount is not critical, because gypsum will not have any adverse effect on the soil and it does not change the pH. Neither is the amount of peat moss or compost critical. The recommended ratio is one shovelful of peat moss to three shovelfuls of soil. This works out to be about 12 cubic feet of peat moss per 100 square feet of soil. The same amount of compost is used in place of the peat moss.

Other additives

Depending on the soil, other materials, such as sharp sand or vermiculite, can be added. If the soil has less than the required amount of phosphorus, then bone meal (15 pounds per 100 square feet) or 20 percent superphosphate (three to four pounds per 100 square feet) can be mixed into the bed. Phosphorus helps a rose bush produce a strong root system.

An Easy Method of Soil Preparation

To a beginner, all of this may seem like a lot of work, but the results pay off handsomely. However, if you are not sure of your ability as a rose grower, here is a procedure that is somewhat simpler.

This method of preparing a bed should be started in July or August. After you have determined the size of your bed, cut the grass and weeds but do not dig them up. If you have clay soil, cover the grass and weeds with gypsum until the ground looks white and then cover it with three or four sheets of newspaper. (If the soil is sandy, leave out the gypsum.) Now cover the newspapers with any kind of organic material available — leaves, decomposable kitchen garbage, grass clippings, or chopped-up weeds. To speed up decomposition, sprinkle a little commercial fertilizer, such as 10-10-10 or 8-8-8, over the surface.

As the weather becomes cooler, turn the compost under, digging it into the soil and dead grass. After spading or tilling the bed, continue to add leaves and other organic matter. In the North, nothing much can be done in winter, so before the ground freezes, add manure — about 150–200 pounds of manure per 100 square feet. In the South, this can be done in January or February by spading or tilling the whole bed once more. By spring, you will have a bed in which roses will grow well, and it will have been done with a minimum of work.

Raised or Sunken Beds

You have probably concluded at this point that the soil level in your bed will be much higher than the surrounding area. Most rosarians prefer raised beds, but some maintain a bed three inches below the grade level to make it easier to mow the grass around the beds. Sunken beds, however, are not recommended for beginners; they must have well-drained soil and are generally quite tricky. They must also be very carefully protected in the winter.

The Importance of Good Drainage

Roses will tolerate many kinds of soil, but poor drainage and lack of aeration — problems encountered by many beginners — will cause your plants to weaken and die.

If winters in your area are usually damp and the soil very wet in the spring, you may have a problem at planting time. Consider covering your rose bed with plastic in the fall. Doing so will keep the bed dry enough for easier planting in the spring.

Preparing Rose Bushes for Planting

Rose bushes are sold either in pots or with bare roots. Bare-root bushes are shipped while dormant, usually between the beginning of November and mid-May. As soon as you receive a shipment of bare-root roses, open the carton and check to see that the roots are still damp. If a shipment is delayed or if the carton has been stored near heat, the roots may have dried out. In any event, you should soak the roots in water before planting, at least overnight or up to 24 hours.

Small potted roses can generally be shipped year-round. If you receive a shipment during the summer, be sure to give the plants a few days of filtered shade after removing them from the carton. Water them well, and gradually expose them to more sunlight. After a week of this conditioning, they will be ready to plant.

Storing Your Rose Bushes

If for some reason you cannot plant immediately, there are several ways to store your roses. Moisten the bush (especially the roots) and wrap it in the plastic shipping bag. Place the bag in the shipping carton and store in a cool, dark place, preferably at a temperature of 35°–40°F. Check the bushes every two or three days and dampen them whenever necessary; they can be kept for as long as two weeks in this manner.

If you need to store the roses longer before planting them, the best thing you can do is to put them in a trench and then cover them with soil. The trench should be at least a foot deep; place the roses close together, lying at a 45° angle. Covering the plants with soil will keep them from drying out, but it is all right for the canes to protrude above the soil. If a hard freeze is forecast, cover the bushes with leaves and plastic, but be sure to remove the plastic if the temperature rises above freezing.

Planting

At planting time, place your rose bushes in a tub of water that covers the canes as well as the roots and let them soak for a couple of hours. When you are ready to plant them, remove the bushes from the water; examine the roots and remove any broken ones, using pruning shears to cut the broken roots just above the break.

Digging the holes

For each bush, dig a hole in your new bed at least 18 inches in diameter and 18 inches deep. If the hole is a little wider, it does not matter. If a plant proves to be too large for the hole, enlarge the hole. If the roots are too long, cut them back so that they fit easily in the hole, but retain as much of the root system as possible.

Before you plant the bush, inspect the canes and be sure to cut off any split or broken ends or any canes broken in shipment. In the North, canes longer than 12 inches are pruned back to 10 or 12 inches before planting. Make the cut approximately one-fourth inch above a bud eye, at a slight downward angle away from the bud eye. In the South, the canes do not need pruning, but broken canes must be trimmed.

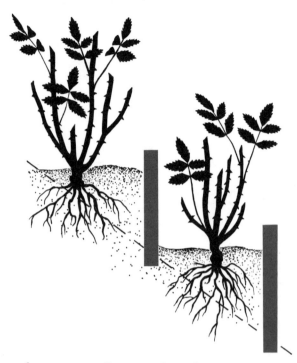

Roses do not grow well on steep slopes, but it is easy to convert a slope into a series of raised beds by terracing. As a rule, terracing will promote good drainage and retard or eliminate the problem of erosion.

Orienting your bushes

Replace most of the soil in the hole, forming a mound or pyramid. Place the plant on this mound, spreading the roots as evenly as possible. The crown, or bud union — the knot of wood between the canes and the roots — should be one or two inches below the level of the bed in the North, where temperatures fall below zero during the winter, and one or two inches above the level of the soil in southern climates. The bud union is usually on the side of the root cane, although it may completely surround the root cane. When planting the bush, place it in the hole so that the sides of the bud union from which most of the canes grow will face north. Orienting the plant this way will help the bud union to cover the root cane completely, causing new canes to form on the south side and producing a more rounded bush.

Fill in the hole until it is about three-fourths full, tamping or firming the soil with your hands so that the soil is packed firmly around the roots. Do not use your feet for this procedure. Tamping with the feet causes the soil to pack so tightly that it

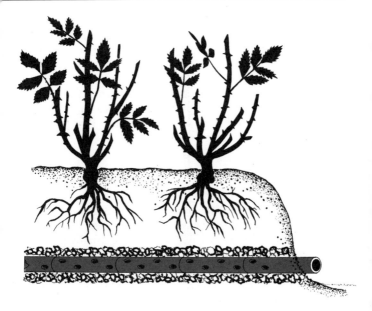

Roses need soil that is very well drained. Some gardeners choose to install a drainage pipe in the soil, several inches below the roots of their rose bushes, to make sure that any excess water in the soil is carried away to a lower level.

becomes difficult for food and water to pass easily through the plant and will destroy the porosity of the soil, which you have worked so hard to achieve.

With the garden hose or a bucket, add water to the hole, filling it to the top and letting it soak into the soil. The soil particles will be packed around the roots as they are carried down by the water, helping to anchor the roots and removing any air pockets in the soil around the roots. If the bed is too dry, thoroughly but gently water the entire bed. When the water has completely soaked in, fill the rest of the hole with the remaining soil.

Protecting bushes

If you live in the North, build a mound of soil over the newly planted bush to a height of 10 to 12 inches (less if the canes are short). If there is not enough soil mixture left, use a mulching material, such as sawdust or well-shredded leaves. The mound should be thoroughly drenched so that it is damp all the way through.

Usually in three or four weeks — sometimes less, depending on the weather — the bud eyes begin to swell on the canes, producing new and tender canes and leaves. The protection can then be removed over a week's time by gently washing the plant down with water. In the South, after the bush is planted, it should be left as is. However, if it has not broken dormancy — that is, if the bud eyes do not swell — you can cover the bush with a plastic bag; a milky white, tan, or light brown bag will do. These bags will also protect the bush if a light freeze occurs. In the Deep South, the early spring is sometimes very warm, so make three or four tiny holes or slits in the top of the plastic so that some of the heat can escape.

Planting Potted Roses

For potted roses, prepare the planting site, protect the canes, and water as you would for a bare-root plant. Because the roots are already in soil, you will have a head start over a bare-root plant. The pots that these roses come in are usually made of plastic, paper-coated plastic, or biodegradable paper. If the rose bushes have been started in a greenhouse during the fall, they may have a well-established root system. But in many instances a nursery does not pot its roses until spring. These roses are usually in a very porous planting mixture, and therefore only feeder roots have begun to develop. Removing the plant from the pot causes the mixture to fall from the roots; this may damage the feeder roots, and the shock of transplanting may be too much for the rose. Thus, it is better to place a potted rose — pot and all — in the hole to the desired depth. Next, fill in around the pot with the soil mix; then remove the plant — pot and all — from the hole. Cut the bottom out of the pot, leaving it momentarily in place. Make two slits in the pot, on opposite sides, starting at the bottom and extending three-quarters of the way to the top. Holding the bottom of the plant with one hand, place it carefully in the fitted hole, removing the bottom piece. Then finish the side cuts, gently remove the two sides of the pot, and firm the loose soil around the potted soil. Now add the remaining soil to bring the hole up to bed level.

1. *Planting a bare-root bush*   2. *Planting a potted bush*

Planting Miniatures

Outdoors in prepared beds, miniatures can be planted as close as 12 inches apart in northern areas and from 14 to 18 inches apart in southern areas. Since miniatures grow on their own roots, they should be planted in the ground slightly deeper than they are in the pots in which they arrive from the nursery. If the soil in the pot is dry, soak the plant thoroughly for several hours before transplanting. If the leaves turn yellow and drop off, this does not necessarily mean that the plant is dead. Placed in the growing environment, the miniature will recover.

Pruning

To have strong, healthy bushes, it is essential to learn how to prune your roses. Pruning is a process that continues throughout the growing season. With newly planted rose bushes, pruning should be kept to a minimum. Many rosarians remove the first blooms, allowing only the second cycle of bloom to develop to maturity. Doing this gives the bush more canes and stronger growth for the summer as well as for the remainder of the year.

Everyone needs a good pair of pruning shears; do not stint on the price, as poor-quality shears can damage your rose bushes. Do not buy anvil shears, which crush the cane. Other pruning shears go by several names: scissors-type, hook-type, or secateurs. The secateur type, if kept sharp, will give a clean cut. Hold the hook edge above the cutting blade, so if there happens to be a little crushing of the cane, it will be on the part of the cane that is being cut off.

Treating New Canes

On the bud union or crown, a new cane, called a basal break, may form. This can occur throughout the year, but generally happens in the spring when the bush breaks dormancy. Then the question is how to treat the new basal breaks. On some bushes the basal breaks may grow only two feet tall, while on others they may grow to six feet. (The tall ones may break off in a windstorm, so it is not a bad idea to tie them to a stake.) You may prefer to pinch the top out when the cane has reached a certain height — 12 inches in the North and 15 to 18 inches in the South. Doing so should make the cane stouter and encourage it to put out two or three new canes.

Deadheading

After a bush has bloomed, the next step is to remove the spent blooms. This is called deadheading. On a new bush, the process of removing the first blooms is a little different from what is done on an older bush. Cut the bloom (using pruning shears) at the stem, about one-quarter inch above the first pair of five-leaflet leaves. (Some rose bushes may have two or three pairs of three-leaflet leaves below a five-leaflet leaf; where this is so, cut off the stem above the second pair of these leaves.) If you want more blooms, continue this practice as your bushes grow older. However, if you want longer stems — particularly on hybrid teas — then you should cut the stem back to the second set of five-leaflet leaves after the first cycle of blooms.

Pruning Older Bushes

All the following information on pruning two-year-old or older bushes is for hybrid teas and grandiflora roses. Depending on where you live, the average heights are also given.

Pruning is essential to rejuvenate two-year-old or older bushes. Dead canes or dead wood caused by winter freezes, dying canes, or diseased wood should be removed. You will also want to remove damaged or broken stems, along with stems that have crossed through the center of the bush and are rub-bing against another cane. First remove weak canes and any that are less than 3/16 of an inch in diameter. Stems growing from pruned canes will grow no larger than the cane from which they have been cut, and are usually smaller.

Pruning of the remaining larger canes depends on whether you live in the North or the South. In the North, the canes are cut back to 12 to 14 inches or less, depending on the amount of winter damage. In the South, the plants are left higher — 18 to 24 inches.

Cutting to an outside eye

When a leaf drops off or is removed from a cane, it leaves a crescent-shaped scar. The area above the scar will produce a swelling, from which a new cane will form; such a swelling is known as an eye or bud eye. These eyes can be found all around the cane where foliage has grown. The first cut should be made

Cut at a 45° angle above a bud eye

as high as possible above an outside, or outward-facing, eye. Cutting to an outside eye gives the bush a better shape: It keeps canes from growing in the center of the bush, helps sun to get to the bud union, and helps keep fungus diseases away from the plant. Depending on a bush's vigor and the number of healthy canes, you will want to retain three to six young canes. Where winter damage has been severe, you will be in good shape if you are able to keep at least three canes with three to four bud eyes each.

Examining the pith

As you prune the cane, be sure to examine the color of the center, or pith. If the pith is white, you have a good live cane. If you have cut it to the desired height, go to the next cane. However, if the cane has a brown pith, cut a little more off the top, continuing to snip off a little at a time until you have located the white center. If this seems drastic, it is — and some rosarians will not cut all the way to a white center, particularly after a severe winter. Instead, they cut back to a bud eye where the center is slightly colored or is a very light tan. The theory is that these canes can produce new wood, helping to keep the bush more productive.

Protecting cut canes

If borers — various types of insects that drill holes in the center of the cane — are a problem in your area, it is advisable to seal all pruning cuts. If borers attack more than one cane, the bush will be weakened and flower production will fall off drastically. Several materials may be used to seal the cut: fingernail polish, Elmer's Glue, carbolated vaseline, or a tree-wound compound.

Pruning Climbers

Climbers are of two types and are pruned differently. The ramblers bloom once during a season with small, clustered flowers. They may be allowed to spread and can even be used as a ground cover by pruning only weak or diseased canes. The ends of the long canes can be snipped to produce more lateral stems and blooms next year. Some rosarians prefer to cut ramblers back to the ground as soon as the bush has finished blooming. Doing this allows new canes to grow during the summer from which blooms are produced during the next year. Nearly all the ramblers produce flowers only on second-year wood.

Large-flowered climbers may be once-bloomers or repeat bloomers. They need pruning only of old, nonproductive canes of winter die-back. The repeat bloomers should have the short flowering stems cut back to the first set of five-leaflet leaves as

Cut here

Second bloom cycle

After the first cycle of blooms, you can increase the number of blossoms produced by a bush if you cut back to the first bud eye below the topmost five-leaflet leaf. When a few weeks have passed, a new stem will grow from the bud eye, and another flowering stem may appear at the base of the lower leaf.

Before pruning

After pruning

In spring, remove any old, weak canes that did not produce good blooms last season; also cut away any canes that cross through the center of the bush. When pruned, the bush has 3 or 4 healthy, strong canes that will soon produce a bounty of colorful blossoms.

soon as the flowers are spent. Because most climbers set hips to produce seed, most of the food and energy goes to producing the seed rather than more flowers. Thus, be sure this deadheading is taken care of, or there will be very little repeat blooming. Don't be surprised if some climbers do not bloom until the third year.

Shaping a Bush

When the pruning is finished, the bush should form a bowl, with the canes radiating from the center like the spokes of a wheel. This leaves the center open to sunlight during the year and encourages basal breaks from the bud union. Canes that form on the inside can be left as long as they are not crossing or rubbing other canes. Weak or small canes should be pruned out. It is best to keep the center open throughout the growing season. If a bush has a spreading habit and takes up too much space, then you can prune back to an inner eye. This causes the new canes to grow straight up, keeping the bush in bounds so that it does not encroach on a neighboring bush. The center will remain open. In the South and the West, young, green basal canes that grew late during the previous year often survive the winter. Only the flower buds should be removed from these canes. Removal of these buds allows the wood to harden, but cutting into the soft green cane will usually cause it to die. In the following spring, after the lateral stems have grown and bloomed, you may cut this basal cane back to just above the lateral growing canes.

Preventing Disease

After pruning, clean up all debris and old leaves to keep diseases from spreading. It is a good idea to spray the bushes and ground with a copper- or sulfur-based dormant oil spray at this time, to kill any dangerous fungus spores that may be present.

Thumb Pruning

The removal of unwanted eyes from rose stems, laterals, and canes with the thumb (instead of shears) is called thumb pruning. This process removes problem stems early; once a stem has produced a bud, it is very hard for most gardeners to remove it.

Unwanted eyes may grow in the wrong place, the wrong direction, or too close together. If you remove them early enough, you can rub them off with your thumb. If the bud eye has already produced a short stem, you can use your thumb and forefinger.

Remove any eyes growing low down on the inside of a cane

or bud union; this will keep the center open and prevent large scars. Frequently a bud eye produces two or three stems, which will become weak as they grow. Thumb prune the excess stems, removing the weakest and leaving the strongest stem — usually the center one — to develop. This process will leave the bush with stronger stems and larger flowers. Sometimes the center eye dies and one stem develops on each side. Thumb prune the weaker one when their comparative strength is evident; should the eyes appear equal, leave the one that will give your bush a better shape.

Winterizing

The removal of a spent bloom is also considered pruning. Therefore, in the fall, three to five weeks before the first frost in your area, you should refrain from cutting the spent heads or blooms on your bushes. Leaving the spent blooms in place is part of winterizing your plants before cold weather arrives. Even though roses in the Deep South may not go dormant, leaving the spent blooms on in November gives the plants a rest from blooming. In the South, the plants retaining spent blooms form seed pods, thereby becoming semidormant. In January, you can begin pruning for the coming year.

You should also withhold any nitrogen-containing fertilizer six to ten weeks before the last blooming cycle. The last blooms could appear by the end of July in the extreme north or the end of September in the extreme south.

The most common way to protect roses is to take soil from a location other than the rose bed and make a mound around the base of the plant to a height of 10 to 12 inches. Where temperatures remain below freezing for some time and the weather becomes stabilized, additional protection is needed. Materials on hand that you can use include leaves, wood chips, pine needles, bark, sawdust, and ground-up corn cobs. Do not apply the protective material too early, as it could cause a late soft growth that will hinder dormancy. Since apricot and yellow roses suffer winter damage the most, they should be given extra winter protection.

Cones and collars

One successful protection device is a rose cone, made of foam plastic, which covers the base of the rose bush. Cones are practical only for growers with just a few bushes, since they are expensive and pose storage problems. Cones must be weighted down to keep them in place during strong winds. You must also prune the bush and tie the canes to fit inside the cones. Provide adequate ventilation, because unseasonable warm spells cause sweating in the containers, and mildew and insects will appear if the cones are not ventilated. Collars can be made from cardboard, metal, plastic-covered wire mesh, plastic, tar paper, or layers of newspapers, folded and stapled. The collar encircles the base of the plant; to hold it in place and permit air to circulate freely, you can fill the collar with soil, leaves, straw, pine needles, and other matter. To accommodate sprawling plants, collars can be contoured, simply by pinning two sections together.

Roses grown in containers, including miniatures, can be buried in soil to the top of the container and treated in the same way as roses growing in beds. Potted roses can be brought indoors and handled like indoor miniatures. Larger plants should be exposed to the outdoors long enough to begin dormancy. Do not allow them to completely dry out because this will cause permanent damage to the plant. If the plants go into active growth indoors without enough light, they will become twiggy or leggy, with light green foliage that will readily be attacked by aphids.

Tree roses that remain outdoors where temperatures fall below 20° F will require extra protection. After the bush has been pruned, remove the soil from one side of the roots to allow the plant to be bent. Dig a trench large and deep enough to completely accommodate the plant and lie it down in the trench; cover it entirely with soil.

Protecting climbers

Climbing roses may need extra protection, at least in the North. Mounding soil on the base will help, and wrapping the canes in burlap will protect them from the drying effect of winter winds. You may also dig a trench next to the bush and bend the canes into the trench, covering them with soil or other material.

Mulching

Another rose-growing practice that you should consider is mulching. Some rosarians do not use mulch; those who live in cool climates maintain that mulching is unnecessary, and that mulch harbors insects and disease. They prefer to leave the soil bare so there can be light cultivation (no more than one and one-half inches deep), because deeper cultivation will injure the feeder roots of the rose bush. Some people also feel that without mulch there is less incidence of crown gall and that fertilizer may be worked into the soil more easily. But keeping unmulched beds free of weeds and grass requires constant care.

If you have less time to devote to weeding, then you will need to consider mulching. Mulching is a convenient way to keep weeds under control, insulate the soil against summer heat, and conserve moisture by slowing down evaporation.

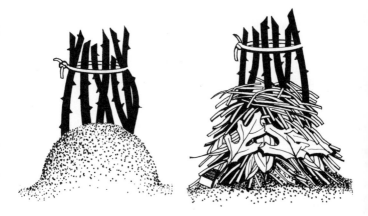

*Mound soil at the base of your bushes to a height of about 12 in.
Tying the canes will keep them from breaking in strong winds.
In especially cold weather you may want to use straw, leaves, or
another mulch to provide insulation.*

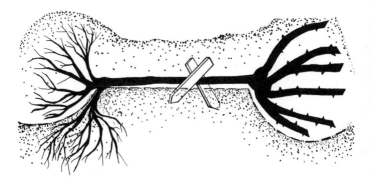

*Protect a tree rose by first digging up half the roots; this will
enable you to lay the plant down on its side. Now cover the
plant with a large mound of soil, and you will have complete
protection.*

The real value in using mulch is found in the soil itself. The
humus resulting from the mulches makes the nutrients already
found in the soil more readily available to the roots of the roses,
improving the soil structure while adding trace elements. Soil
temperature and moisture are consistent, providing favorable
conditions for a continuous growth of fine roses.

The best time to apply mulch is after the soil has warmed. In the South, this can be done before the bushes start growing. Before you mulch, the soil should be soaked by a good rain or water from the garden hose.

Mulching materials

Many materials have been used and tested for use as mulch. It has been found that a depth of four inches is necessary for most mulches to give the desired results. Cost and availability also determine which mulch to use. So that grass and weeds can be easily removed by hand, mulch should be placed no closer to the bush than six inches. Consult your local garden center to determine which mulches will suit you best.

Fertilizer

Beginners will find that there are many materials and methods of fertilizing. What constitutes the best method is a matter of opinion, but it certainly depends on the type of soil and climate. A group of researchers in England has found that a combination of organic fertilizer and chemical fertilizer will grow better roses than either by itself.

When you buy fertilizer, three numbers are printed on the bag or container. The first number indicates the percentage, by weight, of nitrogen included. The second number gives the percentage of phosphorus available as phosphoric acid or P_2O_5 (phosphorus pentoxide). The third number is the percentage of potassium or soluble potash, usually represented by the chemical formula K_2O (potassium oxide). There are many types of formulations: 8-8-8, 10-10-10, 0-20-20, 20-20-20, 18-6-12, 5-10-10, and so on. A soil analysis will tell you what formulation of fertilizer will be best.

When to feed your roses

For newly planted rose bushes, add fertilizer only after the first blooming cycle and thereafter only once a month. Stop feeding your roses by six weeks before the last bloom cycle. Scatter the fertilizer evenly around the bush, at least six inches from the base. Scratch it lightly into the soil, and then water it in. If your soil is dry, water the soil the day before you feed your roses.

On two-year-old or established rose bushes, feeding should start in the spring, about four to six weeks before the first cycle of blooms, with continued feeding as discussed above.

Other kinds of fertilizer

You may want to take advantage of various other products available, including slow-release fertilizers and water-soluble fertilizers. Be sure to read and follow label directions carefully.

Or you may want to make your own organic fertilizers, using a blend of products that are easy to get hold of. Some rosarians like to use a solution of Epsom salts to induce more basal breaks. In the summer, if your roses need an extra boost, consult your local garden center about how to apply fish emulsion.

Creating New Cultivars

Wild roses respond very gradually over time to the demands and pressures of the situation, or ecological niche, in which they grow. Adapting to survival in a dynamic environment is a lengthy process, full of changes so subtle and slow that they may be very nearly impossible for a person to detect. This process of change has come to be known as selection.

Unlike wild roses, most roses in cultivation are bred with the intention, on the part of the breeder, of enhancing or minimizing certain inherited traits, such as color or fragrance, that may have no bearing on the plant's survival. Gardeners want flowers with many petals, blooms of different colors, and a variety of growth habits and sizes. These different forms may be the result of seedling variability, intentional and accidental hybridization, or mutation. Variant forms are produced in the wild, too, but plants under cultivation are subjected to more critical observation, and the variant, if it is desirable, is more likely to be bred again and again. These selected variants are called cultivars, because they develop under cultivation; they are also commonly referred to as varieties.

Mutation

New rose cultivars come about through one of two processes, either mutation or hybridization. Mutation is spontaneous; relatively uncommon, it occurs in the meristem (which is inside the developing stem tip) when a gene in one cell changes, or mutates. The affected cell develops and divides, producing a relatively large body of cells. When these cells mature, the change in traits becomes evident. The most common mutations produce changes in flower color or growth habit; for example, a pink rose may produce red flowers or a bush rose may develop a climbing form. A rarer mutation is the change from once-flowering to repeat-flowering. Most mutations, often called sports, are relatively unstable and may change back, either partially or completely, to the parental form. Almost always, only one trait is involved.

Hybridization

Whether intentional or accidental, hybridization is the principal way to create rose cultivars. The species in the genus *Rosa* are remarkably uniform. The five-petaled flowers have many pistils at the center; the pistils (made up of the stigma, style, and ovary) are surrounded by many stamens — the pollen producers. Each pistil is attached to the inside wall of the receptacle. When fertilization occurs and the resulting egg cell matures, it becomes an achene — a seed enclosed in a woody coating. The receptacle, with its enclosed achenes, enlarges as it matures, and when ripe (a "hip") turns from green to yellow, orange, orange-red, or purplish black.

A factor complicating hybridization in roses is the varying number of chromosomes in the different species. It is the interplay among these chromosomes that determines the appearance and other traits of the offspring. Rose chromosomes are divided into groups called genomes, with seven chromosomes each. Hybridization between cultivars with the same number of genomes is relatively uncomplicated and usually produces fertile progeny. Hybridization between cultivars with different numbers of genomes usually succeeds, but the progeny will be relatively infertile.

Artificial Pollination

Once you have learned to grow roses, you may discover that you are interested in cross-breeding some of your own varieties. The techniques you need to master in order to produce seeds by artificial pollination are relatively simple.

To provide the pollen, choose a flower that is just starting to open. Remove the sepals and petals. Examine the stamens to be sure they have not started to shed pollen; if they have, choose a younger flower. With a pair of small scissors or forceps, remove the stamens and place them on a small sheet of wax paper. Put the wax paper and stamens in a shaded, calm place, where the stamens will ripen and shed pollen (which looks like fine yellow dust).

Now select a flower to pollinate. Choose one at the same stage of development as the rose you have selected to be the pollen parent. With a pair of scissors, a small knife, or forceps, remove the sepals, petals, and stamens. Using a small brush, place pollen on the pistils. Cover the pollinated flower with a small paper bag, secured to the stem with a twist-tie; this will prevent unwanted pollination by insects and keep it from drying out.

If you are attempting to make more than one cross, it is vital to use a clean brush when changing pollen parents. You can sterilize a pollen brush by dipping it in ethanol and then drying it. Put a label on the pollinated flower showing the name of the seed and pollen parents — for example, Crimson Glory × Peace. (It is customary to list the seed parent first.) Pollen may not be available when the seed parent flower has been prepared, but if the prepared flower has been protected from drying out, it should remain usable for two to three days. Discard it if the pistils begin to discolor.

If your attempt has been successful, you will begin to see the effects in about two weeks. The receptacle, or hip, will start to enlarge; when it is ripe and ready to harvest, it will have changed color — usually about three months after pollination. Remove the ripe hips before the first frost sets in; cut them open and remove the seeds. If you have a warm greenhouse or other suitable facility, you can plant the seeds at this time. Otherwise, keep them in a cool place (at a temperature of 35–40° F), make sure they stay moist, and plant them when spring comes.

It is a good practice to keep a permanent record of one's hybridizing work. Such a record should include not only the names of the parents but the number of flowers pollinated, the dates of pollination, and the number of seeds obtained.

Hardiness

Gardeners accustomed to referring to the Department of Agriculture's Plant Hardiness Zone Map may be surprised to see that the map does not appear in this book. The reason is that plant hardiness zones, which are based on the average minimum winter temperatures in each region, are of less use in growing roses than in growing most other ornamental perennial plants. With roses, the actual degrees of cold are less important than wide temperature fluctuations and the drying effects of wind and sun.

When you select a rose for hardiness, a general rule is that tender roses will survive where the average minimum winter temperature ranges from 10° to 20°F. Winter-hardy roses should flourish where the minimum temperatures do not fall below −10° F, and some will survive even colder temperatures. When you read the hardiness factor in the caption accompanying the picture of the rose, you will see that some are described as winter hardy, some as moderately winter hardy, some as extremely winter hardy, and some as hardy with protection. Even hardy roses can be made hardier with winter protection.

Surviving the Winter

One factor that helps roses through a severe winter is the presence of a good snow cover all winter long. Growers of roses in snowy northern regions suffer fewer losses than those in milder regions where snow cover is spotty. Roses are also more likely to come through very cold temperatures if the change is gradual.

In areas where freezes and thaws alternate, some gardeners use foam rose cones or build foam housing over their rose plants. If you object to the look of Styrofoam and don't want to store the cones or plastic over the growing season, a less expensive method is to staple several layers of newspaper around and over each rose bush. Whatever winter protection you use, be sure that you do not put it in place until the growing season is completely over and the cold weather has arrived.

Rose growers will tell you that good cultural practices during the growing season (see "Getting Started") are the best winter protection, and that choosing hardy varieties is the best way to ensure winter survival. It is also a good idea to refrain from cutting flowers or pruning the bushes in the fall. Instead, let the hips form and remain on the plant. Withhold fertilizers in fall but never withhold water; desiccation is a bigger enemy than cold weather.

Hardiness by Class and Cultivar

Among roses, winter hardiness varies with each different cultivar and is related to the genetic ability of each rose to manufacture its own antifreeze. Although hardiness varies enormously within each group of roses, it is possible to make some generalizations.

Species roses vary from very hardy to very tender and include what is probably the hardiest rose of all, *Rosa acicularis*, the Polar Rose, found growing around the Arctic Circle and over wide areas of Asia and North America.

Most old garden roses, such as the gallicas, the damasks, and the albas, are extremely hardy. So are many of the old climbing and rambling roses.

Among modern roses, many of the shrub roses are very hardy. Otherwise, hardiness varies widely. Hybrid teas, grandifloras, and floribundas are likely to be tender. Of this group, the floribundas are hardier than the other two.

This said, it is important to remember that there are many exceptions to these guidelines — and that every garden has not only a climate but probably several microclimates that affect the ability of a rose to survive the winter.

The Color Plates

Visual Key

Species Roses

These are the roses found in the wild. The ancestors of all our cultivars, they have 5 to 12 petals. After blooming, they set brightly colored hips.

Climbers

Climbing roses have long canes and can be trained up a trellis or wall. Some are forms of bush roses. There are 7 groups, each with a different heritage.

Shrub Roses

The shrub roses comprise 8 groups. They include neat little bushes with clusters of flowers; ground covers; tall, arching plants; and large, billowy bushes that are perfect for hedges.

Old Garden Roses

The old garden roses are a very large class, made up of 10 groups of roses that have been in cultivation since before 1867. Their flowers are typically large, globular, and very full — some with as many as 200 petals. Old garden varieties are among the most fragrant of all roses. Many of these roses bloom only once, while others — notably the teas and Chinas — are dependable repeat bloomers.

Floribundas

With their abundant large blossoms, borne singly or in clusters, the floribundas were developed by crossing repeat-blooming hybrid teas with many-flowered polyanthas, which are one group of shrub roses.

Grandifloras

A recently established class, the grandifloras are the result of a cross between hybrid teas and floribundas. These big, vigorous plants bear large, fine flowers.

Hybrid Teas

A product of crossing two old garden types — hybrid perpetuals and teas — hybrid teas are the most popular of all roses. Grown today almost everywhere in the world, these hardy roses bloom early in the season and continue to produce flowers until fall. The blossoms are borne singly on long stems; they have a classic spiral shape, with the petals unfurling evenly from a high center. Some are very fragrant.

Miniatures

Perfect for small gardens, terraces, and indoor pots, these petite plants are uncannily like their large relatives. They are tremendously popular today.

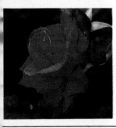

Species Roses

Rosa laevigata

Plant height: 6–20 ft.
Blossom width:
2½–3½ in.
Blooms early in season
with no repeat

Fragrant
Not winter hardy
Disease resistant
p. 264

Rosa rugosa alba

Plant height: 3–5 ft.
Blossom width:
2½–3½ in.
Blooms continuously

Strong clove
fragrance
Winter hardy
Disease free
p. 268

Rosa multiflora

Plant height: 7–12 ft.
Blossom width: ¹/₂ in.
Blooms early to
midseason with no
repeat

Honey fragrance
Winter hardy in all
but severe climates
Disease free
p. 265

Rosa soulieana

Plant height: to 12 ft.
Blossom width:
1¹/₂ in.
Blooms early to
midseason with no
repeat

Little or no fragrance
Not reliably winter
hardy
Disease free
p. 269

Rosa wichuraiana   Plant height: 10–20 ft.   Fragrant
Blossom width: Hardy in all but
1½–2 in.   severe climates
Blooms late in season   Disease free
with no repeat   p. 270

Rosa carolina   Plant height: 3–6 ft.   Fragrant
Blossom width: 2 in.   Winter hardy except
Blooms in midseason   in severe climates
Disease free
p. 262

Rosa spinosissima | Plant height: 3–4 ft. | Light, sweet
| Blossom width: | fragrance
| 1¼–2 in. | Winter hardy
| Blooms very early in | Disease resistant
| season with no repeat | p. 269

Rosa palustris | Plant height: 6–12 ft. | Very sweet fragrance
| Blossom width: | Winter hardy
| 2½ in. | Disease free
| Blooms late in season | p. 265
| with no repeat |

Rosa roxburghii normalis

Plant height: 7–9 ft.
Blossom width:
3½–4 in.
Blooms early in season
with no repeat

Light, sweet
fragrance
Not entirely winter
hardy
Disease free
p. 267

Rosa rubrifolia

Plant height: 4–8 ft.
Blossom width: ½ in.
Blooms early in season
with no repeat

Fragrant
Winter hardy in all
but severe climates
Disease free
p. 267

Rosa pendulina

Plant height: to 4 ft.
Blossom width: 2 in.
Blooms in midseason
or later

Light, sweet
fragrance
Winter hardy
Disease free
p. 266

Rosa eglanteria

Plant height: 8–10 ft.
Blossom width:
1–1½ in.
Blooms early in season
with no repeat

Light, sweet
fragrance
Winter hardy
Disease free
p. 262

Rosa pomifera

Plant height: 5–7 ft.
Blossom width: 2 in.
Blooms early in season
with no repeat

Fragrant
Winter hardy
Disease free
p. 266

Rosa rugosa rubra

Plant height: 3–5 ft.
Blossom width:
2½–3½ in.
Blooms continuously
all season

Strong fragrance
Winter hardy
Disease free
p. 268

Rosa rugosa

Plant height: 3–5 ft.
Blossom width:
2½–3½ in.
Blooms continuously
all season

Strong fragrance
Winter hardy
Disease free
p. 268

Rosa roxburghii

Plant height: 6–7 ft.
Blossom width:
2–2½ in.
Blooms in midseason
with no repeat

Slight fragrance
Not winter hardy
Disease resistant
p. 266

Rosa × highdownensis Plant height: 9–12 ft.   Fragrant
Blossom width: Winter hardy
1½ in.   Disease resistant
Blooms early in season p. 263

Rosa foetida bicolor Plant height: 4–5 ft.   Heavy fragrance
Blossom width: Not reliably winter
2–2½ in.   hardy
Blooms early in season   Susceptible to black
with no repeat   spot
p. 263

Rosa moyesii

*Plant height: to 10 ft.
Blossom width:
1¾–2½ in.
Blooms early in season
with no repeat*

*Slight fragrance
Winter hardy
Disease free
p. 264*

Rosa foetida persiana

*Plant height: 4–5 ft.
Blossom width:
2½–3 in.
Blooms early with no
repeat*

*Little or no fragrance
Not winter hardy
Susceptible to black
spot
p. 263*

Rosa hugonis

Plant height: to 6 ft.
Blossom width:
1½–2 in.
Blooms early in season
with no repeat

Little or no fragrance
Winter hardy except
in extreme climates
Disease free
p. 264

**Rosa chinensis
viridiflora**

Plant height: 3–4 ft.
Blossom width:
1½–2½ in.
Blooms all season

Not fragrant
Not winter hardy
Disease resistant
p. 262

Rosa spinosissima altaica

Plant height: to 6 ft.
Blossom width:
1½–2½ in.
Blooms very early in
season with no repeat

Slight fragrance
Winter hardy
Disease resistant
p. 269

Rosa banksiae lutea

Plant height: 20–30 ft.
Blossom width: 1 in.
Blooms very early in
season with no repeat

Slight fragrance
Not winter hardy
Disease free
p. 261

Climbers

Albéric Barbier *Wichuraiana Climber*   *Green-apple*
Plant height: to 20 ft.   *fragrance*
Blossom width: *Winter hardy*
3–3½ in.   *Disease free*
Blooms late in season   *p. 273*
with no repeat

Elegance   *Large-flowered*   *Fragrant*
Climber   *Winter hardy*
Plant height: 12–15 ft.   *Disease resistant*
Blossom width: *p. 273*
4½–5½ in.
Blooms abundantly in
midseason with no
repeat

City of York

*Large-flowered
Climber
Plant height: to 20 ft.
Blossom width:
3–3½ in.
Blooms in midseason
for long period with
no repeat*

*Strong fragrance
Winter hardy
Disease free
p. 275*

Paul's Lemon Pillar

*Climbing Hybrid Tea
Plant height: 10–12 ft.
Blossom width:
3½–4 in.
Blooms well all season*

*Strong lemon
fragrance
Not winter hardy
Disease resistant
p. 282*

Leverkusen

Kordesii Climber
Plant height: 8–10 ft.
Blossom width:
3–3½ in.
Blooms well in
midseason with good
repeat

Slight fragrance
Winter hardy
Disease free
p. 280

Silver Moon

Wichuraiana Climber
Plant height: to 20 ft.
Blossom width:
3½–4½ in.
Blooms in midseason
for long period with
no repeat

Fragrant
Winter hardy
Disease free
p. 284

Mermaid

Hybrid Bracteata
Plant height: to 20 ft.
Blossom width:
4¹/₂–5¹/₂ in.
Blooms in midseason
for long period with
no repeat

Fragrant
Not winter hardy
Disease resistant
p. 281

Royal Sunset

Large-flowered
Climber
Plant height: 6 ft.
Blossom width:
4¹/₂–5 in.
Blooms in midseason
with good repeat

Fragrant
Not reliably winter
hardy in severe
climates
Disease resistant
p. 283

Golden Showers   *Large-flowered Climber*
Plant height: 8–10 ft.
Blossom width:
3½–4 in.
Blooms abundantly all season

Fragrant
Winter hardy except in severe winter climates
Disease resistant
p. 279

Joseph's Coat   *Large-flowered Climber*
Plant height: 8–10 ft.
Blossom width:
3–4 in.
Blooms well in midseason with fair repeat

Slight fragrance
Not dependably winter hardy
Disease resistant
p. 280

Lawrence Johnston

*Large-flowered Climber
Plant height: to 20 ft.
Blossom width:
3–3½ in.
Blooms early to
midseason with no
repeat*

*Fragrant
Winter hardy
Disease resistant
p. 280*

Handel

*Large-flowered Climber
Plant height: 12–15 ft.
Blossom width:
3½ in.
Blooms well in
midseason with good
repeat*

*Slight fragrance
Winter hardy
Disease resistant
p. 279*

Veilchenblau

Rambler
Plant height: to 12 ft.
Blossom width:
1¼ in.
Blooms midseason to
late season with no
repeat

Green-apple
fragrance
Winter hardy
Disease resistant
p. 284

Blossomtime

Large-flowered
Climber
Plant height: 7–9 ft.
Blossom width:
3½–4 in.
Blooms well in
midseason with sparse
repeat

Strong fragrance
Winter hardy
Disease resistant
p. 275

American Pillar

Rambler
Plant height: 15–20 ft.
Blossom width:
2–3 in.
Blooms very
abundantly late in
season for long period

Little or no fragrance
Winter hardy
Disease resistant
p. 274

New Dawn

Wichuraiana Climber
Plant height: 12–15 ft.
Blossom width:
3–3½ in.
Blooms well in
midseason with good
repeat

Fragrant
Winter hardy
Disease resistant
p. 281

Baltimore Belle   *Large-flowered Climber*
Plant height: 8–10 ft.
Blossom width:
2–2½ in.
Blooms late in season
with no repeat

Little or no fragrance
Winter hardy
Disease resistant
p. 274

May Queen   *Wichuraiana Climber*
Plant height: 15 ft.
Blossom width:
3–3½ in.
Blooms in midseason
for long period with
no repeat

Green-apple
fragrance
Winter hardy
Disease free
p. 281

Dr. J. H. Nicolas

Large-flowered Climber
Plant height: 8–10 ft.
Blossom width: 4½–5 in.
Blooms profusely in midseason with good repeat

Strong fragrance
Winter hardy
Disease resistant
p. 278

Clair Matin

Large-flowered Climber
Plant height: 10–12 ft.
Blossom width: 2½–3 in.
Blooms profusely in midseason for long period with no repeat

Fragrant
Winter hardy
Disease resistant
p. 276

Aloha

*Climbing Hybrid Tea
Plant height: 8–10 ft.
Blossom width:
3½ in.
Blooms well all season*

*Strong fragrance
Winter hardy
Disease resistant, but
slightly susceptible to
mildew
p. 273*

Viking Queen

*Large-flowered
Climber
Plant height: 12–15 ft.
Blossom width:
3–4 in.
Blooms in midseason
with good repeat*

*Strong fragrance
Winter hardy
Disease resistant
p. 284*

Dorothy Perkins

Rambler
Plant height: 10–12 ft.
Blossom width: ¾ in.
Blooms late in season
with no repeat

Little or no fragrance
Winter hardy
Disease resistant, but
susceptible to mildew
p. 277

Rosarium Uetersen

Kordesii Climber
Plant height: 10–12 ft.
Blossom width:
3½–4 in.
Blooms profusely in
midseason with good
repeat

Fragrant
Very winter hardy
Disease resistant
p. 283

Excelsa

Rambler
Plant height: 12–18 ft.
Blossom width: ¼ in.
Blooms late in season
with no repeat

Little or no fragrance
Winter hardy
Disease resistant, but
susceptible to mildew
p. 279

Dr. Huey

Large-flowered
Climber
Plant height: 12–18 ft.
Blossom width:
3–3½ in.
Blooms in midseason
for long period with
no repeat

Fragrant
Winter hardy
Disease resistant
p. 277

America

Large-flowered Climber
Plant height: 9–12 ft.
Blossom width:
3½–4½ in.
Blooms well in midseason with fair repeat

Fragrant
Winter hardy
Disease resistant
p. 274

Don Juan

Large-flowered Climber
Plant height: 8–10 ft.
Blossom width:
4½–5 in.
Blooms profusely in midseason with good repeat

Strong fragrance
Not reliably winter hardy
Disease resistant
p. 276

Paul's Scarlet Climber   *Large-flowered*   *Slight fragrance*
Climber   *Winter hardy*
Plant height: 12–15 ft. *Disease resistant*
Blossom width: *p. 282*
3–3½ in.
Blooms profusely in
midseason with no
repeat

Dublin Bay   *Large-flowered*   *Fragrant*
Climber   *Winter hardy*
Plant height: 8–14 ft. *Disease resistant*
Blossom width: *p. 278*
4½ in.
Blooms profusely in
midseason with good
repeat

Blaze

*Large-flowered
Climber
Plant height: 7–9 ft.
Blossom width:
2½–3 in.
Blooms well in
midseason with
excellent repeat*

*Slight fragrance
Winter hardy
Disease resistant
p. 275*

Dortmund

*Kordesii Climber
Plant height: 10–12 ft.
Blossom width:
3–3½ in.
Blooms profusely in
midseason with good
repeat*

*Fragrant
Winter hardy
Disease free
p. 277*

Pierre de Ronsard

Large-flowered Climber
Plant height: 8–10 ft.
Blossom width: 5–5½ in.
Blooms profusely in midseason with fair repeat

Little fragrance
Winter hardy
Disease resistant
p. 282

Rhonda

Large-flowered Climber
Plant height: 7–9 ft.
Blossom width: 3½–4 in.
Blooms well all season

Slight fragrance
Winter hardy
Disease resistant
p. 283

Compassion

*Large-flowered
Climber
Plant height: 8–10 ft.
Blossom width:
4½–5 in.
Blooms well all season*

*Strong fragrance
Winter hardy
Disease resistant
p. 276*

Altissimo

*Large-flowered
Climber
Plant height: 10–12 ft.
Blossom width:
4–5 in.
Blooms well all season*

*Slight fragrance
Winter hardy
Disease resistant
p. 273*

Shrub Roses

Penelope

Hybrid Musk
Plant height: 5–7 ft.
Blossom width: 3 in.
Blooms in midseason
with good repeat

Very fragrant
Winter hardy
Disease resistant
p. 309

Blanc Double de Coubert

Hybrid Rugosa
Plant height: 4–6 ft.
Blossom width:
2½–3 in.
Blooms early to
midseason with fair
repeat

Very fragrant
Very winter hardy
Disease free
p. 291

Alba Meidiland

Ground Cover
Plant spread: 6 ft.
Blossom width: 2 in.
Blooms profusely in
midseason with good
repeat in the fall

Not fragrant
Winter hardy
Disease resistant
p. 288

Sea Foam

Shrub
Plant height: 8–12 ft.
Blossom width:
2–2½ in.
Blooms in midseason
with excellent repeat

Slight fragrance
Winter hardy
Disease resistant
p. 314

Hebe's Lip   *Eglanteria*
Plant height: to 4 ft.
Blossom width: 3 in.
Blooms early in season
with no repeat

Moderately strong
fragrance
Winter hardy
Disease free
p. 303

Frau Dagmar Hastrup   *Hybrid Rugosa*
Plant height: 2½–3 ft.
Blossom width:
3–3½ in.
Blooms early to
midseason with good
repeat

Very strong clove
fragrance
Winter hardy
Disease free
p. 300

Nevada

Shrub
Plant height: 6–8 ft.
Blossom width:
3¹/₂–4 in.
Blooms in midseason
with excellent repeat

Little or no fragrance
Winter hardy
Disease resistant
p. 308

Frühlingsmorgen

Hybrid Spinosissima
Plant height: 5–7 ft.
Blossom width:
3–3¹/₂ in.
Blooms profusely,
early in season, with
no repeat

Slight, sweet
fragrance
Winter hardy
Disease free
p. 301

Ballerina

Hybrid Musk
Plant height: 3–4 ft.
Blossom width: 2 in.
Blooms in midseason
with good repeat

Slight sweet-pea
fragrance
Winter hardy
Disease resistant
p. 289

Cornelia

Hybrid Musk
Plant height: 6–8 ft.
Blossom width: 1 in.
Blooms in midseason
with good repeat

Fragrant
Winter hardy
Disease resistant
p. 295

Sarah Van Fleet

Hybrid Rugosa
Plant height: 6–8 ft.
Blossom width:
3–3½ in.
Blooms early to
midseason with good
repeat

Very fragrant
Winter hardy
Disease resistant
p. 313

Conrad Ferdinand Meyer

Hybrid Rugosa
Plant height: 9–12 ft.
Blossom width:
3½–4½ in.
Blooms early to
midseason with no
repeat

Strong fragrance
Not reliably winter
hardy
Disease free
p. 295

Cécile Brunner

Polyantha
Plant height: 2½–3 ft.
Blossom width:
1½ in.
Blooms profusely late
in season with
excellent repeat

Slight fragrance
Not reliably winter
hardy in severe
climates
Disease resistant
p. 294

Sparrieshoop

Shrub
Plant height: to 5 ft.
Blossom width: 4 in.
Blooms well in
midseason with fair
repeat

Very fragrant
Winter hardy
Disease resistant
p. 314

Pink Grootendorst

Hybrid Rugosa
Plant height: 5–6 ft.
Blossom width:
1½ in.
Blooms profusely in
midseason with good
repeat

Not fragrant
Winter hardy
Disease resistant
p. 309

The Fairy

Polyantha
Plant height: 1½–2 ft.
Blossom width:
1–1½ in.
Blooms late in season
with excellent repeat

Little or no fragrance
Winter hardy
Disease resistant
p. 315

Boy Crazy

Dwarf Shrub
Plant height: 2–2½ ft.
Blossom width:
1½–2 in.
Heavy midseason
bloom with excellent
repeat

Not fragrant
Winter hardy
Disease resistant, but
may require
protection from
black spot
p. 292

Constance Spry

Shrub
Plant height: 5–6 ft.
Blossom width:
4½–5 in.
Blooms in midseason
with no repeat

Strong myrrh scent
Winter hardy
Disease resistant
p. 295

Bonica

Shrub
Plant height: 3–5 ft.
Blossom width:
1–2 in.
Long midseason
bloom with excellent
repeat

Not fragrant
Winter hardy
Disease resistant
p. 291

China Doll

Polyantha
Plant height: to 1½ ft.
Blossom width:
1–2 in.
Blooms late in season
continuously until
frost

Slight fragrance
Winter hardy
Disease resistant
p. 294

Robin Hood

Hybrid Musk
Plant height: 5–7 ft.
Blossom width: ³/₄ in.
Blooms in midseason
with excellent repeat

Moderate fragrance
Winter hardy
Disease resistant
p. 311

Marguerite Hilling

Shrub
Plant height: 6–8 ft.
Blossom width: 4 in.
Blooms in midseason
with excellent repeat

Little or no fragrance
Winter hardy
Disease resistant
p. 306

Erfurt

Hybrid Musk
Plant height: 5–6 ft.
Blossom width:
3½ in.
Blooms well all season

Strong fragrance
Winter hardy
Disease resistant
p. 298

Belinda

Hybrid Musk
Plant height: 4–6 ft.
Blossom width: ¾ in.
Blooms in midseason
with good repeat

Light fragrance
Winter hardy
Disease resistant
p. 290

Baby Faurax

Polyantha
Plant height: 8–12 in.
Blossom width: 2 in.
Blooms in midseason
or later

Little or no fragrance
Winter hardy with
some protection
Disease resistant
p. 289

Birdie Blye

Shrub
Plant height: 4–5 ft.
Blossom width:
3½–4 in.
Blooms in midseason
with fair repeat

Slight fragrance
Winter hardy
Disease resistant
p. 291

Delicata

Hybrid Rugosa
Plant height:
3½–4½ ft.
Blossom width:
3–3½ in.
Blooms abundantly in
early to midseason
with good repeat

Very strong clove
fragrance
Winter hardy
Disease free
p. 296

Belle Poitevine

Hybrid Rugosa
Plant height: 7–9 ft.
Blossom width:
3½–4 in.
Blooms profusely in
early season with good
repeat

Strong clove
fragrance
Winter hardy
Disease resistant
p. 290

Hansa

Hybrid Rugosa
Plant height: to 5 ft.
Blossom width:
3–3½ in.
Blooms early to
midseason with good
repeat

Clove fragrance
Winter hardy
Disease resistant
p. 303

Gartendirektor
Otto Linne

Shrub
Plant height:
3½–4½ ft.
Blossom width:
1½–2 in.
Blooms in midseason
with good repeat

Little or no fragrance
Winter hardy
Disease resistant
p. 301

Roseraie de l'Haÿ

Hybrid Rugosa
Plant height: 7–9 ft.
Blossom width:
4–4½ in.
Blooms very early in
season with
occasional repeat

Strong fragrance
Winter hardy
Disease free
p. 312

Lavender Lassie

Hybrid Musk
Plant height: 5–7 ft.
Blossom width: 3 in.
Blooms in midseason
with good repeat

Strong fragrance
Winter hardy
Disease resistant
p. 305

Elmshorn

Shrub
Plant height: 5–6 ft.
Blossom width:
1½ in.
Blooms in midseason
with good repeat

Slight fragrance
Winter hardy
Disease resistant
p. 297

F. J. Grootendorst

Hybrid Rugosa
Plant height: 6–8 ft.
Blossom width:
1½ in.
Blooms profusely in
midseason with good
repeat

Not fragrant
Winter hardy
Disease resistant
p. 298

All That Jazz

Shrub
Plant height: 5 ft.
Blossom width:
5–5½ in.
Blooms well all season

Fragrant
Winter hardy
Disease free
p. 289

Esprit

Shrub
Plant height: 3–3½ ft.
Blossom width:
3–3½ in.
Excellent all-season
bloom

Not fragrant
Winter hardy
Disease resistant
p. 298

Will Scarlet

*Hybrid Musk
Plant height: to 6 ft.
Blossom width: 3 in.
Blooms in midseason
with good repeat*

*Moderately strong
fragrance
Winter hardy
Disease resistant
p. 318*

Margo Koster

*Polyantha
Plant height: to 1 ft.
Blossom width:
1–1½ in.
Blooms late in season
with excellent repeat*

*Slight fragrance
Winter hardy
Disease resistant
p. 306*

Fred Loads

Shrub
Plant height: 4½–5 ft.
Blossom width:
3–3½ in.
Blooms well all season

Little or no fragrance
Winter hardy
Disease resistant
p. 300

Alchymist

Shrub
Plant height: 8–12 ft.
Blossom width:
3½–4 in.
Blooms early to
midseason with no
repeat

Fragrant
Winter hardy
Disease resistant
p. 288

Buff Beauty

Hybrid Musk
Plant height: to 6 ft.
Blossom width: 3 in.
Blooms in midseason
with good repeat

Fragrant
Winter hardy
Disease resistant
p. 292

Westerland

Shrub
Plant height: 5–6 ft.
Blossom width: 3 in.
Blooms in midseason
with no repeat

Strong fragrance
Winter hardy
Disease resistant
p. 317

Agnes

Hybrid Rugosa
Plant height: to 5 ft.
Blossom width:
3–3½ in.
Blooms early to
midseason

Strong fragrance
Winter hardy
Disease resistant
p. 288

Goldbusch

Shrub
Plant height: to 5 ft.
Blossom width:
2½–3 in.
Blooms midseason or
later with good repeat

Fragrant
Winter hardy
Disease resistant
p. 302

Maigold

*Shrub
Plant height: to 5 ft.
Blossom width: 4 in.
Blooms early to
midseason with no
repeat*

*Strong fragrance
Winter hardy
Disease resistant
p. 306*

Golden Wings

*Shrub
Plant height:
4½–5½ ft.
Blossom width:
4–5 in.
Blooms profusely all
season*

*Slight fragrance
Winter hardy except
in very severe
climates
Disease resistant
p. 302*

Harison's Yellow

Shrub
Plant height: 5–7 ft.
Blossom width:
2–2½ in.
Blooms very early in
season with no repeat

Light, sweet
fragrance
Winter hardy
Disease resistant
p. 303

Frühlingsgold

Hybrid Spinosissima
Plant height: 5–7 ft.
Blossom width:
3–3½ in.
Blooms early in season
with no repeat

Fragrant
Winter hardy
Disease free
p. 300

Cocktail

Shrub
Plant height: 5–6 ft.
Blossom width:
2–2½ in.
Blooms in midseason
with good repeat

Light fragrance
May require winter
protection in extreme
climates
Disease resistant
p. 294

Morgenrot

Shrub
Plant height: 3 ft.
Blossom width:
2½–3 in.
Blooms in midseason
with excellent repeat

Slight fragrance
Winter hardy
Disease resistant
p. 307

Ralph's Creeper

Ground Cover
Plant spread: 4–6 ft.
Blossom width:
1½–2 in.
Blooms in midseason
with good repeat

Fragrant
May need winter
protection in severe
climates
Disease resistant
p. 310

Robusta

Hybrid Rugosa
Plant height: 6–8 ft.
Blossom width:
2½ in.
Blooms early in season
with excellent repeat

Slight fragrance
Winter hardy
Disease resistant
p. 311

La Sevillana

*Shrub/Ground Cover
Plant height and
spread: 3 ft.
Blossom width:
2–2½ in.
Profuse midseason
bloom with excellent
repeat*

*Little or no fragrance
Winter hardy
Disease resistant
p. 304*

The Squire

*English Rose
Plant height: 3–4 ft.
Blossom width: 4 in.
Blooms in midseason
with fair repeat*

*Fragrant
Winter hardy
Disease resistant
p. 316*

Stretch Johnson

Shrub
Plant height: 4–5 ft.
Blossom width: 3 in.
Blooms in midseason
with good repeat

Slight fragrance
Winter hardy
Disease resistant
p. 314

Scarlet Meidiland

Ground Cover
Plant spread: 6 ft.
Blossom width:
1–2 in.
Profuse bloom in
midseason with
intermittent repeat

Not fragrant
Winter hardy
Disease resistant
p. 313

Fisherman's Friend   *English Rose*
Plant height: 3–4 ft.   *Fragrant*
Blossom width: *Winter hardy*
5–6 in.   *Disease resistant*
Blooms in midseason   *p. 299*
with good repeat

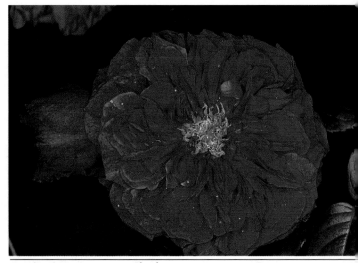

Cardinal Hume   *Shrub*
Plant height: 4 ft.   *Fragrant*
Blossom width: *Winter hardy*
1½ in.   *Disease resistant*
Excellent all-season   *p. 293*
bloom

Othello

English Rose
Plant height: 5–6 ft.
Blossom width:
5–6 in.
Blooms in midseason
with excellent repeat

Very fragrant
Winter hardy
Disease resistant
p. 308

Linda Campbell

Hybrid Rugosa
Plant height: 3–5 ft.
Blossom width: 3 in.
Blooms in midseason
with good repeat

Not fragrant
Winter hardy
Disease resistant
p. 305

Carefree Beauty

Shrub
Plant height: 5–6 ft.
Blossom width:
4–4½ in.
Excellent all-season
bloom

Fragrant
Winter hardy
Disease resistant
p. 293

Raubritter

Shrub/Ground Cover
Plant spread: 7–10 ft.
Blossom width:
1½ in.
Long midseason
bloom with occasional
repeat

Little fragrance
Extremely winter
hardy
Disease resistant, but
may need protection
from mildew
p. 311

Carefree Wonder

Shrub
Plant height: 4–5 ft.
Blossom width:
4–5 in.
Heavy midseason
bloom with good
repeat

Slight fragrance
Winter hardy
Disease resistant
p. 293

Ferdy

Ground Cover
Plant spread: 5–7 ft.
Blossom width: 1 in.
Long, abundant
early-season bloom
with very little repeat

Not fragrant
Winter hardy
Disease free
p. 299

Heritage

English Rose
Plant height: 5–6 ft.
Blossom width:
4½–5 in.
Blooms in midseason
with good repeat

Very fragrant
Winter hardy
Disease resistant
p. 304

Sweet Juliet

English Rose
Plant height: 3½ ft.
Blossom width:
3–3½ in.
Blooms in midseason
with good repeat

Fragrant
Winter hardy
Disease resistant
p. 315

The Reeve

English Rose
Plant height: 3–4 ft.
Blossom width:
3–4 in.
Blooms in midseason
with good repeat

Very fragrant
Winter hardy
Disease resistant
p. 316

Bredon

English Rose
Plant height: 2½–3 ft.
Blossom width:
2½ in.
Good midseason
bloom with fair repeat

Fragrant
Winter hardy
Disease resistant, but
may need protection
from mildew
p. 292

Mary Rose

English Rose
Plant height: 4–6 ft.
Blossom width:
4–4½ in.
Excellent all-season
bloom

Fragrant
Winter hardy
Disease resistant
p. 307

Morden Centennial

Shrub
Plant height: 3 ft.
Blossom width:
3½–4 in.
Blooms in midseason
with good repeat

Light fragrance
Winter hardy
Disease resistant
p. 307

Romanze

Shrub
Plant height: 4–6 ft.
Blossom width:
3½–4 in.
Good all-season
bloom

Slight fragrance
Winter hardy
Disease resistant
p. 312

William Baffin

Shrub
Plant height: 8–12 ft.
Blossom width:
3–4 in.
Blooms in midseason
with excellent repeat

Not fragrant
Very winter hardy
Disease free
p. 317

David Thompson

Hybrid Rugosa
Plant height: 4 ft.
Blossom width:
2½ in.
Excellent all-season
bloom

Very fragrant
Winter hardy
Disease resistant
p. 296

Lavender Dream

Shrub
Plant height: 4–5 ft.
Blossom width:
2–2½ in.
Blooms in midseason
with excellent repeat

Not fragrant
Winter hardy
Disease resistant
p. 305

Gertrude Jekyll

English Rose
Plant height: 5–8 ft.
Blossom width:
4¹/₂–5 in.
Blooms in midseason
with sporadic repeat

Very fragrant
Winter hardy
Disease resistant
p. 301

Wife of Bath

English Rose
Plant height: 2–3 ft.
Blossom width:
2¹/₂–3 in.
Blooms in midseason
with good repeat

Very fragrant
Winter hardy
Disease resistant
p. 317

Pearl Drift

Shrub
Plant height: 3 ft.
Blossom width:
3–3½ in.
Blooms in midseason
with good repeat

Slight fragrance
Winter hardy
Disease resistant
p. 308

The Countryman

English Rose
Plant height: to 5 ft.
Blossom width:
3½–4 in.
Blooms in midseason;
repeat bloom
unreliable

Very fragrant
Winter hardy
Disease resistant
p. 315

Distant Drums   *Shrub*   *Very fragrant*
                     Plant height: 4–5 ft.   *Winter hardy*
                     Blossom width: *Disease resistant*
                     4–4½ in.   *p. 296*
                     Blooms late in season,
                     with excellent repeat

Dove   *English Rose*   *Strong fragrance*
                     Plant height: 2½–3 ft.   *Winter hardy*
                     Blossom width: *Disease resistant*
                     2–2½ in.   *p. 297*
                     Blooms in midseason
                     with good repeat

Prosperity

Hybrid Musk
Plant height: 6–8 ft.
Blossom width:
1–1½ in.
Blooms late in season
with reliable repeat

Fragrant
Winter hardy
Disease resistant
p. 310

Fair Bianca

English Rose
Plant height: 2½–3 ft.
Blossom width:
3–3½ in.
Blooms in midseason
with good repeat

Strong fragrance
Winter hardy
Disease resistant
p. 299

Abraham Darby

English Rose
Plant height: 5–6 ft.
Blossom width:
4½–5 in.
Blooms in midseason
with good repeat

Very fragrant
Moderately winter
hardy
Disease resistant but
requires protection
from black spot
p. 287

Belle Story

English Rose
Plant height: 3–4 ft.
Blossom width: 4 in.
Blooms in midseason
with good repeat

Fragrant
Winter hardy
Disease resistant
p. 290

Windrush

Shrub
Plant height: 4–6 ft.
Blossom width: 5 in.
Blooms early in season
with excellent repeat

Fragrant
Winter hardy
Disease resistant
p. 318

Sally Holmes

Shrub
Plant height: 7–10 ft.
Blossom width:
3½ in.
Excellent all-season
bloom

Slight fragrance
Winter hardy
Disease resistant
p. 313

Topaz Jewel
Hybrid Rugosa
Plant height: 5 ft.
Blossom width:
3½–4 in.
Good all-season
bloom

Fragrant
Winter hardy
Disease resistant
p. 316

Graham Thomas
English Rose
Plant height: 5–7 ft.
Blossom width:
3½–4 in.
Blooms late in season
with fair repeat

Very fragrant
Winter hardy
Disease resistant
p. 302

Perdita

English Rose
Plant height: 2½–3 ft.
Blossom width:
2½–3 in.
Blooms in midseason
with good repeat

Variable fragrance
Winter hardy
Disease resistant
p. 309

Rosy Carpet

Ground Cover
Plant spread: 4 ft.
Blossom width: 1 in.
Profuse bloom in
midseason with
autumn repeat

Fragrant
Winter hardy
Disease resistant
p. 312

English Garden

English Rose
Plant height: 2½–3 ft.
Blossom width:
3½ in.
Blooms in midseason
with fair repeat

Fragrant
Winter hardy
Disease resistant
p. 297

Pink Meidiland

Shrub
Plant height: 4 ft.
Blossom width:
2–2½ in.
Blooms well in
midseason, repeats in
autumn

Not fragrant
Winter hardy
Disease resistant
p. 310

Old Garden

Roses

Rosette Delizy

Tea
Plant height: 3½–4 ft.
Blossom width:
3½–4 in.
Blooms in midseason
with good repeat

Spicy fragrance
Not winter hardy
Disease resistant
p. 351

Lady Hillingdon

Tea
Plant height: 2½–3 ft.
Blossom width:
3½ in.
Blooms early in season
with good repeat

Fragrant
Not winter hardy
Disease resistant
p. 338

Gloire de Dijon

Tea
Plant height: 10–12 ft.
Blossom width: 4 in.
Blooms early in season
with good repeat

Fragrant
Not winter hardy
Disease resistant
p. 334

Celine Forestier

Noisette
Plant height: 10–15 ft.
Blossom width:
2–2½ in.
Blooms in midseason
with excellent repeat

Very fragrant
Not winter hardy
Disease resistant
p. 328

Madame Alfred Carrière

Noisette
Plant height: 10–15 ft.
Blossom width:
2½–3 in.
Blooms in midseason
with excellent repeat

Fragrant
Moderately winter hardy
Disease resistant
p. 341

Madame Legras de St. Germain

Alba
Plant height: 6–7 ft.
Blossom width:
3½ in.
Blooms early in season
with no repeat

Very sweet fragrance
Winter hardy
Disease resistant
p. 343

Frau Karl Druschki

Hybrid Perpetual
Plant height: 5–7 ft.
Blossom width:
4–4½ in.
Blooms in midseason
with good repeat in
fall

Little or no fragrance
Winter hardy
Disease resistant
p. 333

Maxima

Alba
Plant height: 6–8 ft.
Blossom width:
2½–3 in.
Blooms profusely,
early to midseason
with no repeat

Very fragrant
Winter hardy
Disease free
p. 346

Madame Hardy

Damask
Plant height: 5–5½ ft.
Blossom width:
3–3½ in.
Blooms in midseason
with no repeat

Fragrant
Winter hardy
Disease free
p. 342

Sombreuil

Tea
Plant height: 12–15 ft.
Blossom width:
3½–4 in.
Blooms early to
midseason with good
repeat

Fragrant
Moderately winter
hardy
Disease resistant
p. 351

Boule de Neige

Bourbon
Plant height: 4–5 ft.
Blossom width:
2½–3½ in.
Blooms in midseason
with good repeat

Fragrant
Winter hardy
Disease resistant
p. 327

Madame Plantier

Alba
Plant height: 5–6 ft.
Blossom width:
2½–3 in.
Blooms profusely in
midseason with no
repeat

Very fragrant
Winter hardy
Disease free
p. 344

Mabel Morrison

Hybrid Perpetual
Plant height: 4–4½ ft.
Blossom width:
3½–4 in.
Blooms well in
midseason with good
repeat in fall

Fragrant
Winter hardy
Disease resistant
p. 341

Champneys' Pink Cluster

Noisette
Plant height: 8–12 ft.
Blossom width: 2 in.
Blooms in midseason
with excellent repeat

Very fragrant
Not winter hardy
Disease resistant
p. 329

Félicité et Perpétue

Hybrid Sempervirens
Plant height: to 20 ft.
Blossom width:
1½ in.
Blooms long, late in
season, with no repeat

Fragrant
Not winter hardy
Disease free
p. 333

Blush Noisette

Noisette
Plant height: 8–12 ft.
Blossom width: 2 in.
Blooms in midseason
with excellent repeat

Very fragrant
Not winter hardy
Disease resistant
p. 326

Mary Washington

Noisette
Plant height: 8–12 ft.
Blossom width:
2½ in.
Blooms in midseason
with good repeat

Fragrant
Winter hardy
with protection
Disease resistant
p. 346

Stanwell Perpetual

Hybrid Spinosissima
Plant height: to 5 ft.
Blossom width:
3½ in.
Blooms early in season
with good repeat

Fragrant
Winter hardy
Disease resistant
p. 352

Souvenir de la Malmaison

Bourbon
Plant height: to 2 ft.
Blossom width:
4½–5 in.
Blooms sparsely in midseason or later with sparse fall repeat

Strong, spicy fragrance
Winter hardy with some protection
Disease resistant
p. 352

Alfred de Dalmas

Moss
Plant height: 2½–3 ft.
Blossom width:
2½–3 in.
Blooms in midseason with fair repeat

Fragrant
Winter hardy
Disease resistant
p. 323

Duchesse de Montebello

Gallica
Plant height: to 5 ft.
Blossom width:
2½–3 in.
Blooms midseason or
later with no repeat

Fragrant
Winter hardy
Disease resistant
p. 332

Général Kléber

Moss
Plant height: to 5 ft.
Blossom width:
2½–3 in.
Blooms midseason or
later with no repeat

Very fragrant
Winter hardy
Disease resistant
p. 334

Maiden's Blush

Alba
Plant height: 5–6 ft.
Blossom width:
2½–3 in.
Blooms very
profusely, early to
midseason, with no
repeat

Very fragrant
Winter hardy
Disease free
p. 344

York and Lancaster

Damask
Plant height: 3–4 ft.
Blossom width:
2½–3 in.
Blooms in midseason
with no repeat

Fragrant
Winter hardy
Disease free
p. 355

Chloris

Alba
Plant height: 5–6 ft.
Blossom width:
3½ in.
Blooms early in season
with no repeat

Intense, sweet
fragrance
Winter hardy
Disease free
p. 329

Gloire de Guilan

Damask
Plant height: 3–5 ft.
Blossom width: 3 in.
Blooms profusely,
early to midseason,
with no repeat

Intensely fragrant
Winter hardy
Disease free
p. 335

Marchioness of Londonderry

Hybrid Perpetual
Plant height: 5–7 ft.
Blossom width:
4½–5 in.
Blooms profusely in
midseason with
occasional repeat in
fall

Very fragrant
Winter hardy
Disease resistant
p. 345

Gloire des Mousseuses

Moss
Plant height: 2½–3 ft.
Blossom width: 3 in.
Blooms in midseason
with no repeat

Very fragrant
Winter hardy
Disease resistant
p. 335

Belle Amour

Alba
Plant height: 5–6 ft.
Blossom width:
3½ in.
Blooms profusely,
early in season

Intense, spicy scent
mixed with a faint
bitterness
Winter hardy
Disease free
p. 325

Ispahan

Damask
Plant height: 3–4 ft.
Blossom width:
2½–3 in.
Blooms for long
period in midseason
with no repeat

Very fragrant
Winter hardy
Disease free
p. 337

Belle Isis

Gallica
Plant height: 2½–3 ft.
Blossom width:
2½–3 in.
Blooms in midseason
with no repeat

Fragrant
Winter hardy
Disease resistant
p. 326

Rose des Peintres

Centifolia
Plant height: 5–7 ft.
Blossom width:
3–3½ in.
Blooms in midseason
with no repeat

Fragrant
Winter hardy
Disease resistant
p. 350

Duchesse de Brabant   *Tea*
Plant height: 3–5 ft.
Blossom width:
4–5 in.
Blooms early to
midseason with
excellent repeat

Very fragrant
Not reliably winter
hardy
Disease resistant
p. 331

Madame Pierre Oger   *Bourbon*
Plant height:
4½–5½ ft.
Blossom width:
3–3½ in.
Blooms abundantly in
midseason with good
repeat in fall

Very fragrant
Winter hardy
Disease resistant
p. 344

Georg Arends

Hybrid Perpetual
Plant height: 4–5 ft.
Blossom width:
4–4½ in.
Blooms in midseason
with good repeat in
fall

Very fragrant
Winter hardy
Disease resistant
p. 334

Louis Gimard

Moss
Plant height: 4–5 ft.
Blossom width:
3–3½ in.
Blooms in midseason
with no repeat

Very fragrant
Winter hardy
Disease resistant
p. 341

Gloire de France

Gallica
Plant height: 2–2½ ft.
Blossom width:
2½–3 in.
Blooms in midseason
with no repeat

Fragrant
Winter hardy
Disease resistant
p. 335

Salet

Moss
Plant height: 4–5 ft.
Blossom width:
2½–3 in.
Blooms in midseason
with fair repeat in fall

Fragrant
Winter hardy
Disease resistant
p. 351

Madame Louis Lévêque

Moss
Plant height: 4–5 ft.
Blossom width:
3–3½ in.
Blooms in midseason;
some repeat in fall

Very fragrant
Winter hardy
Disease resistant
p. 343

Celestial

Alba
Plant height: 4½–5 ft.
Blossom width:
3½ in.
Blooms early in season
with no repeat

Very sweet fragrance
Winter hardy
Disease free
p. 328

Celsiana

Damask
Plant height: 3½–4 ft.
Blossom width:
3½–4 in.
Blooms for long
period in midseason
with no repeat

Intensely fragrant
Winter hardy
Disease free
p. 328

Common Moss

Moss
Plant height: 5–7 ft.
Blossom width: 3 in.
Blooms in midseason
with no repeat

Very fragrant
Winter hardy
Disease resistant
p. 330

Baroness Rothschild

*Hybrid Perpetual
Plant height: 4–6 ft.
Blossom width:
5½–6 in.
Blooms profusely in
midseason with fair
repeat in fall*

*Very fragrant
Winter hardy
Disease resistant
p. 324*

Old Blush

*China
Plant height: 3–4 ft.
Blossom width: 3 in.
Blooms well all season*

*Little or no fragrance
Not winter hardy
Disease resistant
p. 347*

Fantin-Latour

Centifolia
Plant height: 5–6 ft.
Blossom width:
3–3½ in.
Blooms profusely in
midseason with no
repeat

Very fragrant
Winter hardy
Disease resistant
p. 332

Petite de Hollande

Centifolia
Plant height: 3½–4 ft.
Blossom width:
2–2½ in.
Blooms in midseason
for a long period with
no repeat

Very fragrant
Winter hardy
Disease resistant
p. 348

Comte de Chambord *Portland*
Plant height: 3½–4 ft.
Blossom width: 3 in.
Blooms in midseason
with good repeat

Very fragrant
Winter hardy
Disease resistant
p. 331

La Ville de Bruxelles *Damask*
Plant height: to 5 ft.
Blossom width:
3½–4 in.
Blooms abundantly in
midseason with no
repeat

Very fragrant
Winter hardy
Disease free
p. 339

Louise Odier

Bourbon
Plant height:
4½–5½ ft.
Blossom width:
3½ in.
Blooms abundantly in
midseason with good
repeat

Very fragrant
Winter hardy
Disease resistant
p. 340

Archduke Charles

China
Plant height: 2–3 ft.
Blossom width:
2½–3 in.
Blooms well all season

Fruity fragrance
Not winter hardy
Disease resistant
p. 324

Empress Josephine

Gallica
Plant height: 3–4 ft.
Blossom width:
3–3½ in.
Blooms in midseason
with no repeat

Slight fragrance
Winter hardy
Disease resistant
p. 332

Maman Cochet

Tea
Plant height: 3–3½ ft.
Blossom width:
3½–4 in.
Blooms in midseason
with excellent repeat

Fragrant
Not winter hardy
Disease resistant
p. 345

Königin von Dänemark

Alba
Plant height: to 6 ft.
Blossom width: 3½ in.
Blooms early in season with no repeat

Intense, sweet fragrance
Winter hardy
Disease free
p. 338

Hermosa

China
Plant height: 3–4 ft.
Blossom width: 3 in.
Blooms well all season

Fragrant
Not winter hardy
Disease resistant
p. 337

La Reine Victoria

Bourbon
Plant height:
4½–5½ ft.
Blossom width:
3–3½ in.
Blooms abundantly in
midseason with good
repeat in fall

Very fragrant
Winter hardy
Disease resistant
p. 339

Maréchal Davoust

Moss
Plant height: to 5 ft.
Blossom width: 3 in.
Blooms in midseason
with no repeat

Very fragrant
Winter hardy
Disease resistant
p. 346

Madame Lauriol de Barny

Bourbon
Plant height: to 6 ft.
Blossom width:
3½–4 in.
Blooms in midseason
with occasional repeat

Fruity fragrance
Winter hardy
Disease resistant
p. 343

La Noblesse

Centifolia
Plant height: to 5 ft.
Blossom width:
3–3½ in.
Blooms profusely,
midseason or later,
with no repeat

Extremely fragrant
Winter hardy
Disease free
p. 339

Little Gem

Moss
Plant height: to 4 ft.
Blossom width: 2 in.
Blooms in midseason
with no repeat

Fragrant
Winter hardy
Disease resistant
p. 340

Crested Moss

Moss
Plant height: 5–7 ft.
Blossom width:
3–3½ in.
Blooms in midseason
with no repeat

Very fragrant
Winter hardy
Disease resistant
p. 331

**Madame de la
Roche-Lambert**

*Moss
Plant height: 4–5 ft.
Blossom width: 3 in.
Blooms in midseason
with no repeat*

*Very fragrant
Winter hardy
Disease resistant
p. 342*

Madame Isaac Pereire

*Bourbon
Plant height: 5–6 ft.
Blossom width:
3½–4 in.
Blooms profusely in
midseason with fair
repeat*

*Intense fragrance
Winter hardy
Disease resistant
p. 342*

Baronne Prévost

Hybrid Perpetual
Plant height: 4–6 ft.
Blossom width:
3½–4 in.
Blooms well in
midseason with good
repeat in fall

Fragrant
Winter hardy
Disease resistant
p. 325

Ulrich Brunner Fils

Hybrid Perpetual
Plant height: 5–7 ft.
Blossom width:
3½–4 in.
Blooms in midseason
with occasional repeat
in fall

Very fragrant
Winter hardy
Disease resistant
p. 354

Rosa gallica officinalis

Gallica
Plant height: 3–3½ ft.
Blossom width:
3–3½ in.
Blooms in midseason
with no repeat

Fragrant
Winter hardy
Disease resistant
p. 349

Zéphirine Drouhin

Bourbon
Plant height: 8–12 ft.
Blossom width:
3½–4 in.
Blooms well all season

Very fragrant
Winter hardy
Disease resistant
p. 356

Complicata
Gallica
Plant height: to 5 ft.
Blossom width:
4–4¹/₂ in.
Blooms in midseason
with no repeat

Fragrant
Winter hardy
Disease resistant
p. 330

American Beauty
Hybrid Perpetual
Plant height: 5–6 ft.
Blossom width:
5–6 in.
Blooms in midseason
with fair repeat in fall

Very fragrant
Winter hardy
Disease resistant
p. 324

Paul Neyron

Hybrid Perpetual
Plant height: 5–6 ft.
Blossom width:
4¹/₂–5¹/₂ in.
Blooms in midseason
with fair repeat in fall

Fragrant
Winter hardy
Disease resistant
p. 347

Tour de Malakoff

Centifolia
Plant height: 6–7 ft.
Blossom width:
3–3¹/₂ in.
Blooms in midseason
with no repeat

Very fragrant
Winter hardy
Disease free
p. 353

Reines des Violettes

*Hybrid Perpetual
Plant height: 5–6 ft.
Blossom width: 3 in.
Blooms profusely in
midseason with
occasional sparse
repeat*

*Very fragrant
Winter hardy
Disease resistant
p. 348*

Cardinal de Richelieu

*Gallica
Plant height: 2½–3 ft.
Blossom width:
2½–3 in.
Blooms in midseason
with no repeat*

*Fragrant
Winter hardy
Disease resistant
p. 327*

The Bishop

Centifolia
Plant height: 4–5 ft.
Blossom width:
2½–3 in.
Blooms early to
midseason with no
repeat

Fragrant
Winter hardy
Disease resistant
p. 353

Rose du Roi

Portland
Plant height: 3–4 ft.
Blossom width:
2½ in.
Blooms in midseason
with good repeat

Very fragrant
Winter hardy
Disease resistant
p. 350

Belle de Crècy

Gallica
Plant height:
3¹/₂–4¹/₂ ft.
Blossom width:
2¹/₂–3 in.
Blooms for long
period in midseason
with no repeat

Very fragrant
Winter hardy
Disease resistant
p. 326

Tuscany Superb

Gallica
Plant height: 3–4 ft.
Blossom width:
3¹/₂–4 in.
Blooms in midseason
with no repeat

Very fragrant
Winter hardy
Disease resistant
p. 354

Tuscany

Gallica
Plant height: 3–4 ft.
Blossom width:
3–3½ in.
Blooms in midseason
with no repeat

Very fragrant
Winter hardy
Disease resistant
p. 354

Roger Lambelin

Hybrid Perpetual
Plant height: 2–2½ ft.
Blossom width:
2½–3 in.
Blooms in midseason
with fair repeat in fall

Fragrant
Winter hardy
Disease resistant
p. 348

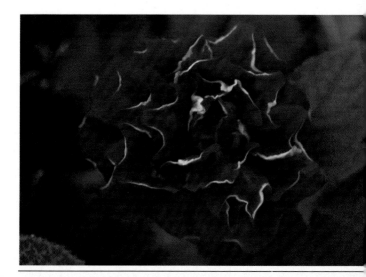

Nuits de Young

Moss
Plant height: to 5 ft.
Blossom width:
2½ in.
Blooms in midseason
with no repeat

Very fragrant
Winter hardy
Disease resistant
p. 347

Baron Girod de l'Ain

Hybrid Perpetual
Plant height: 4–5 ft.
Blossom width: 4 in.
Blooms well in
midseason with fair
repeat in fall

Fragrant
Winter hardy
Disease resistant
p. 325

Gloire des Rosomanes

China
Plant height:
3½–4½ ft.
Blossom width: 3 in.
Blooms well all season

Little or no fragrance
Moderately hardy
Disease resistant
p. 336

Rose de Rescht

Damask
Plant height:
2½–3½ ft.
Blossom width:
2–2½ in.
Blooms in midseason
with good repeat

Very fragrant
Winter hardy
Disease resistant
p. 350

Grüss an Teplitz

Bourbon
Plant height: 5–6 ft.
Blossom width:
3–3½ in.
Blooms profusely in
midseason with good
repeat

Strong, spicy
fragrance
Winter hardy
Disease resistant
p. 336

Henry Nevard

Hybrid Perpetual
Plant height: 4–5 ft.
Blossom width:
4–4½ in.
Blooms well in
midseason with good
repeat in fall

Very fragrant
Winter hardy
Disease resistant
p. 337

Henri Martin

Moss
Plant height: to 5 ft.
Blossom width:
2½ in.
Blooms midseason or
later with no repeat

Fragrant
Winter hardy
Disease resistant
p. 336

John Hopper

Hybrid Perpetual
Plant height: 5–7 ft.
Blossom width: 4 in.
Blooms well in
midseason with
occasional repeat in
fall

Very fragrant
Winter hardy
Disease resistant
p. 338

William Lobb

Moss
Plant height: 4–5 ft.
Blossom width: 3 in.
Blooms in midseason
with no repeat

Very fragrant
Winter hardy
Disease resistant
p. 355

Charles de Mills

Gallica
Plant height: 4½–5 ft.
Blossom width:
3–3½ in.
Blooms in midseason
with no repeat

Fragrant
Winter hardy
Disease resistant
p. 329

Ferdinand Pichard   *Hybrid Perpetual*   *Fragrant*
                        Plant height: 4–5 ft.   *Winter hardy*
                        Blossom width: *Disease resistant*
                        3–3½ in.   *p. 333*
                        Blooms well in
                        midseason with fair
                        repeat

Rosa Mundi   *Gallica*   *Fragrant*
                 Plant height: 3–3½ ft.   *Winter hardy*
                 Blossom width: *Disease resistant*
                 3–3½ in.   *p. 349*
                 Blooms in midseason
                 with no repeat

**Commandant
Beaurepaire**

*Bourbon
Plant height: 4–5 ft.
Blossom width:
3–3½ in.
Blooms in midseason
with sparse repeat
bloom*

*Fragrant
Winter hardy
Disease resistant
p. 330*

Camaieux

*Gallica
Plant height: 3–3½ ft.
Blossom width:
3–3½ in.
Blooms in midseason
with no repeat*

*Fragrant
Winter hardy
Disease resistant
p. 327*

Striped Moss

Moss
Plant height: 5–6 ft.
Blossom width:
1½–2 in.
Blooms in midseason
with no repeat

Fragrant
Winter hardy
Disease resistant
p. 353

*Rosa centifolia
variegata*

Centifolia
Plant height: 5–7 ft.
Blossom width:
3–3½ in.
Blooms profusely in
midseason with no
repeat

Fragrant
Winter hardy
Disease resistant
p. 349

Variegata di Bologna

Bourbon
Plant height: 5–7 ft.
Blossom width:
3½–4 in.
Blooms in midseason
with no repeat

Fragrant
Winter hardy
Disease resistant
p. 355

Leda

Damask
Plant height: 2½–3 ft.
Blossom width:
2½–3 in.
Blooms in midseason
with no repeat

Fragrant
Winter hardy
Disease free
p. 340

Floribundas

Sunsprite

*Plant height: 2½–3 ft.
Blossom width: 3 in.
Blooms well in
midseason with good
repeat*

*Very fragrant
Winter hardy
Disease resistant
p. 373*

Princess Alice

*Plant height: 3½–5 ft.
Blossom width:
2½–3 in.
Blooms well late in
season with regular
repeat*

*Slight fragrance
Winter hardy
Disease resistant
p. 370*

H. C. Anderson

Plant height: 3–4 ft.
Blossom width:
2½–3 in.
Blooms very well in
midseason with good
repeat

Slight fragrance
Winter hardy
Disease resistant
p. 365

Ivory Fashion

Plant height: 3½–4 ft.
Blossom width:
3½ in.
Blooms abundantly in
midseason with good
repeat

Fragrant
Winter hardy
Disease resistant
p. 367

French Lace

*Plant height: 3–3½ ft.
Blossom width:
3½–4 in.
Blooms well in
midseason with good
repeat*

*Moderate fragrance
Winter hardy
Disease resistant
p. 364*

Iceberg

*Plant height: to 4 ft.
Blossom width: 3 in.
Blooms early to
midseason with
continuous repeat*

*Fragrant
Winter hardy
Disease resistant, but
susceptible to black
spot
p. 366*

Class Act

Plant height: 3–4 ft.
Blossom width:
3–3½ in.
Blooms in midseason
with good repeat

Slight fragrance
Winter hardy
Disease resistant
p. 360

Margaret Merril

Plant height:
3½–4½ ft.
Blossom width:
4–4½ in.
Excellent all-season
bloom

Powerful fragrance
Winter hardy
Disease resistant
p. 368

Evening Star

*Plant height: 3–3½ ft.
Blossom width:
4–4½ in.
Blooms in midseason
with fair repeat*

*Slight fragrance
Not winter hardy
Disease resistant
p. 362*

Grüss an Aachen

*Plant height: 2–2½ ft.
Blossom width:
3–3½ in.
Blooms early to
midseason with good
repeat*

*Fragrant
Winter hardy
Disease resistant
p. 365*

| **Lavender Pinocchio** | *Plant height: 2½–3 ft.* *Blossom width:* *3–3½ in.* *Blooms well in midseason with fair repeat* | *Fragrant* *Winter hardy* *Disease resistant* *p. 367* |

| **Poulsen's Pearl** | *Plant height: 2½–3 ft.* *Blossom width:* *2½–3 in.* *Blooms in midseason with good repeat* | *Fragrant* *Winter hardy* *Disease resistant* *p. 370* |

Escapade

Plant height: 2½–3 ft.
Blossom width: 3 in.
Blooms very well in
midseason with
excellent repeat

Fragrant
Winter hardy
Disease resistant
p. 362

Pleasure

Plant height: 3 ft.
Blossom width: 4 in.
Blooms profusely in
midseason, with
excellent repeat

Slight fragrance
Winter hardy
Disease resistant
p. 369

Gene Boerner | Plant height: 4–5 ft. Blossom width: 3–3½ in. Blooms very well in midseason with excellent repeat | Little or no fragrance Winter hardy Disease resistant p. 365

Angel Face | Plant height: 2½–3 ft. Blossom width: 3½–4 in. Blooms in midseason with good repeat | Strong fragrance Winter hardy Disease resistant p. 359

Simplicity

Plant height:
2½–3½ ft.
Blossom width:
3–4 in.
Blooms abundantly all
season

Little or no fragrance
Winter hardy
Disease resistant
p. 373

Little Darling

Plant height:
2½–3½ ft.
Blossom width:
2½–3 in.
Blooms abundantly,
early to midseason,
with continuous
repeat

Spicy fragrance
Winter hardy
Disease resistant
p. 368

Dicky

*Plant height: 3–3½ ft.
Blossom width:
3–3½ in.
Abundant midseason
bloom with excellent
repeat*

*Slight fragrance
Winter hardy
Disease resistant
p. 361*

Hannah Gordon

*Plant height: 4–6 ft.
Blossom width:
4–4½ in.
Blooms abundantly in
midseason with
autumn repeat*

*Slight fragrance
Winter hardy
Disease resistant
p. 366*

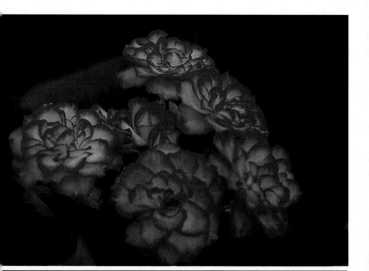

Betty Prior

Plant height: 5–7 ft.
Blossom width:
3–3½ in.
Blooms abundantly in
midseason with
excellent repeat

Fragrant
Winter hardy
Disease resistant
p. 359

First Edition

Plant height: 3½–4 ft.
Blossom width:
2½–3 in.
Blooms well in
midseason with fair
repeat

Slight fragrance
Not winter hardy
without protection
Disease resistant
p. 363

Fashion

Plant height:
3½–4½ ft.
Blossom width:
3–3½ in.
Blooms in midseason
with excellent repeat

Slight fragrance
Winter hardy
Disease resistant
p. 363

Circus

Plant height: 2½–3 ft.
Blossom width: 3 in.
Blooms in midseason
with good repeat

Spicy fragrance
Winter hardy
Disease resistant, but
needs protection
from black spot
p. 360

Playboy

*Plant height: 2½–3 ft.
Blossom width:
3½ in.
Blooms in midseason
with good repeat*

*Slight fragrance
Winter hardy
Disease resistant
p. 369*

Playgirl

*Plant height: 3–3½ ft.
Blossom width:
3–3½ in.
Blooms profusely
early to midseason,
with good repeat*

*Slight fragrance
Winter hardy
Disease resistant
p. 369*

Redgold

Plant height: 3–3½ ft.
Blossom width:
2½–3 in.
Blooms well in
midseason with fair
repeat

Slightly fruity
fragrance
Winter hardy
Disease resistant
p. 371

Orangeade

Plant height: 2½–3 ft.
Blossom width:
3–3½ in.
Blooms *abundantly in*
midseason with good
repeat

Slight fragrance
Not winter hardy
without protection
Disease resistant, but
needs protection
from mildew
p. 368

Sarabande

*Plant height: to 2½ ft.
Blossom width:
2½ in.
Blooms profusely in
midseason with
excellent repeat*

*Slight, spicy
fragrance
Winter hardy with
some protection
Disease resistant
p. 372*

Trumpeter

*Plant height:
3½–4½ ft.
Blossom width:
3½ in.
Blooms extremely
well in midseason with
excellent repeat*

*Slight fragrance
Winter hardy
Disease resistant
p. 374*

Impatient

Plant height: 3–3½ ft.
Blossom width: 3 in.
Blooms well in midseason with fair repeat

Slight fragrance
Winter hardy
Disease resistant
p. 366

Anabell

Plant height: 2½–3 ft.
Blossom width: 3–3½ in.
Blooms in midseason with good repeat

Fragrant
Winter hardy
Disease resistant
p. 359

Frensham

*Plant height: 2½–3 ft.
Blossom width: 3 in.
Blooms extremely
well in midseason with
good repeat*

*Slight fragrance
Winter hardy
Disease resistant
p. 364*

Eye Paint

*Plant height: 3–4 ft.
Blossom width:
2½ in.
Blooms in midseason
with good repeat*

*Slight fragrance
Winter hardy
Disease resistant, but
needs protection
from black spot
p. 363*

ropeana

Plant height: 2½–3 ft.
Blossom width: 3 in.
Blooms abundantly in
midseason with good
repeat

Very slight fragrance
Winter hardy
Disease resistant
p. 362

owbiz

Plant height: 2½–3 ft.
Blossom width:
2½–3 in.
Blooms well all season

Slight fragrance
Winter hardy
Disease resistant
p. 373

Dusky Maiden

*Plant height: 2–3 ft.
Blossom width:
3–3½ in.
Blooms abundantly in
midseason with
excellent repeat*

*Fragrant
Winter hardy
Disease resistant
p. 361*

Intrigue

*Plant height: to 3 ft.
Blossom width: 3 in.
Blooms well in
midseason with good
repeat*

*Strong fragrance
Not winter hardy
without protection
Disease resistant
p. 367*

Purple Tiger

Plant height: 1½–2 ft.
Blossom width:
3–4 in.
Good all-season
bloom

Fragrant
Winter hardy
Disease resistant
p. 371

Priscilla Burton

Plant height: 3½–4 ft.
Blossom width:
2½ in.
Good all-season
bloom

Fragrant
Winter hardy
Disease resistant
p. 370

Fragrant Delight

*Plant height: 3½–4 ft.
Blossom width: 3 in.
Blooms in midseason
with good repeat*

*Very fragrant
May require winter
protection in severe
climates
Disease resistant
p. 364*

Regensberg

*Plant height: 1½–2 ft.
Blossom width:
3–3½ in.
Good all-season
bloom*

*Fragrant
Winter hardy
Disease resistant
p. 371*

Sexy Rexy

*Plant height: 3–4 ft.
Blossom width:
3½–4 in.
Blooms profusely late
in season with good
repeat*

*Slight fragrance
Winter hardy
Disease resistant
p. 372*

Cherish

*Plant height: 3–3½ ft.
Blossom width: 3–4 in.
Blooms in midseason
with good repeat*

*Fragrant
May require winter
protection in severe
climates
Disease resistant
p. 360*

Grandifloras

Gold Medal

Plant height:
4½–5½ ft.
Blossom width:
3½ in.
Blooms well all season

Slight, fruity
fragrance
Not winter hardy;
needs protection
Disease resistant but
needs protection
from black spot
p. 377

Prominent

Plant height:
3½–4½ ft.
Blossom width:
3½ in.
Blooms extremely
well all season

Slight fragrance
Winter hardy
Disease resistant
p. 379

Tournament of Roses *Plant height: 3 ft.* *Not fragrant*
Blossom width: *Winter hardy*
3½–4 in. *Disease resistant*
Blooms abundantly all *p. 380*
season

Lagerfeld *Plant height:* *Intensely fragrant*
4½–5½ ft. *Winter hardy*
Blossom width: *Disease resistant*
4½–5½ in. *p. 378*
Blooms well all season

Shreveport *Plant height: 4½–5 ft.* *Slight fragrance*
Blossom width: *Winter hardy*
3½–4 in. *Disease resistant*
Blooms fairly well all *p. 380*
season

Queen Elizabeth *Plant height: 5–7 ft.* *Fragrant*
Blossom width: *Winter hardy*
3½–4 in. *Disease resistant*
Abundant midseason *p. 379*
bloom; excellent
repeat bloom

Montezuma

Plant height: 4½–5 ft.
Blossom width:
3½–4 in.
Blooms well all season

Slight fragrance
Winter hardy
Disease resistant
p. 378

Aquarius

Plant height: 4½–5 ft.
Blossom width:
3½–4½ in.
Blooms well all season

Slight fragrance
Winter hardy
Disease resistant
p. 377

Pink Parfait

*Plant height:
3½–4½ ft.
Blossom width:
3½–4 in.
Blooms abundantly at
midseason with good
repeat*

*Slight fragrance
Winter hardy
Disease resistant
p. 379*

Camelot

*Plant height: 5–5½ ft.
Blossom width:
3½–4 in.
Good all-season
bloom*

*Spicy fragrance
Winter hardy
Disease resistant
p. 377*

Love

Plant height: 3–3½ ft.
Blossom width:
3½ in.
Blooms well all season

Very slight fragrance
Winter hardy
Disease resistant
p. 378

White Lightnin'

Plant height: 4½–5 ft.
Blossom width:
3½–4 in.
Blooms well
all-season

Very fragrant
Winter hardy
Disease resistant
p. 380

Hybrid Teas

Kaiserin Auguste Viktoria

Plant height: 5–7 ft.
Blossom width:
4–4½ in.
Blooms profusely,
early to midseason,
with fair repeat

Strong fragrance
Winter hardy
Disease resistant
p. 392

Honor

Plant height: 5–5½ ft.
Blossom width:
4–5 in.
Blooms well all season

Slight fragrance
Not winter hardy
without protection
Disease resistant
p. 391

White Masterpiece

Plant height: to 3 ft.
Blossom width:
5–5¹/₂ in.
Blooms sparsely all
season

Slight fragrance
Not winter hardy
without protection
Disease resistant
p. 405

Pascali

Plant height: 3¹/₂–4 ft.
Blossom width:
4–4¹/₂ in.
Blooms extremely
well all season

Very slight fragrance
Winter hardy
Disease resistant
p. 398

Pristine

Plant height: 4–4½ ft.
Blossom width:
4½–6 in.
Blooms well all season

Slight fragrance
Winter hardy
Disease resistant
p. 400

Garden Party

Plant height: 5–6 ft.
Blossom width:
5–5½ in.
Blooms profusely in
midseason with good
repeat

Fragrant
Winter hardy
Disease resistant, but
susceptible to mildew
p. 390

La France

*Plant height: 4–5 ft.
Blossom width:
4–4½ in.
Blooms profusely,
early to midseason,
with good repeat*

*Very fragrant
Winter hardy
Disease resistant
p. 394*

Peace

*Plant height: 5–6 ft.
Blossom width:
5½–6 in.
Blooms well all season*

*Slight fragrance
Winter hardy
Disease resistant
p. 398*

Kordes' Perfecta

Plant height: 4–5 ft.
Blossom width:
4½–5 in.
Blooms well all season

Very fragrant
Winter hardy
Disease resistant
p. 393

Granada

Plant height: 5–6 ft.
Blossom width:
4–5 in.
Blooms abundantly all season

Spicy fragrance
Needs winter protection in severe climates
Disease resistant, but needs protection from mildew
p. 391

Touch of Class

Plant height: 4–5 ft.
Blossom width:
5–5½ in.
Blooms extremely
well all season

Slight fragrance
Winter hardy
Disease resistant
p. 404

Chicago Peace

Plant height:
4½–5½ ft.
Blossom width:
5–5½ in.
Blooms well all season

Slight to moderately
strong fragrance
Winter hardy
Disease resistant
p. 385

Duet

Plant height:
4½–5½ ft.
Blossom width: 4 in.
Good midseason
bloom with excellent
repeat

Fragrant
Winter hardy
Disease resistant
p. 388

Medallion

Plant height:
4½–5½ ft.
Blossom width:
5–5½ in.
Blooms profusely in
midseason with good
repeat

Fruity fragrance
Not reliably winter
hardy without
protection
Disease resistant
p. 394

Folklore

Plant height: 6–8 ft.
Blossom width:
4½–5 in.
Good bloom in late
season, with autumn
repeat

Fragrant
Winter hardy
Disease resistant
p. 389

Summer Dream

Plant height: to 5 ft.
Blossom width:
4–5 in.
Blooms profusely all
season

Slight fragrance
Winter hardy
Disease resistant
p. 402

Tiffany

Plant height: 4–4½ ft.
Blossom width:
4–5 in.
Blooms well all season

Very fragrant
Winter hardy
Disease resistant
p. 404

Royal Highness

Plant height: 4½–5 ft.
Blossom width:
5–5½ in.
Blooms well all season

Very fragrant
Not winter hardy
Disease resistant
p. 401

Charlotte Armstrong

Plant height: 4–5 ft.
Blossom width:
3½–4½ in.
Blooms in early
summer with good
repeat

Fragrant
Winter hardy with
some protection
Disease resistant
p. 385

Dainty Bess

Plant height: 3½–4 ft.
Blossom width:
3½ in.
Blooms well all season

Fragrant
Winter hardy
Disease resistant
p. 387

Lady X

Plant height: 5–7 ft.
Blossom width:
4½–5 in.
Blooms well all season

Fragrant
Winter hardy
Disease resistant
p. 393

Sterling Silver

Plant height: 2½–3 ft.
Blossom width:
3½ in.
Blooms fairly well all season

Strong lemon fragrance
Winter hardy
Disease resistant, but susceptible to black spot and mildew
p. 402

Paul Shirville

Plant height: 3–4 ft.
Blossom width: 4 in.
Blooms profusely all
season

Very fragrant
Winter hardy
Disease resistant
p. 398

Century Two

Plant height: 4–5 ft.
Blossom width: 5 in.
Blooms profusely all
season

Fragrant
Winter hardy
Disease resistant
p. 384

Peter Frankenfeld

Plant height: to 5 ft.
Blossom width:
4–5 in.
Blooms profusely all
season

Slight fragrance
Winter hardy
Disease resistant
p. 399

Marijke Koopman

Plant height:
4½–5½ ft.
Blossom width:
4–5 in.
Blooms profusely all
season

Fragrant
Winter hardy
Disease resistant
p. 394

Sweet Surrender

Plant height: 3½–5 ft.
Blossom width:
3½–4½ in.
Blooms fairly well all season

Strong fragrance
Not reliably winter hardy
p. 403

Pink Peace

Plant height:
4½–5½ ft.
Blossom width:
4½–6 in.
Blooms well all season

Very fragrant
Winter hardy
Disease resistant
p. 399

Friendship

*Plant height: 5–6 ft.
Blossom width:
5½ in.
Blooms well all season*

*Very fragrant
Winter hardy
Disease resistant
p. 390*

Double Delight

*Plant height: 3½–4 ft.
Blossom width:
5½ in.
Blooms extremely
well all season*

*Spicy fragrance
Winter hardy
Disease resistant, but
susceptible to mildew
in some regions
p. 387*

Color Magic

Plant height: 3½–4 ft.
Blossom width: 5 in.
Blooms continuously
all season

Slight fragrance
Not winter hardy
without protection
Disease resistant
p. 386

Mon Cheri

Plant height: 2½–3 ft.
Blossom width:
4½ in.
Blooms well all season

Moderate fragrance
Winter hardy
Disease resistant
p. 396

First Prize

Plant height: to 5 ft.
Blossom width:
5–5½ in.
Blooms well in
midseason with good
repeat

Fragrant
Not winter hardy
Disease prone; needs
protection from
mildew and black
spot
p. 389

Paradise

Plant height: 4–4½ ft.
Blossom width:
3½–4½ in.
Blooms well all season

Fragrant
Winter hardy
Disease resistant, but
susceptible to mildew
in cool, wet climates
p. 397

Seashell

Plant height: 3½–4 ft.
Blossom width:
4–5 in.
Blooms fairly well all
season

Fragrant
Winter hardy
Disease resistant
p. 401

Pink Favorite

Plant height: 4–4½ ft.
Blossom width:
3½–4 in.
Blooms profusely in
midseason with good
repeat

Slight fragrance
Winter hardy
Disease resistant
p. 399

Electron

*Plant height:
2½–3½ ft.
Blossom width: 5 in.
Blooms abundantly all
season*

*Very fragrant
Winter hardy
Disease resistant
p. 388*

Oklahoma

*Plant height: 5–6 ft.
Blossom width:
4–5½ in.
Blooms abundantly all
season*

*Very fragrant
Winter hardy
Disease resistant
p. 397*

Ingrid Bergman

Plant height: 4 ft.
Blossom width:
4–4½ in.
Blooms abundantly all
season

Slight fragrance
Winter hardy
Disease resistant
p. 391

Crimson Glory

Plant height: 3½–4 ft.
Blossom width:
4–4½ in.
Blooms well all season

Very fragrant
Winter hardy
Disease resistant
p. 386

Mirandy

Plant height: 4–5 ft.
Blossom width:
4½–5 in.
Blooms well all season

Strong true-rose
fragrance
Winter hardy
Disease resistant
p. 395

Precious Platinum

Plant height: to 4 ft.
Blossom width:
3½ in.
Blooms abundantly all
season

Slight fragrance
Winter hardy
Disease resistant
p. 400

Mister Lincoln

Plant height:
4¹/₂–5¹/₂ ft.
Blossom width:
5–5¹/₂ in.
Blooms well all season

Very fragrant
Winter hardy
Disease resistant
p. 396

Chrysler Imperial

Plant height: 4–5 ft.
Blossom width:
4¹/₂–5 in.
Blooms profusely in
midseason with good
repeat

Very fragrant
Winter hardy
Disease resistant, but
susceptible to mildew
in cool, wet climates
p. 385

Elizabeth Taylor

Plant height: 4–5 ft.
Blossom width:
4–5 in.
Blooms well all season

Slight fragrance
Winter hardy
Disease resistant
p. 389

Mikado

Plant height: 4–5 ft.
Blossom width:
4½–5 in.
Blooms well all season

Light fragrance
Winter hardy
Disease resistant
p. 395

Kardinal | Plant height: to 4½ ft. | Slight fragrance
| Blossom width: | Winter hardy
| 4–4½ in. | Disease resistant
| Blooms well all season | p. 392

Olympiad | Plant height: 4–5 ft. | Slight fragrance
| Blossom width: | Winter hardy
| 4–4½ in. | Disease resistant
| Blooms well all season | p. 397

American Pride　　　*Plant height: 5–5½ ft.*　　*Little or no fragrance*
　　　　　　　　　　　　Blossom width:　　　　　*Winter hardy*
　　　　　　　　　　　　4½–5½ in.　　　　　　　*Disease resistant*
　　　　　　　　　　　　Blooms best in early　　　*p. 383*
　　　　　　　　　　　　summer and fall

Fragrant Cloud　　　*Plant height: 4–5 ft.*　　　*Intense true-rose*
　　　　　　　　　　　　Blossom width: 5 in.　　　*fragrance*
　　　　　　　　　　　　Blooms well all season　　*Winter hardy*
　　　　　　　　　　　　　　　　　　　　　　　　Disease resistant
　　　　　　　　　　　　　　　　　　　　　　　　p. 390

Miss All-American Beauty

Plant height: 4–5 ft.
Blossom width: 5 in.
Blooms abundantly in midseason with good repeat

Very fragrant
Winter hardy
Disease resistant
p. 396

Tropicana

Plant height: 4–5 ft.
Blossom width: 5 in.
Blooms extremely well all season

Very strong, fruity fragrance
Winter hardy
Disease resistant
p. 404

Polarstern

Plant height:
4½–5½ ft.
Blossom width:
4–5½ in.
Blooms profusely all
season

Little or no fragrance
Winter hardy
Disease resistant
p. 400

Sutter's Gold

Plant height: 4–4½ ft.
Blossom width:
4–5 in.
Blooms well all season

Strong, fruity
fragrance
Moderately winter
hardy
Disease resistant
p. 402

Crystalline

Plant height: 4–5 ft.
Blossom width:
4½–5 in.
Blooms abundantly all
season

Fragrant
Winter hardy
Disease resistant
p. 387

Brandy

Plant height: 4–5 ft.
Blossom width:
4–4½ in.
Blooms profusely all
season

Moderately strong,
fruity fragrance
Winter hardy with
some protection
Disease resistant, but
susceptible to black
spot
p. 384

Elina

*Plant height: 5 ft.
Blossom width:
5½–6 in.
Blooms profusely all
season*

*Slight fragrance
Winter hardy
Disease resistant
p. 388*

Just Joey

*Plant height: 3–3½ ft.
Blossom width:
4–5 in.
Blooms well all season*

*Strong fragrance
Winter hardy in all
but most severe
climates
Disease resistant
p. 392*

King's Ransom

Plant height: 4½–5 ft.
Blossom width:
5–6 in.
Blooms profusely in
midseason with good
repeat

Fragrant
Not reliably winter
hardy in severe
climates
Disease resistant, but
susceptible to mildew
p. 393

Bride's Dream

Plant height:
4½–5½ ft.
Blossom width:
4½–5½ in.
Blooms abundantly all
season

Slight fragrance
Winter hardy
Disease resistant
p. 384

Sheer Elegance

Plant height: 4–5 ft.
Blossom width:
4½–6 in.
Blooms well all season

Light fragrance
Winter hardy
Disease resistant
p. 401

Milestone

Plant height: 4–5 ft.
Blossom width:
5–5½ in.
Blooms well all season

Slight fragrance
Winter hardy
Disease resistant
p. 395

Swarthmore

Plant height: 4–5 ft.
Blossom width:
4–5 in.
Blooms well all season

Slight fragrance
Winter hardy
Disease resistant, but
susceptible to mildew
in cool, wet climates
p. 403

The Temptations

Plant height:
3½–4½ ft.
Blossom width:
4–5 in.
Blooms well all season

Light fragrance
May need winter
protection in severe
climates
Disease resistant
p. 403

Miniatures

Snow Bride

Plant height:
10–14 in.
Blossom width: 1 1/2 in.
Blooms in midseason
with good repeat

Slight fragrance
Winter hardy
Disease resistant
p. 416

Simplex

Plant height:
15–18 in.
Blossom width:
1 1/4 in.
Blooms in midseason
with excellent repeat

Slight fragrance
Winter hardy
Disease resistant
p. 416

Popcorn

Plant height: 12–14 in.
Blossom width: ³/₄ in.
Blooms in midseason
with excellent repeat

Honey fragrance
Winter hardy
Disease resistant
p. 414

Olympic Gold

Plant height:
18–24 in.
Blossom width:
2–2¹/₂ in.
Blooms in midseason
with good repeat

Slight fragrance
Winter hardy
Disease resistant
p. 413

Green Ice

*Plant height: 8–16 in.
Blossom width:
1¼ in.
Blooms in midseason
with good repeat*

*Slight fragrance
Winter hardy
Disease resistant
p. 410*

Sweet Chariot

*Plant height: 18 in.
Blossom width:
1½ in.
Blooms profusely in
midseason and
autumn*

*Very fragrant
Very winter hardy
Disease resistant
p. 417*

Jean Kenneally

Plant height:
10–14 in.
Blossom width:
1½ in.
Blooms in midseason
with excellent repeat

Slight fragrance
Winter hardy
Disease resistant
p. 411

Black Jade

Plant height:
14–18 in.
Blossom width: ¾ in.
Blooms in midseason
with good repeat

Not fragrant
Winter hardy
Disease resistant
p. 408

Party Girl

Plant height: 12–14 in.
Blossom width:
1¼ in.
Blooms in midseason
with good repeat

Sweet, spicy
fragrance
Winter hardy
Disease resistant
p. 413

Scarlet Moss

Plant height:
10–14 in.
Blossom width: 1 in.
Blooms in midseason
with good repeat

Not fragrant
Winter hardy when
well established
Disease resistant
p. 416

Rise 'n' Shine

Plant height:
10–14 in.
Blossom width:
1½–1¾ in.
Blooms in midseason
with good repeat

Slight fragrance
Winter hardy
Disease resistant
p. 415

Rainbow's End

Plant height:
10–14 in.
Blossom width:
1½ in.
Blooms in midseason
with good repeat

Little or no fragrance
Winter hardy
Disease resistant
p. 414

Cinderella

Plant height: 8–10 in.
Blossom width: ¾ in.
Blooms very well in
midseason with
excellent repeat

Very spicy fragrance
Winter hardy
Disease resistant
p. 409

Pierrine

Plant height: 12–16 in.
Blossom width:
1½ in.
Blooms in midseason
with good repeat

Slight fragrance
Winter hardy
Disease resistant
p. 413

Minnie Pearl

Plant height:
10–14 in.
Blossom width:
1½ in.
Blooms in midseason
with good repeat

Slight fragrance
Winter hardy
Disease resistant
p. 412

Giggles/KINgig

Plant height:
15–18 in.
Blossom width:
1½ in.
Blooms profusely all
season

Little or no fragrance
Winter hardy
Disease resistant
p. 410

Pompon de Paris

Plant height: 8–10 in.
Blossom width: ¾ in.
Blooms in midseason
with good repeat

Little or no fragrance
Winter hardy
Disease resistant
p. 414

Rosa roulettii

Plant height:
15–18 in.
Blossom width:
¾–1 in.
Blooms in midseason
with good repeat

Little or no fragrance
Winter hardy
Disease resistant
p. 415

Jeanne Lajoie

Plant height: 4–8 ft.
Blossom width: 1 in.
Blooms profusely all
season

Slight fragrance
Winter hardy
Disease resistant
p. 411

Little Jackie

Plant height:
14–18 in.
Blossom width:
1½ in.
Blooms in midseason
with excellent repeat

Very fragrant
Winter hardy
Disease resistant
p. 411

Mary Marshall

*Plant height:
10–14 in.
Blossom width:
1½ in.
Blooms in midseason
with good repeat*

*Slight fragrance
Winter hardy
Disease resistant
p. 412*

Angel Darling

*Plant height: 12–18 in.
Blossom width:
1½ in.
Blooms in midseason
with good repeat*

*Slight fragrance
Winter hardy
Disease resistant, but
susceptible to fungus
diseases, black spot,
and mildew
p. 408*

Stars 'n' Stripes
Plant height:
10–14 in.
Blossom width:
1¾ in.
Blooms in midseason
with good repeat

Little or no fragrance
Winter hardy
Disease resistant
p. 417

Magic Carrousel
Plant height:
15–18 in.
Blossom width:
1¾–2 in.
Blooms in midseason
with good repeat

Little or no fragrance
Winter hardy
Disease resistant
p. 412

Dreamglo

*Plant height:
18–24 in.
Blossom width: 1 in.
Blooms extremely
well in midseason with
good repeat*

*Slight fragrance
Winter hardy
Disease resistant
p. 409*

Starina

*Plant height: 12–16 in.
Blossom width:
1½ in.
Blooms in midseason
with excellent repeat*

*Little or no fragrance
Winter hardy
Disease resistant
p. 417*

Beauty Secret

Plant height:
10–18 in.
Blossom width:
1½ in.
Blooms extremely
well in midseason with
excellent repeat

Very fragrant
Winter hardy
Disease resistant
p. 408

Red Beauty

Plant height:
10–12 in.
Blossom width:
1½ in.
Blooms in midseason
with good repeat

Slight fragrance
Winter hardy
Disease resistant
p. 415

Encyclopedia of Roses

Natural wild roses, commonly called species roses, grow throughout the Northern Hemisphere, from North America to Europe, China, and Japan. They are known to thrive in a very wide range of habitats and climates, flourishing from the far north down to the northern reaches of Africa.

A Matter of Debate

What constitutes a species rose is a matter of continuing academic debate. According to the usual concept, there are about 200 wild roses, but some authorities claim to be able to distinguish many times that number. Linnaeus himself commented that those who had examined just a few species could explain them a great deal better than those who had examined many.

While the debate rages on among the experts, most gardeners are satisfied to define a species rose as one that bears a single (five-petaled) flower that sets self-pollinated hips and produces seedlings resembling the parent in every particular.

Living History

The group of species roses described in this book is by no means exhaustive; the roses included here were chosen for their particular beauty and for the contributions that they have made to the heritage of the many rose cultivars that exist today. *Rosa spinosissima*, for example, is the ancestor of many fine horticultural varieties, including Frühlingsgold and Frühlingsmorgen, which belong to the shrub rose class. *Rosa multiflora* forms part of the background of the polyantha roses — shrub roses that bear their flowers in clusters — and, by extension, of all roses descended from the polyanthas, including the entire floribunda class. *Rosa wichuraiana* is included in the parentage of many notable climbers, including Silver Moon and Albéric Barbier. And the list goes on, making it easy to see why it is not only interesting but also helpful to have some understanding of these beautiful roses that grow in the wild.

Even in the wild, species roses are known to hybridize very

freely. This fact accounts, at least in part, for the rather inde-
terminate boundaries that exist between some species, and for
the extent to which the exact number of species roses is still in
dispute. What is more, many species roses have over the centuries developed strains that can appear very different. *Rosa
multiflora*, for example, has many very thorny strains, yet also
occurs with canes that are almost thornless.

Abundant Blooms

Species roses are for the most part once-blooming, and most of
them flower early in the season, in May or June. They produce
an enormous crop of blossoms each year. In most instances, the
flowers are followed by brightly colored fruits, known as seed
hips, which prolong the beauty of the plants and provide feed
for birds. Rose hips also make attractive subjects for flower and
foliage arrangements.

Wild Roses in Your Garden

Species roses require little care in the garden. Many of these
vigorous roses are also extremely hardy, although it is well to
remember, if you are considering using species roses in your
garden, that some are more naturally cold-tolerant than others.
The kind of environment that suits them in the wild will also
suit them admirably in your backyard.

If you do decide to plant species roses in your garden, make
certain that you have allowed enough room for these vigorous
plants. Many of them are extremely bushy and will grow up to
eight or nine feet tall and just as wide.

As garden subjects, species roses are delightful and varied.
Some — especially the larger varieties — are ideally suited for
hedges, while others, such as *Rosa wichuraiana*, are very
sprawling in their growth and make a good ground cover. Individual bushes or a row of species roses will make a very fine
backdrop for many other plants, including other types of roses.

Any species roses that are sold commercially or that can (with
proper permission) be collected in the wild can be used in some
way in a garden setting. They offer something of interest at all
times of the year, with flowers, hips, foliage, thorns, and canes
all contributing in some way, expected or unexpected, to the
visual appeal of your garden.

ROSA BANKSIAE LUTEA, *p. 57*
(J. D. Parks, 1824)

Also called the Yellow Lady Banks Rose, this early bloomer was
named for Lady Banks, the wife of the director of Kew Gardens

at the time of its introduction. It is not quite as vigorous or fragrant as the white form, *Rosa banksiae albo-plena.*

FLOWERS   1 in. wide. Light to medium yellow. Double; perhaps 45–50 petals. The very early-season blooms are not recurrent. Slight fragrance. The very full, old rose form gives it a rather raggedy look, like a double-flowering cherry.

FOLIAGE   20–30 ft. tall. Very long canes, very vigorous growth, not winter hardy. Disease resistant. Almost thornless. Leaves small, long, light green.

ROSA CAROLINA, p. 48
(1826)

A native American rose, this pink species is sometimes called the Pasture Rose.

FLOWERS   2 in. wide. Medium pink. Single; 5 petals. Midseason bloom followed by bright red hips. Blooms mostly single, sometimes in clusters. Fragrant.

FOLIAGE   3–6 ft. tall. Upright, spreading by means of suckers. Disease free. Winter hardy except in severe winter climates. Canes fairly smooth, with few thorns. Leaves medium green, glossy

ROSA CHINENSIS VIRIDIFLORA, p. 56
(Before 1845)

Also known as the Green Rose, this flower is a curiosity. Its petals have been transformed into sepals, giving them a deformed look.

FLOWERS   1½–2½ in. wide. Green. Double. Continuous bloom. No fragrance.

FOLIAGE   3–4 ft. tall. Upright. Can be grown in a pot. Disease resistant. Not winter hardy. Leaves medium to dark green.

ROSA EGLANTERIA, p. 51
(Before 1551)

The Sweetbriar, or Shakespeare's Eglantine, has a sweet, true-rose fragrance; the foliage is strongly apple-scented, especially when it is wet.

FLOWERS   1–1½ in. wide. Light to medium pink. Single; 5 petals. Blooms early; not recurrent. Has a light, sweet, true-rose fragrance. Blooms in clusters, with blossoms opening flat to reveal showy yellow stamens. Clusters of bright red oval hips appear later in the season.

FOLIAGE   8–10 ft. tall. Upright, vigorous. Disease free and winter hardy. Canes very thorny. Leaves small, abundant, medium green, and glossy, with a fragrance of apples.

ROSA FOETIDA BICOLOR, p. 54
(Before 1590)

Also called the Austrian Copper, this sport, or mutation, of *Rosa foetida* shares that rose's heavy aroma.

FLOWERS   2–2½ in. wide. Orange-red with yellow reverse. Single; 5 petals. Early-season bloom, not recurrent. The fragrance has been called heavy but not unpleasant; to some, it is reminiscent of boiled linseed oil.

FOLIAGE   4–5 ft. tall. Upright, irregularly branched, and rather gaunt. Prone to black spot. Not reliably winter hardy. Canes moderately thorny with small, dull, medium green, and rather sparse leaves.

ROSA FOETIDA PERSIANA, p. 55
(1837)

Also called the Persian Yellow, this rose is the ancestor of many of our yellow and bicolor varieties.

FLOWERS   2½–3 in. wide. Medium to deep yellow. Semi-double; 24–30 petals. Early-season bloom, not recurrent. Loose, cupped form.

FOLIAGE   4–5 ft. tall. Upright. Moderately vigorous; much more so in very warm climates. Susceptible to black spot. Leaves small, ferny, and medium green.

ROSA × HIGHDOWNENSIS, p. 54
(1796)

This rose is widely distributed in this country as Geranium, another variety or possible hybrid of *Rosa moyesii*.

FLOWERS   1½ in. wide. Medium red, fading to deep cerise pink. Single; 5 petals. Early-season bloom is followed by bright orange, vase-shaped hips. Fragrant. Blossoms open flat, occurring singly and in clusters.

FOLIAGE   9–12 ft. tall. Strong, arching, moderately thorny canes. Disease free and winter hardy. Leaves small, blue-green to dark green.

ROSA HUGONIS, p. 56
(Father Hugh Scanlon, 1899)

This species is also called Father Hugo's Rose and the Golden Rose of China. It does best in poor soil.

FLOWERS   1½–2 in. wide. Pale yellow. Single; 5 petals. Very early bloom, not recurrent. Little or no fragrance. Opens to cup shape, with showy golden stamens. The small maroon hips that develop later are not conspicuous.

FOLIAGE   Up to 6 ft. tall and as wide, with arching canes. Disease free. Winter hardy except in extreme climates. Leaves small, light to medium green, and ferny.

ROSA LAEVIGATA, p. 46
(1759)

Originally from China, *Rosa laevigata* had become naturalized in the southeastern part of North America by 1759. It is also known as the Cherokee Rose.

FLOWERS   2½–3½ in. wide. Single; 5 petals. Usually white; sometimes (but rarely) pink. Early-season bloom; does not repeat. Fragrant. Large, open flowers with yellow stamens are followed by large, decorative, bristly red hips.

FOLIAGE   6–20 ft. tall. Upright, arching, and bushy. Disease resistant. Not winter hardy. Canes very thorny. Leaves fine, bright medium green, glossy. Almost evergreen in very mild climates.

ROSA MOYESII, p. 55
(Discovered by Hemsley and Wilson; introduced in 1894, again in 1903)

This extraordinary deep blood-red species from western China is named for the Reverend E. J. Moyes, a missionary in that country. *Rosa moyesii* is grown for its spectacular hip display as well as for its flowers.

FLOWERS   1¾–2½ in. wide. Deep blood-red, although lighter shades have occurred in the wild. Single; 5 petals. Early to midseason bloom, not recurrent. Little fragrance. Blooms singly and in small clusters. Long, vase-shaped hips with retentive sepals; brilliant red, with some bristles.

FOLIAGE   10 ft. tall or taller. Canes somewhat sparse, upright, treelike. Disease resistant and winter hardy, with moderately thorny canes. Leaves small, delicate, ferny; medium to dark green, dull to semiglossy.

ROSA MULTIFLORA, *p. 47*
(Before 1868)

Often sold as a "living fence," this many-flowered rose has become a noxious weed in some regions of the country. Widely used as an understock, *Rosa multiflora* is the ancestor of many popular polyantha and floribunda varieties.

FLOWERS   ½ in. wide, in large clusters. White. Single; 5 petals. Honey-scented. Early to midseason bloom, not recurrent. Blossoms appear in large, airy clusters. Tiny, round red hips follow later in the season.

FOLIAGE   7–12 ft. tall. Upright, arching canes. Disease free, and winter hardy in all but the most severe winter climates. Many strains are thorny, but there are some thornless *multifloras*. Leaves light to medium green; long, narrow, and glossy.

ROSA PALUSTRIS, *p. 49*
(1726)

This sweetly fragrant pink species, also called the Swamp Rose, grows in wet, swampy soil, where it forms dense thickets.

FLOWERS   2½ in. wide. Medium pink. Single; 5 petals. Late-season bloom, not recurrent. Very sweet fragrance. Blossoms open flat, showing bright golden stamens. Blooms singly and in clusters.

FOLIAGE   6–12 ft. tall or taller. Upright, in dense thickets. Disease free and winter hardy. Light green canes very smooth, with few thorns. Soft, dull leaves, pale to medium green.

ROSA PENDULINA, *p. 51*
(1683)

Known as the Alpine Rose, this pink species bears conspicuous pear-shaped hips later in the season.

FLOWERS   2 in. wide. Medium pink to deep pink, sometimes mauve. Single; 5 petals. Light, sweet fragrance. Mid- to late-season bloom. Blossoms open flat, showing bright yellow stamens. Blooms singly and in clusters. Hips bright red, pear-shaped.

FOLIAGE   4 ft. tall. Arching, graceful growth. Disease free and winter hardy. Canes very smooth, almost thornless. Leaves finely divided, medium green, glossy.

ROSA POMIFERA, *p. 52*
(1771)

This mauve-pink species is also called the Apple Rose, in reference to the large hips that appear later in the season.

FLOWERS   2 in. wide. Mauve-pink. Single; 5 petals. Fragrant. Early-season bloom, not recurrent. Large, round reddish hips follow later in the season.

FOLIAGE   5–7 ft. tall. Very upright. Disease free, winter hardy. Canes somewhat thorny. Leaves medium-size, blue-green.

ROSA ROXBURGHII, *p. 53*
(1814)

This rose is also known as the Burr Rose and the Chestnut Rose, and is more correctly called *R. roxburghii plena*. It is the double form of the species *roxburghii*, but it was discovered 94 years before the true species (which was named *R. roxburghii normalis*) and given the species name in error.

FLOWERS   3–3½ in. wide. Light pink. Double; probably 45–55 petals. Early-season bloom; a long blooming season in the South, where it is essentially a repeat bloomer. Little or no fragrance. Outer petals open wide to reveal a mass of shorter central petals; all petals have a papery feel.

FOLIAGE   5–6 ft. tall. Upright, irregularly branched growth. Not as vigorous as *Rosa roxburghii normalis*. Gray, peeling canes. Disease resistant. Tender. Leaves long and narrow; light to medium green and very evenly spaced, giving a ladderlike effect.

ROSA ROXBURGHII NORMALIS, *p. 50*
(1908)

This rose is the true *roxburghii* species. It is more vigorous than the double form (*Rosa roxburghii*), which ironically has been known for nearly a century longer.

FLOWERS   3½–4 in. wide. Light pink. Single; 5 petals. Early-season bloom, not recurrent. Light, sweet fragrance. Large, crinkly petals open flat, revealing showy golden stamens. The petals have a papery quality. Bristly hips later in the season.

FOLIAGE   7–9 ft. tall. Upright, irregularly branched growth. Gray, peeling canes. Disease free and borderline hardy (cannot survive harsh winters). Leaves long, narrow, and very evenly spaced, giving unusual ladderlike effect; light to medium green.

ROSA RUBRIFOLIA, *p. 50*
(Before 1830)

There are several strains of this species, some producing smaller plants and others growing into very large bushes. Its Latin name refers to the plant's red leaves; *Rosa rubrifolia* is worth growing for its foliage alone.

FLOWERS   ½ in. wide. Light pink with a white eye. Single; 5 petals. Early-season bloom, not recurrent. Fragrant. Blossoms open flat and occur in small clusters. Small, dark red, shiny hips appear in fall.

FOLIAGE   4–8 ft. tall. Upright, open, arching canes. Disease free. Winter hardy in all but severe winter climates. Canes red, very smooth, and almost thornless. Leaves are an unusual dark maroon.

ROSA RUGOSA, p. 53
(1845)

Originally discovered in northeastern Asia, this species has become naturalized in the northeastern United States, and it is found along beaches in New England. It can lend architectural quality to a garden, and it makes a good hedge. Its large hips look like cherry tomatoes; edible, they are an excellent source of vitamin C.

FLOWERS   2½–3½ in. wide. Medium mauve-pink. Single; 5–12 petals (variable). Continuously in bloom during the entire growing season. Intensely fragrant. Blossom opens its wide, crinkly, cupped petals to reveal golden stamens. Continues to bloom even after its large red hips form.

FOLIAGE   3–5 ft. tall. Upright, vigorous, and spreading, forming a dense bush. Disease free and winter hardy. Canes very thorny. Dark green, leathery leaves, deeply etched (rugose) and glossy.

ROSA RUGOSA ALBA, p. 46
(1845)

This white rose is a sport of *Rosa rugosa*, which it resembles in everything but color.

FLOWERS   2½–3½ in. wide. White. Single; 5–12 petals (variable). Continuously in bloom. Intense clove fragrance. Large, bright orange-red hips, resembling cherry tomatoes, appear later in the season.

FOLIAGE   3–5 ft. tall. Upright, vigorous, and spreading, forming a dense bush. Disease free and winter hardy. Dark green leathery leaves, deeply etched (rugose) and glossy.

ROSA RUGOSA RUBRA, p. 52
(1845)

This is a color sport, or mutation, of *Rosa rugosa*. Its pink flowers, present all season long, are intensely fragrant.

FLOWERS   2½–3½ in. wide. Deep mauve-pink. Single; 5 to 12 petals (variable). Continuously in bloom. Intensely fragrant. Bright red hips form later in the season.

FOLIAGE   3–5 ft. tall. Upright, vigorous, spreading, and dense. Disease free and winter hardy, with very thorny canes. The glossy, leathery leaves are dark green and deeply etched (rugose).

ROSA SOULIEANA, *p. 47*
(1896)

This species from western China is very thorny. It often grows in a climbing or trailing fashion.

FLOWERS   1½ in. wide. White. Single; 5 petals. Early- to mid-season bloom, not recurrent. Little or no fragrance. Blooms occur in large clusters. Tiny orange-red hips appear later in the season.

FOLIAGE   12 ft. tall. Upright, arching growth. Disease free. Not reliably winter hardy. Canes very thorny. Leaves gray-green.

ROSA SPINOSISSIMA, *p. 49*
(Cultivated prior to 1600)

Also known as the Scotch Rose or Burnet Rose, this species is sometimes referred to as *Rosa pimpinellifolia*. It is the ancestor of several cultivated forms.

FLOWERS   1¼–2 in. wide. Cream, white, or light yellow; pink and purple forms have also been found in the wild. Single; 5 petals. Slight fragrance. Very early bloom; does not recur. Small, round hips, purple or black.

FOLIAGE   3–4 ft. tall. Bushy, spreading. Disease resistant and winter hardy. Canes very thorny. Small, ferny leaves are a dull medium green.

ROSA SPINOSISSIMA ALTAICA, *p. 57*
(1820)

Originating in western Asia, this variety of *Rosa spinosissima* was introduced into cultivation in 1820. It closely resembles *Rosa spinosissima*, but is considerably more vigorous.

FLOWERS   1½–2½ in. wide. Single; 5 petals. Pale yellow to white. Very early bloom; not recurrent. Blossoms open wide, with petals that do not overlap, to reveal thick bright stamens. Slight fragrance. Globular hips are maroon to purple.

FOLIAGE   6 ft. tall and as wide. Upright, bushy. Disease resistant and winter hardy, with thorny canes. Leaves small, dull, gray-green.

ROSA WICHURAIANA, *p. 48*
(1891)

Also known as the Memorial Rose, this species is the parent of many climbing roses. It makes a good ground cover.

FLOWERS   1½–2 in. wide. White. Single; 5 petals. Late-season bloom, not recurrent. Fragrant. Blooms occur in clusters. Small, red, oval hips appear later in season.

FOLIAGE   10–20 ft. tall. Procumbent, but can be trained to grow upward. Disease free. Hardy in all but very severe winter climates. Canes moderately thorny. Leaves medium-size, dark green, and very glossy.

Climbers

Left to grow on their own, climbing roses do not actually climb at all — they lack the tendrils that other climbing plants, such as vines, use to attach themselves to structures. There are several different kinds of climbing roses, some of them actually sports, or chance mutations, of bush roses. But all climbing roses have long supple or sturdy canes that support the growth of blossoms along their lengths.

Climbing roses must be tied to a support, such as a trellis or a wall. There they serve a variety of purposes, covering ugly structures or forming beautiful arbors.

Here we recognize seven different groups of climbing roses: hybrid bracteatas, hybrid giganteas, climbing hybrid teas, kordesii climbers, large-flowered climbers, hybrid wichuraiana climbers, and ramblers.

Hybrid Bracteatas

There are only a very few hybrid bracteata climbers in commerce today, perhaps because they require a lot of space. Mermaid is a popular one. It will cover a large trellis, the roof of a low building, or a rough bank.

Cerise Bouquet, another commercially available variety, forms an upright small tree in just three or four years. For both of these roses, plenty of space must be allocated, for there is no hope of pruning them to a smaller area.

Hybrid Giganteas

The hybrid gigantea climbers are very tender and can be grown only in regions with mild winters, where they are almost evergreen. They have very large blooms, sweetly perfumed. With a long season of bloom, they are perfect for arbors and trellises. The variety found most often in this country, notably in California, is Belle of Portugal.

Climbing Hybrid Teas

Mostly sports of the bush varieties, climbing hybrid tea roses are usually classed along with the bush forms. There are, however, a few climbing hybrid teas for which there is no bush form. They resemble other hybrid teas in every way, being medium-size, upright, rather stiffly caned plants.

Kordesii Climbers

Every once in a while the rose helps the hybridizer out by spontaneously changing something in its genetic makeup; this is what happened for Wilhelm Kordes, a well-known 20th-century rose specialist. A new species, called *Rosa kordesii* in his honor, came into being, and Kordes used this species to develop many new varieties. The kordesii roses are medium-size climbers. They come in an assortment of colors, in intense hues, with well-shaped blooms and dark, hollylike foliage. Kordesii climbers make wonderful pillar roses, and they are perfect for planting along a fence. They tend to be quite winter hardy.

Large-flowered Climbers

A catch-all class of climbing roses, the large-flowered climbers do not belong in any other group. These roses have medium-size to large blooms, usually in small clusters. Some large-flowered climbers are repeat bloomers, but others are not. Some of them, on the basis of their parentage, might well be considered climbing hybrid teas for which there is no bush form. Others are of mixed or even unknown parentage.

Hybrid Wichuraiana Climbers

Derived from the Memorial Rose, *Rosa wichuraiana,* the hybrid wichuraiana climbers are large, strong climbers, with canes reaching as long as 20 feet or more. Foliage is shining, dark green, and disease proof. The sweetly scented blooms are large and well shaped, in shades of white and pink. Wichuraiana climbers are once-blooming, and some varieties have a pleasing hip display later in the fall.

Ramblers

The last of the climbers to come into bloom are the rambler roses. Without exception, they are once-blooming, but they extend the rose season with very bright colors of pink, red, and purple. Many of them are derived from *Rosa multiflora,* although some ramblers are based on other species.

Ramblers have long, pliable canes that can easily be trained to a trellis or fence. They are not the best choices for walls, being very susceptible to mildew. (There is one shining exception, the variety Chevy Chase.) Good air circulation is a must.

The best rambler blooms are made up of tiny flowers in huge clusters. These usually come on second-year canes, so it is a good idea to prune away the oldest canes each year. It is generally recommended that this pruning be done after flowering, but unless you are a very experienced pruner, it is best to wait for the late winter or early spring, when the plants are just coming out of dormancy and there is no foliage to hide the canes.

ALBÉRIC BARBIER, *p. 60*
(Barbier, 1900)

This is a wichuraiana climber; therefore, it is extremely vigorous, with large flowers that occur in small clusters.

FLOWERS   3–3½ in. wide. Light yellow, fading to white at edges. Double; perhaps 45–55 petals. A long period of bloom occurs late in the season; not recurrent. Fragrance reminiscent of green apples. Blossoms cupped, in clusters.

FOLIAGE   20 ft. tall. Vigorous, spreading. Disease free and winter hardy. Canes moderately thorny. Dark green, glossy leaves.

ALOHA, *p. 70*
(Boerner, 1949)

This fragrant pink rose is a climbing hybrid tea for which there is no bush form. It is a good pillar rose, and also does well on a small to medium-size trellis.

FLOWERS   3½ in. wide. Medium pink with lavender-pink reverse. Double; 55–60 petals. Good all-season bloom. Very fragrant. Buds are short and appear malformed when first opening, but become somewhat cupped and globular.

FOLIAGE   8–10 ft. tall. Upright, vigorous. Disease resistant, but slightly prone to mildew unless planted where there is good air circulation. Winter hardy. Leaves dark green, leathery.

ALTISSIMO, *p. 77*
(Delbard-Chabert, 1966)

A single-petaled rose often showing 7 petals instead of the usual 5, Altissimo displays prominent yellow stamens. Well suited for use on a trellis or pillar, this rose can also be pruned to grow as a shrub.

FLOWERS   4–5 in. wide. Blood-red. Single; 5–7 petals. Good all-season bloom. Slight fragrance. Cupped to flat blooms in small clusters.

FOLIAGE   10–12 ft. tall. Vigorous, somewhat spreading. Disease resistant and winter hardy. Leaves dark green, serrated.

AMERICA, *p. 73*
(Warriner, 1976)

An All-America Rose Selection for 1976. This fragrant rose is one of the very few climbers to receive this distinction.

FLOWERS   3½–4½ in. wide. Coral salmon. Double; 40–45 petals. Good midseason bloom, followed by fair repeat bloom. Fragrant. Very full, evenly petaled, high-centered bloom, becoming cupped.

FOLIAGE   9–12 ft. tall. Upright, vigorous, and bushy. Disease resistant and winter hardy. Leaves medium green, semiglossy.

AMERICAN PILLAR, *p. 67*
(Van Fleet, 1902)

Like its wild ancestors, *Rosa wichuraiana* and *Rosa setigera,* American Pillar is vigorous and disease free.

FLOWERS   2–3 in. wide. Deep pink with white eye. Single; 5 petals. Very abundant, long, late-season bloom with little or no fragrance. Blossoms occur in immense clusters, and red hips appear later in the fall.

FOLIAGE   15–20 ft. tall. Upright, vigorous growth. Disease resistant, but subject to mildew in the South. Winter hardy. Canes moderately thorny. Leaves medium green, leathery, glossy.

BALTIMORE BELLE, *p. 68*
(Feast, 1843)

This large-flowered climber is descended from *Rosa setigera,* a vigorous native American species.

FLOWERS 2–2½ in. wide. Light pink, fading to white. Double; 45–55 petals. Late-season bloom, not recurrent, with little or no fragrance. The very full blossom sometimes has a button center. Blooms in clusters.

FOLIAGE 8–10 ft. tall. Upright, sturdy, and pliable. Disease resistant and winter hardy. Canes moderately thorny, with dark green, leathery, semiglossy leaves.

BLAZE, *p. 75*
(Kallay, 1932)

Perhaps the most floriferous of the short climbers, Blaze remains in bloom for most or all of the growing season. It is reported to be descended from Paul's Scarlet Climber crossed with Grüss an Teplitz.

FLOWERS 2½–3 in. wide. Medium red. Semidouble; perhaps 18–24 petals. Good midseason bloom and excellent repeat. Slight fragrance. Cupped blossoms, in clusters.

FOLIAGE 7–9 ft. tall. Upright, vigorous. Disease resistant and winter hardy. Leaves medium green, semiglossy.

BLOSSOMTIME, *p. 66*
(O'Neal, 1951)

This very fragrant large-flowered climber makes a good pillar or trellis rose.

FLOWERS 3½–4 in. wide. Medium pink with deeper pink reverse. Double; 35–40 petals. Very fragrant. Good midseason bloom with sparse repeat bloom. The high-centered, classic blossoms occur in clusters.

FOLIAGE 7–9 ft. tall. Upright, vigorous, bushy. Disease resistant and winter hardy. Canes thorny, with medium green, semiglossy leaves.

CITY OF YORK, *p. 61*
(Tantau, 1945)

This very fragrant white climber won the American Rose Society National Gold Medal Certificate in 1950.

FLOWERS 3–3½ in. wide. White. Semidouble; 15 petals. Long midseason bloom, not recurrent. Very fragrant. Flower opens to become saucer-shaped, revealing bright golden stamens. The blossoms have several central petaloids.

FOLIAGE 20 ft. tall. Upright, very vigorous. Disease free. Winter hardy. Canes moderately thorny, with light to medium green, glossy leaves.

CLAIR MATIN, *p. 69*
(Meilland, 1963)

This profusely blooming pink climber was awarded the Bagatelle Gold Medal in 1960.

FLOWERS 2½–3 in. wide. Medium pink. Semidouble; 12–18 petals. Profuse, long midseason bloom, not recurrent. Fragrant. Blooms in clusters, with cupped to flat blossoms.

FOLIAGE 10–12 ft. tall. Upright, vigorous, and bushy. Disease resistant and winter hardy. Canes moderately thorny. Leaves dark green, leathery.

COMPASSION, *p. 77*
(Harkness, 1973)

Winner of gold medals in France, Germany, and Switzerland and the Edland Fragrance Medal in England, Compassion has set the standard for climbing roses in the latter part of the 20th century. There is a pale yellow sport called Highfield.

FLOWERS 4½–5 in. wide. Pink, shaded apricot, varying with the weather. Double; 36 petals. Excellent all-season bloom. Strong, sweet fragrance. The hybrid-tea-shaped blooms appear singly and in small clusters.

FOLIAGE 8–10 ft. tall. Stiff, branching growth. Disease resistant. Winter hardy. Succulent canes have large red thorns and dark green, semiglossy foliage.

DON JUAN, *p. 73*
(Malandrone, 1958)

This deep red climber makes an excellent pillar or trellis rose, particularly in areas with mild winter climates.

FLOWERS 4½–5 in. wide. Dark red. Double; 35 petals. Profuse midseason bloom with good repeat bloom. Very fragrant. The blossoms have a classic high-centered form.

FOLIAGE 8–10 ft. tall. Upright, vigorous. Disease resistant, but not dependably winter hardy. Leaves dark green, leathery, and glossy.

DOROTHY PERKINS, *p. 71*
(Jackson & Perkins, 1901)

This popular rambler was once one of the most overplanted roses in America, and in some areas it continues to flourish despite conditions of neglect.

FLOWERS ¾ in. wide. Medium pink. Double; perhaps 35–40 petals. Late-season bloom, not recurrent, with little or no fragrance. Blooms occur in large clusters.

FOLIAGE 10–12 ft. tall. Very vigorous, but susceptible to mildew. Winter hardy. Canes moderately thorny. Leaves small, dark green, glossy.

DORTMUND, *p. 75*
(Kordes, 1955)

This kordesii climber makes a wonderful pillar rose, and its brilliant red, white-centered blossom is spectacular.

FLOWERS 3–3½ in. wide. Medium red with white eye at center. Single; 5 petals. Profuse midseason bloom followed by good repeat bloom. Fragrant. Blossoms, which occur in large clusters, open flat to reveal showy stamens. Large bright red hips appear later in the fall.

FOLIAGE 10–12 ft. tall. Upright, vigorous. Disease free and winter hardy, with dark green, glossy leaves.

DR. HUEY, *p. 72*
(Thomas, 1914)

Dr. Huey was awarded the American Rose Society's Gertrude M. Hubbard Gold Medal in 1924. It is widely used as an understock, and may persist long after the death of the rose that was originally budded onto it.

FLOWERS   3–3½ in. wide. Dark, deep maroon. Semidouble; 15 petals. Long midseason bloom, not recurrent. Fragrant. Blossoms open to become saucer-shaped, contrasting with bright golden stamens. Blooms in clusters.

FOLIAGE   12–18 ft. tall. Upright, vigorous, arching. Disease resistant and winter hardy, with moderately thorny canes. Leaves dark green, semiglossy.

DR. J. H. NICOLAS, *p. 69*
(Nicolas, 1940)

This excellent pillar rose is also suitable for a trellis of low to medium height.

FLOWERS   4½–5 in. wide. Medium pink. Double; 50 petals. Profuse midseason bloom followed by good repeat bloom. Very fragrant. Blossoms have a classic high-centered form.

FOLIAGE   8–10 ft. tall. Upright, vigorous. Disease resistant and winter hardy, with dark green, leathery leaves.

DUBLIN BAY, *p. 74*
(McGredy, 1975)

This large-flowered climber puts out profuse, fragrant red blooms at midseason, and usually follows up with a good repeat bloom.

FLOWERS   4½ in. wide. Medium red. Double; 25 petals. Profuse midseason bloom, good repeat. Blossoms fragrant and cupped.

FOLIAGE   8–14 ft. tall. Upright, vigorous, and well branched. Disease resistant. Winter hardy. Canes moderately thorny, with medium to dark green, leathery leaves.

ELEGANCE, *p. 60*
(Brownell, 1937)

The abundant yellow flowers of this handsome climber make an attractive accent for a wall or large trellis.

FLOWERS   4½–5½ in. wide. Medium yellow. Double; 45–50 petals. Abundant midseason bloom, not recurrent. Fragrant blossoms have a cupped form.

FOLIAGE   12–15 ft. tall. Upright, very vigorous. Disease resistant and winter hardy, with medium green, semiglossy leaves.

EXCELSA, p. 72
(Walsh, 1909)

Also known as the Red Dorothy Perkins, this rambler won the American Rose Society's Gertrude M. Hubbard Gold Medal in 1914.

FLOWERS   ¾ in. wide. Medium red. Double; perhaps 35–40 petals. Late-season bloom, not recurrent. With little or no fragrance. Cupped blossoms occur in large clusters.

FOLIAGE   12–18 ft. tall. Very vigorous and winter hardy, although susceptible to mildew. Canes moderately thorny. Leaves small, medium green, glossy.

GOLDEN SHOWERS, p. 64
(Lammerts, 1956)

An All-America Rose Selection for 1957 and winner of the Portland Gold Medal in 1957. Golden Showers is the most floriferous of the shorter climbers within its color range.

FLOWERS   3½–4 in. wide. Medium yellow. Double; 20–35 petals. Blooms abundantly throughout the growing season. Fragrant, cupped blossoms.

FOLIAGE   8–10 ft. tall. Upright, vigorous, and bushy. Disease resistant. Winter hardy except in severe winter climates. Canes moderately thorny, with dark green, glossy leaves.

HANDEL, p. 65
(McGredy, 1965)

Excellent for a wall or large trellis, Handel produces abundant cream-colored blossoms with a bright pink edge.

FLOWERS   3½ in. wide. Cream, edged in pink. Double; 22 petals. Good midseason bloom followed by good repeat bloom. Slight fragrance. Blossoms have a high-centered to cupped form.

FOLIAGE   12–15 ft. tall. Upright, vigorous. Disease resistant. Winter hardy. Canes moderately thorny. Leaves medium green, glossy.

JOSEPH'S COAT, p. 64
(Armstrong & Swim, 1964)

This kaleidoscopic climber was the winner of the Bagatelle Gold Medal in 1964. A "changing-colors" rose in a climber.

FLOWERS   3–4 in. wide. Double; 24–30 petals. Blossoms are yellow, gradually turning red. Good midseason bloom followed by fair repeat bloom. Slight fragrance. Blossoms have open, cupped form; occur in clusters.

FOLIAGE   8–10 ft. tall. Upright, vigorous. Disease resistant. Not dependably winter hardy. Leaves dark green, glossy.

LAWRENCE JOHNSTON, p. 65
(Pernet-Ducher; date uncertain)

Also called Hidcote Yellow, Lawrence Johnston is a vigorous climber that requires plenty of space.

FLOWERS   3–3½ in. wide. Medium yellow. Semidouble; 18–24 petals. Early to midseason bloom, not recurrent. Fragrant. Cupped blossoms occur in clusters.

FOLIAGE   20 ft. tall. Upright, very vigorous. Disease resistant in some areas; highly prone to black spot in the South. Winter hardy. Thorny canes and medium green, glossy leaves.

LEVERKUSEN, p. 62
(Kordes, 1954)

This pale yellow kordesii climber is an excellent rose for a pillar or trellis.

FLOWERS   3–3½ in. wide. Light yellow. Double; 24–30 petals. Good midseason bloom is followed by a good repeat bloom.

Slight fragrance. The high-centered, hybrid-tea-type forms occur in clusters.

FOLIAGE   8–10 ft. tall. Upright and vigorous. Disease free, winter hardy, with dark green, glossy leaves.

MAY QUEEN, *p. 68*
(Manda, 1898)

May Queen is a little less vigorous and spreading than many other wichuraianas and can be used in a variety of situations.

FLOWERS   3–3½ in. wide. Medium pink. Double; 45–55 petals. Long midseason bloom, not recurrent. Fragrant scent, like that of green apples. Full blooms, slightly cupped, quartered, with a button center.

FOLIAGE   15 ft. tall. Upright, vigorous. Disease free and winter hardy. Moderately thorny canes bear glossy leaves.

MERMAID, *p. 63*
(Paul, 1918)

Mermaid was the winner of the Royal National Rose Society Gold Medal in 1917. This hybrid bracteata climber or trailer should not be pruned any more than is absolutely necessary. It will form a ground cover and can be used to cover an arbor.

FLOWERS   4½–5½ in. wide. Medium yellow, fading to light yellow. Single; 5 petals. Fragrant. Very long midseason bloom. Blossoms open to become cupped.

FOLIAGE   20 ft. plus. Vigorous and very lax, but can be trained up. Disease resistant. Tender, not winter hardy. Canes are rather brittle. Leaves dark green, glossy.

NEW DAWN, *p. 67*
(Dreer, 1930)

This rose was the world's first patented plant. An everblooming sport of Dr. W. Van Fleet, New Dawn's flower form is not quite as fine, and some find it less vigorous than its relative.

FLOWERS   3–3½ in. wide. Light pink. Semidouble; 18–24 petals. Good midseason bloom with good repeat bloom. Fragrant. Cupped blooms show bright yellow stamens.

FOLIAGE   12–15 ft. tall. Upright, vigorous, and bushy. Disease free and winter hardy, with moderately thorny canes and medium green, glossy leaves.

PAUL'S LEMON PILLAR, *p. 61*
(Paul, 1915)

A climbing hybrid tea, Paul's Lemon Pillar won the Royal National Rose Society Gold Medal in 1915. The word "Lemon" refers to the rose's fragrance, not to its color.

FLOWERS   3½–4 in. wide. White. Double; 35–45 petals. Good all-season bloom. Very fragrant; lemon scent. Blossoms have the classic hybrid tea form.

FOLIAGE   10–12 ft. tall. Upright, vigorous. Disease resistant, but tender. Abundant dark green, glossy leaves.

PAUL'S SCARLET CLIMBER, *p. 74*
(Paul, 1916)

This popular large-flowered climber won the National Rose Society Gold Medal in 1915 and the Bagatelle Gold Medal in 1918.

FLOWERS   3–3½ in. wide. Medium red. Double; 24–30 petals. Profuse midseason bloom, not recurrent. Slight fragrance. Cupped blossoms occur in clusters.

FOLIAGE   12–15 ft. tall. Upright, vigorous. Disease resistant and winter hardy, with moderately thorny canes and dark green, semiglossy leaves.

PIERRE DE RONSARD, *p. 76*
(Meilland, 1987)

The classic old-garden-rose form of this variety makes it a suitable climbing companion for David Austin's English Roses. Like many climbers, Pierre de Ronsard requires several years to become well established and give its best.

FLOWERS   5–5½ in. wide. Cream suffused with lavender pink. Double; 40–50 petals. Profuse midseason bloom with sporadic repeat. Little fragrance. Fully cupped blooms appear singly and in nodding clusters.

FOLIAGE   8–10 ft. tall. Upright, vigorous. Disease resistant and winter hardy. Leaves are light green and semiglossy.

RHONDA, *p. 76*
(Lissemore, 1968)

Raised by an amateur rose breeder in New Jersey, this climber is dependable and easy to grow in all climates.

FLOWERS   3½–4 in. wide. Carmine-rose. Double; 35 petals. Good all-season bloom. Slight fragrance. Globular blooms usually appear in clusters.

FOLIAGE   7–9 ft. tall. Upright, vigorous, bushy. Disease resistant and winter hardy. Leaves dark green, glossy.

ROSARIUM UETERSEN, *p. 71*
(Kordes, 1977)

Named for the rose garden at Uetersen in northern Germany, this kordesii climber is one of the most heavily petaled of all modern roses. It is particularly good for growing on a wall.

FLOWERS   3½–4 in. wide. Deep coral pink. Extremely double; 142 petals. Profuse mid-season bloom with steady repeat bloom. Fragrance like that of sweet green apples. Rounded petals open flat. Blooms occur singly and in clusters.

FOLIAGE   10–12 ft. tall. Vigorous, upright, pliant growth. Disease resistant and very winter hardy. Abundant, glossy leaves are light to medium green.

ROYAL SUNSET, *p. 63*
(Morey, 1960)

Apricot climbers often suffer from awkward, leggy growth, but Royal Sunset is well clothed with foliage. It was awarded the Portland Gold Medal in 1960.

FLOWERS   4½–5 in. wide. Apricot. Semidouble; 20 petals. Midseason bloom followed by good repeat bloom. Fruity fragrance. Cupped blossoms occur singly and in clusters.

FOLIAGE   6 ft. tall. Vigorous, bushy, stiff growth. Disease resistant. Requires winter protection. Foliage is bronze-green and leathery.

SILVER MOON, *p. 62*
(Van Fleet, 1910)

Descended in part from *Rosa wichuraiana,* Silver Moon is a magnificent rose requiring plenty of space.

FLOWERS   3½–4½ in. wide. White. Semidouble; 12–20 petals. Long midseason bloom, not recurrent. Fragrant. Cupped blossoms open to saucer shape.

FOLIAGE   20 ft. tall. Upright, vigorous, arching. Disease free and winter hardy. Moderately thorny canes bear dark green, glossy leaves.

VEILCHENBLAU, *p. 66*
(Schmidt, 1909)

This rose can sometimes be found as a surviving understock in old gardens.

FLOWERS   1¼ in. wide. Violet with a white center. Semidouble; perhaps 18–24 petals. Mid- to late-season bloom, not recurrent. Fragrance like that of green apples. Petals open flat. Blossoms occur in clusters.

FOLIAGE   12 ft. tall. Upright, vigorous. Disease resistant and winter hardy. Canes smooth, almost thornless. Leaves long and pointed, medium green.

VIKING QUEEN, *p. 70*
(Phillips, 1963)

Bred for winter hardiness, this large-flowered climber is suitable for a wall or large trellis.

FLOWERS   3–4 in. wide. Medium to deep pink. Double; 60 petals. Midseason bloom followed by good repeat bloom. Very fragrant. Full, globular blossoms in clusters.

FOLIAGE   12–15 ft. tall. Upright, vigorous. Disease resistant and winter hardy, with dark green, leathery, glossy leaves.

Shrub Roses

 Like many terms used in horticulture, the word "shrub" is open to several different interpretations. For the purposes of this discussion, the shrub roses include the following subclasses: the English roses, ground covers, hybrid eglantines, hybrid musks, hybrid rugosas, hybrid spinosissimas (in part), polyanthas, and shrub roses. This last group is a catch-all class, also known as modern shrubs, whose members include roses that have come into cultivation since the mid-19th century but do not fit into any of the seven categories named above.

English Roses

The newest class of roses, developed since the 1960s by the British rose breeder David Austin, English roses combine the soft colors, rich fragrance, and intricate form of old garden roses with the bushy habit and repeat bloom characteristic of modern roses. Eventually we will see English roses from other hybridizers as well. It should also be noted that not all of Austin's introductions are English roses; Windrush is one example.

Ground Covers

This is an evolving class of roses whose members exhibit low, spreading growth and low-maintenance characteristics. Most ground covers are descendants of the species *Rosa wichuraiana* and could be thought of as climbers and ramblers with a procumbent habit. Ideal for planting on embankments and in other difficult areas, they have revealed a whole new way in which to use roses in the landscape. While they will not smother existing weeds, most ground covers will grow densely enough to prevent new weed growth during the summer.

The Meidiland roses have been the most widely distributed ground covers in America, although some Meidilands — most notably Pink Meidiland — grow upright and cannot be considered ground covers.

Hybrid Eglantines

The hybrid eglantines, descended from *Rosa eglanteria*, were developed by Lord Penzance in the late 1800s and are usually classified with the shrub roses.

These hybrids are upright, treelike shrubs, with flowers a little larger than those produced by the species. The improvement, however, is only slight when you consider that the foliage is not usually as fragrant; what is more, because the cross was made with *R. foetida*, a proclivity for black spot was bred in. Nonetheless, these hybrids offer a range of colors, and there are undoubtedly good uses for them in the garden. Hebe's Lip, a later development by William Paul, may be the most refined of the group.

Hybrid Musk Roses

A 20th-century development, the hybrid musk roses are really like big, blowsy, overgrown floribundas. They are so far removed from the influence of the Musk Rose (*Rosa moschata*) that they really should be called hybrid multifloras, for their immediate background is *Rosa multiflora*.

Hybrid musks can be used as big, freestanding bushes or hedges or trained as low climbers. The blooms are mostly delicate shades that quickly fade to white and give a white effect in the garden even before the color fades. There are a few in deeper tones. As a class these roses are fragrant, and a few of them have the sweet-pea fragrance of *Rosa moschata*.

Hybrid musks have an exceptionally good repeat bloom if they are planted in full sun; when planted in partial shade, they will usually repeat sparingly in the fall. A few varieties have attractive fall hips.

Hybrid Rugosas

Another 20th-century group, the hybrid rugosas are a varied lot. Some have the deeply etched foliage typical of the wild roses, while others do not. Some produce good repeat blooms, while others have neither repeat blooms nor good hip displays. None of them has the quality of the species *Rosa rugosa*, from which they are derived, but some are nonetheless outstanding in their own right. Some of the most unusual varieties in the group are borderline winter hardy, which is a great disappointment to those gardeners who live in severe winter climates and are accustomed to depending on this class when all else fails.

Hybrid Spinosissimas

There are two categories of hybrid spinosissimas. The first includes ancient varieties (notably Stanwell Perpetual) and is grouped with the old garden roses. The second includes the modern shrub hybrid spinosissimas, particularly the Frühlings series developed by Wilhelm Kordes.

These hybrid spinosissimas are upright, arching bushes, rather open and gaunt in habit, with very early blooms. The very large, sweetly fragrant flowers are mostly single, but some varieties are fully double.

The ancient spinosissimas grow in low mounds of ferny foliage, but the modern ones form arching hoops of seven to nine feet, making a tremendous display in early spring.

Polyantha Roses

The early polyantha roses were derived from *Rosa multiflora* and various forms of *Rosa chinensis*. The polyanthas (from the Greek for "many-flowered") started out as everblooming dwarf forms of once-blooming climbing and rambling roses. They are very hardy, and though they are among the last of the rose varieties to come into bloom, they then continue to flower until frost. Polyanthas are neat little shrubs, and they come in many colors of white, pink, red, coral, and orange. They make a bright accent in the garden and can always be depended upon. Some of them are borderline hardy in really severe winter climates, but many of them are rock hardy. Eventually, the polyanthas came to be crossed with various hybrid teas. The resulting roses — the floribundas — soon surpassed the polyanthas in popularity, and the latter tended to be neglected. Because of the recent popularity of the miniature roses, polyanthas continue to be neglected today. Fortunately, however, a great many polyanthas have been preserved, and luckily, they do still have their champions among discriminating gardeners.

ABRAHAM DARBY, p. 121
(Austin, 1985)

Also known by its code name of AUScot, Abraham Darby has long arching canes that can be trained to climb. This is an English rose raised from two modern roses, the floribunda Yellow Cushion and the climbing hybrid tea Aloha.

FLOWERS 4½–5 in. wide. Apricot pink with a yellow base. Double; 45 petals. Midseason bloom with repeat in regular cycles. Very fragrant. Blossom has cupped form.

FOLIAGE   5–6 ft. tall, but will grow taller if trained up a wall. Vigorous, arching. Very resistant to mildew; may require protection from black spot. Moderately winter hardy. Canes are armed with thorns up to 1 in. in length. Leaves deep green, glossy.

AGNES, p. 101
(Saunders, 1900)

Agnes is a cross of *Rosa rugosa* with *Rosa foetida persiana* (Persian Yellow), an attempt to breed the yellow color into the rugosa hybrids. This strong bush may repeat bloom when very well established.

FLOWERS   3–3½ in. wide. Light yellow. Double; 24–30 petals. Very fragrant. Early to midseason bloom, sometimes recurrent. Cupped form.

FOLIAGE   5 ft. tall. Upright, vigorous, bushy. Disease resistant and winter hardy. Canes very thorny; leaves dull, dark green.

ALBA MEIDILAND, p. 81
(Meilland, 1985)

A low-maintenance ground-cover rose, Alba Meidiland is also a good source of cut-flower sprays.

FLOWERS   2 in. wide. White. Double; 40-plus petals. Profuse bloom in midseason with another good display in the fall. No fragrance. Blossoms cupped, in clusters.

FOLIAGE   2 ft. tall by 6 ft. wide. Vigorous, spreading. Disease resistant and winter hardy. Small, medium green, glossy leaves.

ALCHYMIST, p. 99
(Kordes, 1956)

The apricot-colored Alchymist can be used as a climber, as it is an excellent pillar rose and also does well on a trellis.

FLOWERS   3½–4 in. wide. Apricot blend. Very double; 65–75 petals. Early to midseason bloom, not recurrent. Fragrant. Blossoms have an old-garden-rose form; sometimes quartered.

FOLIAGE   8–12 ft. tall. Upright, vigorous, and arching. Disease resistant, winter hardy. Very thorny canes bear large, dark green, glossy leaves.

ALL THAT JAZZ, *p. 97*
(Twomey, 1991)

An All-America Rose Selection in 1991, All That Jazz is considered a breakthrough rose for its disease-free growth. It has such attractive foliage that it is a garden ornament even when not in bloom.

FLOWERS   5–5½ in. wide. Bright coral salmon. Semidouble; 12–13 petals. Early to midseason bloom with steady repeat bloom. Moderate damask fragrance. Blossoms are loose and cupped, in clusters of 3–5.

FOLIAGE   5 ft. tall. Upright, vigorous, bushy. Disease free. Winter hardy. Dark green, very glossy leaves.

BABY FAURAX, *p. 92*
(Lille, 1924)

This polyantha variety is good for edgings and accents in the garden, where its deep violet color makes an attractive accent.

FLOWERS   2 in. wide. Mauve. Double; 18–24 petals. Blooms first at midseason or later, continuous bloom thereafter until frost. Little or no fragrance. Blossoms cupped, in clusters.

FOLIAGE   8–12 in. tall. A bushy, dense dwarf plant. Disease resistant and winter hardy with dark green, glossy leaves.

BALLERINA, *p. 84*
(Bentall, 1937)

With its arching growth, this hybrid musk makes a good "weeping" standard. The shape of the plant is reminiscent of a ballerina's skirt, hence the name.

FLOWERS   2 in. wide. Pink with a deeper pink edge and a white center. Yellow stamens turn dark rather quickly. Single; 5 petals. Midseason bloom with good repeat bloom. Slight musky fragrance, like sweet peas. Blooms in clusters.

FOLIAGE   3–4 ft. tall. Arching growth, about as wide as high. Disease resistant and winter hardy. Canes smooth, with few thorns. Leaves light green, semiglossy.

BELINDA, *p. 91*
(Bentall, 1936)

The vigorous Belinda grows dense and bushy, and it makes a good hedge rose.

FLOWERS   ¾ in. wide. Medium pink. Semidouble; 12–15 petals. Midseason bloom with good repeat bloom. Light fragrance. Blooms in clusters.

FOLIAGE   4–6 ft. tall. Upright, vigorous, bushy, and dense. Disease resistant; winter hardy. Fairly smooth canes with few thorns bear light green, semiglossy leaves.

BELLE POITEVINE, *p. 93*
(Bruant, 1894)

Belle Poitevine is a big, billowing shrub. Almost always in bloom, it is intensely fragrant, with an aroma of cloves.

FLOWERS   3½–4 in. wide. Medium pink with a mauve tint. Semidouble; 18–24 petals. Profuse early-season bloom followed by good repeat bloom. Very fragrant; clove-scented. Blossoms have a cupped form.

FOLIAGE   7–9 ft. tall and as wide. Upright, vigorous, spreading. Disease free and winter hardy. Very thorny canes bear medium green, leathery, deeply etched (rugose) leaves.

BELLE STORY, *p. 121*
(Austin, 1984)

This English rose has an excellent habit and can be planted in the front of the border. The semidouble blooms resemble those of a peony and come on long stems.

FLOWERS   4 in. wide. Warm light pink, fading slightly. Semidouble; 20 petals. Midseason bloom with good repeat bloom. Good fragrance. Cup-shaped blooms appear singly and in wide clusters.

FOLIAGE   3–4 ft. tall. Bushy. Disease resistant and winter hardy. Medium green, semiglossy leaves.

BIRDIE BLYE, *p. 92*
(Van Fleet, 1904)

This pink shrub rose has an interesting parentage; it is the product of tea and multiflora ancestors.

FLOWERS   3½–4 in. wide. Medium pink. Double; 24–30 petals. Midseason bloom with fair repeat bloom. Slight fragrance. Blossoms cupped, in clusters.

FOLIAGE   4–5 ft. tall. Upright, vigorous, arching. Disease resistant and winter hardy, with light green, glossy leaves.

BLANC DOUBLE DE COUBERT, *p. 80*
(Cochet-Cochet, 1892)

One of the most popular of the shrub roses. Deadheading will encourage more blooms, and removing only the spent petals will make it possible to enjoy the hips.

FLOWERS   2½–3 in. wide. White. Semidouble; 18–24 petals. Good early to midseason bloom, followed by fair repeat bloom. Very fragrant. Rather raggedy spent blooms hang on, looking limp and dirty. Good hips later in season.

FOLIAGE   4–6 ft. tall. Upright, moderately vigorous. Disease free and very winter hardy. Leaves light green and leathery, turning bright yellow in the fall.

BONICA, *p. 89*
(Meilland, 1982)

In 1987, Bonica became the first shrub ever to be named an All-America Rose Selection. In 1983, it received Germany's prestigious ADR award, an indication that it is exceptionally winter hardy and disease resistant. It is sometimes sold under its code name, MEIdomonac.

FLOWERS   1–2 in. wide. Medium pink, lighter at edges. Double; 40-plus petals. Long midseason bloom with excellent repeat bloom. No fragrance. Rosette form, in clusters.

FOLIAGE   3–5 ft. tall. Spreading, vigorous, arching. Disease resistant and winter hardy. Leaves are small, dark green, semi-glossy.

BOY CRAZY, *p. 88*
(Dickson, 1992)

A dwarf shrub that could also be called a patio rose, Boy Crazy has a profuse bloom that provides an excellent alternative to annual bedding plants.

FLOWERS   1½–2 in. wide. Raspberry pink with creamy eye. Semidouble; 15–20 petals. Heavy midseason bloom with excellent repeat bloom. No fragrance. Blossoms cupped, in clusters.

FOLIAGE   2–2½ ft. tall. Bushy. Very resistant to mildew; may require protection from black spot. Winter hardy. Plentiful dark green, glossy leaves.

BREDON, *p. 113*
(Austin, 1984)

An English rose that could well have been classified as a floribunda, Bredon makes a good low hedge. Deadheading is required for best repeat bloom.

FLOWERS   2½ in. wide. Apricot. Double; 40-plus petals. Good midseason bloom, repeats. Sharp tea fragrance. Blossoms have rosette form, in clusters.

FOLIAGE   2½–3 ft. tall. Upright, bushy. Generally disease resistant, but may need protection from mildew. Winter hardy. Leaves small, light green, leathery.

BUFF BEAUTY, *p. 100*
(Pemberton, 1922)

There is very little influence of *Rosa moschata* in the hybrid musk roses, and they might better be called hybrid multifloras. Like any rose, Buff Beauty will grow nicely in partial shade, but it will bloom well only when provided with a half-day's sunlight.

FLOWERS   3 in. wide. Apricot, blended with deep yellow and gold. Double; perhaps 30–40 petals. Midseason bloom with good repeat bloom. Fragrant. Fully double blooms reflex into balls.

FOLIAGE   6 ft. tall. Vigorous, bushy. Disease resistant. Winter hardy. Canes moderately thorny. Leaves light to medium green, semiglossy.

CARDINAL HUME, *p. 108*
(Harkness, 1984)

A fascinating shrub in an unusual color, Cardinal Hume grows wider than it does tall but holds its canes too far off the ground to be classified as a ground cover. David Austin considers this variety akin to his English roses.

FLOWERS   1½ in. wide. Rich purple, fading to deep red-purple. Double; 31 petals. Abundant midseason bloom with excellent repeat bloom. Good fragrance; musky scent. Cup-shaped blossoms appear in wide sprays.

FOLIAGE   4 ft. tall by 6 ft. wide. Vigorous, spreading. Disease resistant and winter hardy. Canes have small thorns. Leaves medium green, matte.

CAREFREE BEAUTY, *p. 110*
(Buck, 1977)

Free-blooming and tough, this rose makes an excellent hedge. Carefree Beauty is the best-known of the many worthwhile "prairie" roses developed by the late Dr. Griffith J. Buck at Iowa State University.

FLOWERS   4–4½ in. wide. Rose-pink. Semidouble; 15–20 petals. Abundant midseason bloom with excellent repeat bloom. Fragrant. Blossoms have ovoid form, in clusters.

FOLIAGE   5–6 ft. tall. Upright, vigorous. Disease resistant and winter hardy. Smooth, olive-green leaves.

CAREFREE WONDER, *p. 111*
(Meilland, 1990)

This rose combines the disease resistance of Dr. Buck's prairie roses with the color interest of Sam McGredy's handpainted strain. In 1990 it became the second shrub rose to receive an All-America Rose Selection award.

FLOWERS   4–5 in. wide. Medium pink, with creamy pink reverse and white eye; petals are etched deeper pink in cool weather. Double; 26 petals. Excellent midseason bloom with very good repeat bloom. Slight fragrance. Cupped blossoms appear singly and in small clusters.

FOLIAGE   4–5 ft. high. Bushy, vigorous. Disease resistant and winter hardy. Canes have narrow reddish thorns and medium green, semiglossy leaves.

CÉCILE BRUNNER, *p. 86*
(Ducher, 1881)

Cécile Brunner is famous as a buttonhole rose. An exceptionally fine climbing form is available.

FLOWERS   1½ in. wide. Light pink. Double. Profuse late-season bloom with excellent repeat bloom. Slight fragrance. Blossoms have a classic hybrid tea form in miniature; borne in clusters.

FOLIAGE   2½–3 ft. tall. Upright, bushy, spreading. Disease resistant. Not dependably winter hardy in severe winter climates. Canes very smooth with few thorns. Abundant dark green leaves are small and semiglossy.

CHINA DOLL, *p. 89*
(Lammerts, 1946)

Blooming late in the season, this pink polyantha makes a good low edging.

FLOWERS   1–2 in. wide. Medium pink. Double; 20–26 petals. Blooms first late in the season, with continuous blooms until frost. Slight fragrance. Blossoms cupped, in clusters.

FOLIAGE   1½ ft. tall. Bushy, spreading, compact. Disease resistant and winter hardy. Leaves medium green, leathery.

COCKTAIL, *p. 104*
(Meilland, 1957)

One of the most spectacular single-petaled roses, Cocktail is a favorite with flower arrangers and photographers.

FLOWERS   2–2½ in. wide. Geranium red with yellow eye. Single; 5 petals. Good midseason bloom with steady repeat bloom. Light, spicy fragrance. Blooms in clusters.

FOLIAGE   5–6 ft. tall. Upright, narrow, semiclimbing. Disease resistant. May require winter protection in extreme climates. Leaves leathery, glossy.

CONRAD FERDINAND MEYER, *p. 85*
(Müller, 1899)

The fragrance of this rose is intense and carrying — it will perfume your whole garden. The plant requires careful placement, but is a wonderful rose when it can be grown.

FLOWERS   3½–4½ in. wide. Light to medium pink. Very double; 65–75 petals. Long early to midseason bloom, not recurrent. Intensely fragrant damask, or true-rose, scent. Full blossoms are globular, sometimes quartered.

FOLIAGE   9–12 ft. tall. Upright and very vigorous, with rather gaunt canes. Disease free but not dependably winter hardy. Very thorny canes with rather sparse gray-green leaves.

CONSTANCE SPRY, *p. 88*
(Austin, 1961)

Named for the English author, floral designer, and collector of old garden roses, Constance Spry is a modern shrub rose with the true old garden rose form and fragrance.

FLOWERS   4½–5 in. wide. Light to medium pink. Double; 45–55 petals. Long midseason bloom, not recurrent. Very fragrant scent, like myrrh. Blossoms full, globular.

FOLIAGE   5–6 ft. tall. Upright, vigorous, arching. Disease resistant and winter hardy. Moderately thorny canes with dark green, semiglossy leaves.

CORNELIA, *p. 84*
(Pemberton, 1925)

It appears that the rose originally introduced by Pemberton under this name is not the same as the rose sold today. Unless further research turns up the modern rose's true name, experts and novices alike must be content to live with this ambiguity.

FLOWERS   1 in. wide. Medium pink with mauve and yellow tints. Double; 20–30 petals. Midseason bloom with good repeat bloom. Fragrant. Rosette form, in clusters.

FOLIAGE   6–8 ft. tall. Vigorous and arching, with a somewhat loose growth habit. Disease resistant and winter hardy. Canes moderately thorny. Leaves medium to dark green, leathery, semiglossy.

DAVID THOMPSON, *p. 116*
(Svejda, 1979)

This is a hybrid rugosa member of the Canadian Explorer family of shrubs. David Thompson the explorer surveyed the headwaters of the Mississippi and discovered the source of the Columbia River. David Thompson the rose is almost never out of bloom.

FLOWERS   2½ in. wide. Cerise-red. Double; 25 petals. Excellent all-season bloom. Very fragrant. Blooms cupped, with yellow stamens.

FOLIAGE   4 ft. tall. Upright, bushy. Disease resistant and winter hardy. Leaves yellow-green, rugose.

DELICATA, *p. 93*
(Cooling, 1898)

This clove-scented, mauve-pink hybrid rugosa is a smaller version of Belle Poitevine.

FLOWERS   3–3½ in. wide. Mauve-pink. Semidouble; 18–24 petals. Abundant early to midseason bloom, followed by good repeat bloom. Very fragrant; clove scent. Blossom has cupped form.

FOLIAGE   3½–4½ ft. tall. Upright, vigorous, well branched, and compact. Disease free and winter hardy. Very thorny canes bear light green, leathery, deeply etched (rugose) leaves.

DISTANT DRUMS, *p. 119*
(Buck, 1985)

This remarkably colored rose displays ever-changing shades of russet and mauve. Especially bred for winter hardiness, Distant Drums is a unique accent plant.

FLOWERS   4–4½ in. wide. Blends of rosy purple, russet, and mauve. Double; 35 petals. Good late-season bloom, with excellent repeat bloom. Very fragrant; myrrh scent. Slightly cupped blooms appear singly and in clusters of up to 10.

FOLIAGE   4–5 ft. tall. Upright, bushy, vigorous. Disease resistant and winter hardy. Moderately thorny canes support dark green, leathery leaves.

DOVE, *p. 119*
(Austin, 1984)

One of the most graceful of David Austin's English roses, Dove is like a modern, compact hybrid musk. It makes excellent stems for cut flowers.

FLOWERS   2–2½ in. wide. Pink buds, opening blush white. Double; 40-plus petals. Good midseason bloom with good repeat bloom. Strongly fragrant; rose and apple scent. Tea-rose-shaped buds open to rosette shape. Blooms in large clusters.

FOLIAGE   2½–3 ft. tall and as wide. Vigorous, loose growth. Disease resistant and winter hardy. Dark green, pointed leaves like those of hybrid musk roses.

ELMSHORN, *p. 96*
(Kordes, 1951)

Many hardy roses have come from the Kordes firm, which has made this quality a special consideration in the roses they develop.

FLOWERS   1½ in. wide. Medium red. Double; 20 petals. Midseason bloom with good repeat bloom. Slight fragrance. Blossoms cupped, occurring in clusters.

FOLIAGE   5–6 ft. tall. Upright, vigorous, bushy. Disease resistant and winter hardy. Moderately thorny canes with long, medium green, semiglossy leaves.

ENGLISH GARDEN, *p. 125*
(Austin, 1986)

The compact growth of this elegantly formed English rose makes it suitable for even the smallest garden. English Garden is also known by its code name, AUSbuff.

FLOWERS   3½ in. wide. Buff yellow. Double; 40-plus petals. Good midseason bloom with fair repeat bloom. Nice tea-rose fragrance. Blossoms open to rosette shape.

FOLIAGE   2½–3 ft. tall. Upright, not vigorous. Disease resistant and winter hardy. Leaves light green.

ERFURT, *p. 91*
(Kordes, 1939)

Erfurt gives somewhat the same garden effect as a single rose without being a true single. The hybrid musks are arching rather than upright, a characteristic that contributes to the abundance of their blossoms.

FLOWERS   3½ in. wide. Wide pink edge, lemon-white in center, with yellow stamens. Semidouble; 10–15 petals. Good continuous bloom throughout the season. Intensely fragrant. Bloom opens to become saucer-shaped. Blossoms occur in clusters.

FOLIAGE   5–6 ft. tall. Very vigorous, bushy. Disease resistant and winter hardy, with moderately thorny canes. Abundant dark green leaves are large, leathery, and wrinkled.

ESPRIT, *p. 97*
(Kordes, 1987)

Sometimes classed as a floribunda, Esprit is truly an international rose, known as City of Birmingham in England, Petit Marquis in France, and Holstein 87 in its native Germany. Because it is sterile and sets no hips, it is able to put all of its energy into flower production.

FLOWERS   3–3½ in. wide. Deep red. Semidouble; 12 petals. Excellent all-season bloom. No fragrance. Cup-shaped blossoms in large clusters.

FOLIAGE   3–3½ ft. tall. Vigorous, compact, bushy. Disease resistant. Winter hardy. Moderately thorny canes bear medium green, semiglossy leaves.

F. J. GROOTENDORST, *p. 96*
(de Goey, 1918)

Like carnations and pinks, this rose has petals with serrated edges. F. J. Grootendorst has several color sports.

FLOWERS 1½ in. wide. Medium red. Double; perhaps 35–45 petals. Profuse midseason bloom followed by good repeat bloom. No fragrance. Petals have serrated edges. Blossoms occur in large clusters.

FOLIAGE 6–8 ft. tall. Upright, vigorous, bushy. Disease resistant and winter hardy. Moderately thorny canes bear small, wrinkled, leathery dark green leaves.

FAIR BIANCA, *p. 120*
(Austin, 1982)

A perfect English rose for the small garden, Fair Bianca displays perfectly quartered, button-eyed blooms reminiscent of the classic damask rose Mme. Hardy.

FLOWERS 3–3½ in. wide. White. Very double; 70 petals. Midseason bloom followed by repeat bloom in regular cycles. Strong fragrance; anise scent. Blooms deeply cupped, quartered, in well-arranged clusters.

FOLIAGE 2½–3 ft. tall. Upright. Disease resistant and winter hardy. Spiny-thorned canes clothed with light green, semiglossy foliage.

FERDY, *p. 111*
(Suzuki, 1984)

This valuable landscaping ground cover provides a mass of bloom over a long period in early summer. Ferdy will cascade over a modest support, creating a flowing, waterfall-like effect in the garden.

FLOWERS 1 in. wide. Coral pink. Semidouble; 18–20 petals. Long, abundant early season bloom, very little repeat bloom. No fragrance. Blossoms cup-shaped, in large clusters.

FOLIAGE 5–7 ft. tall. Vigorous, spreading, procumbent. Disease free and winter hardy. Leaves are small, medium green, matte.

FISHERMAN'S FRIEND, *p. 108*
(Austin, 1987)

Named for the popular brand of throat lozenges, Fisherman's Friend produces gigantic crimson flowers and is a good repeat bloomer.

FLOWERS 5–6 in. wide. Deep crimson. Very double; 60-plus petals. Good midseason bloom, with good repeat bloom. Good fragrance; damask scent. Cup-shaped blooms usually appear singly.

FOLIAGE 3–4 ft. tall. Upright, a somewhat slow grower. Disease resistant, but may require protection under stressful conditions. Winter hardy. Canes are armed with large red-brown thorns and bear dark green, semiglossy leaves.

FRAU DAGMAR HASTRUP, *p. 82*
(Unknown, c. 1914)

Also called Frau Dagmar Hartopp, this pink favorite has an architectural value in the garden landscape, as it makes an excellent low hedge. It is beloved of bees.

FLOWERS 3–3½ in. wide. Light pink. Single; 5 petals. Early to midseason bloom followed by good repeat bloom. Very fragrant; clove scent. Blooms open to become saucer-shaped with bright golden stamens. Large, bright red hips appear later in the season.

FOLIAGE 2½–3 ft. tall. Upright, vigorous, dense, and spreading. Disease free, winter hardy, with very thorny canes. Leaves medium green, deeply etched (rugose).

FRED LOADS, *p. 99*
(Holmes, 1968)

Winner of the Royal National Rose Society Gold Medal in 1967, this big, husky bush is almost always in bloom and is excellent for garden display.

FLOWERS 3–3½ in. wide. Orange. Semidouble; 12–18 petals. Good all-season bloom. Little or no fragrance. Blossoms cupped to saucer-shaped, in clusters.

FOLIAGE 4½–5 ft. tall. Upright, vigorous, well branched. Disease resistant. Winter hardy. Moderately thorny canes bear dark green, glossy leaves.

FRÜHLINGSGOLD, *p. 103*
(Kordes, 1937)

This rose and Frühlingsmorgen are part of a series developed by Kordes, who used *Rosa spinosissima*, the Scotch Rose, as a parent.

FLOWERS   3–3½ in. wide. Light yellow. Single; 5 petals. Early-season bloom, not recurrent. Fragrant. Blossom opens to saucer shape with showy golden stamens.

FOLIAGE   5–7 ft. tall. Upright, arching, vigorous. Disease free, winter hardy, with moderately thorny canes. Leaves soft, dull, light green.

FRÜHLINGSMORGEN, p. 83
(Kordes, 1942)

The name of this hybrid spinosissima means "spring morning." This rose is very similar to Frühlingsgold except in the color of the bloom.

FLOWERS   3–3½ in. wide. Pink with light yellow at base. Single; 5–7 petals. Profuse early-season bloom, not recurrent. Fragrant. Blossom opens to become saucer-shaped with unusual maroon stamens.

FOLIAGE   5–7 ft. tall. Upright, arching, vigorous. Disease free. Winter hardy. Canes moderately thorny; leaves soft, dull, dark green.

GARTENDIREKTOR OTTO LINNE, p. 94
(Lambert, 1934)

This bushy variety makes an excellent hedge, and its deep pink blossoms provide a bright touch of color.

FLOWERS   1½–2 in. wide. Deep pink. Double; 25–35 petals. Midseason bloom followed by good repeat bloom. Little or no fragrance. Blossoms cupped, in clusters.

FOLIAGE   3½–4½ ft. tall. Upright, bushy, spreading. Disease resistant. Winter hardy. Canes smooth, nearly thornless. Leaves light to medium green, semiglossy.

GERTRUDE JEKYLL, p. 117
(Austin, 1986)

A spectacular English rose for the large garden, Gertrude Jekyll exhibits exquisitely formed rich pink blooms of true old-garden-rose character.

FLOWERS   4½–5 in. wide. Rich pink. Very double; 60-plus petals. Good midseason bloom with sporadic repeat bloom. Very fragrant; damask scent. Blooms open to rosette form.

FOLIAGE   5–8 ft. tall. Upright, vigorous, slightly arching. Disease resistant and winter hardy. Thorny canes bear medium green, semiglossy foliage.

GOLDBUSCH, *p. 101*
(Kordes, 1954)

Supposedly a hybrid eglanteria, Goldbusch actually has little affinity with that group and is here classed as a shrub.

FLOWERS   2½–3 in. wide. Medium yellow, becoming paler on edges. Double; 24–30 petals. Mid- to late-season bloom, with good repeat bloom. Fragrant. Open, cupped form. Blossoms occur in clusters.

FOLIAGE   5 ft. tall. Upright, vigorous, bushy. Disease resistant. Winter hardy. Moderately thorny canes bear light green, semiglossy leaves.

GOLDEN WINGS, *p. 102*
(Shepherd, 1956)

Winner of the American Rose Society National Gold Medal Certificate in 1958, Golden Wings is almost the earliest rose to bloom and remains in flower longest of all roses. A favorite of bees, it is also popular with people, and is considered the most valuable of landscape roses.

FLOWERS   4–5 in. wide. Light yellow. Single; 5 petals. Excellent all-season bloom. Slight fragrance. Blooms open to become saucer-shaped, revealing golden stamens.

FOLIAGE   4½–5½ ft. tall. Upright, vigorous, well branched. Disease resistant. Winter hardy except in very severe winter climates. Canes moderately thorny. Leaves dull, light green.

GRAHAM THOMAS, *p. 123*
(Austin, 1983)

Named for the famous British plantsman, Graham Thomas was the first true yellow English Rose.

FLOWERS 3½–4 in. wide. Deep golden yellow. Double; 35 petals. Good late-season bloom; repeat bloom varies with climate, from excellent to sporadic. Very fragrant; tea rose scent. Blossom maintains its cupped form until petals drop.

FOLIAGE 5–7 ft. tall. Upright, vigorous, narrow growth. Disease resistant and winter hardy. Plentiful light green leaves.

HANSA, *p. 94*
(Schaum & Van Tol, 1905)

Growing in a bushy, dense fashion, this hybrid rugosa is popular because of its architectural value in the garden.

FLOWERS 3–3½ in. wide. Red-violet. Double; perhaps 35–45 petals. Early to midseason bloom with good repeat bloom. Fragrant; clove-scented. Bloom form rather loose, cupped. Large red hips appear later in the season.

FOLIAGE 5 ft. tall. Upright, vigorous, bushy, dense. Disease resistant and winter hardy. Canes very thorny. Leaves dark green, deeply etched (rugose).

HARISON'S YELLOW, *p. 103*
(Harison, 1830)

This popular shrub rose has bright yellow flowers that hold their color. After the flowers have bloomed, the ferny foliage remains healthy and attractive.

FLOWERS 2–2½ in. wide. Deep yellow. Double; 20–24 petals. Very early bloom, not recurrent. Blooms cupped, with showy golden stamens. Blossoms occur along arching canes.

FOLIAGE 5–7 ft. tall. Upright, spreading, arching habit. Disease resistant. Winter hardy. Canes dark mahogany brown, very thorny. Leaves small, abundant, light to medium green, ferny.

HEBE'S LIP, *p. 82*
(Paul, 1912)

Also called Reine Blanche and Rubrotincta, this hybrid eglanteria probably has a damask rose in its ancestry. A smaller plant than is typical for its class.

FLOWERS   3 in. wide. Creamy white, margined with red. Semidouble; 12–15 petals. Early, profuse bloom does not repeat. Moderate rose fragrance. Fat, pointed buds are tipped with red, opening to flat white blooms tipped in red on outer petals. Showy golden stamens.

FOLIAGE   4 ft. tall. Upright, bushy, and moderately vigorous. Disease free and winter hardy. Canes moderately thorny. Leaves dull, dark green, with a fragrance of apples.

HERITAGE, p. 112
(Austin, 1985)

David Austin considers this the most beautiful of his English roses. It combines all of the qualities he seeks in a rose: true old-garden-rose form, outstanding fragrance, and dependable repeat bloom.

FLOWERS   4½–5 in. wide. Soft pink. Double; 40-plus petals. Good midseason bloom, followed by good repeat bloom. Very fragrant; lemony scent. Blossoms have cupped form and appear both singly and in clusters.

FOLIAGE   5–6 ft. tall. Upright, vigorous, arching. Disease resistant and winter hardy. Almost thornless canes support small, dark green, semiglossy leaves.

LA SEVILLANA, p. 106
(Meilland, 1978)

Sometimes classified as a floribunda, La Sevillana should not be confused with Sevilliana, a pink blend shrub from Griffith Buck. La Sevillana produces autumn bloom every bit as spectacular as its early summer display, a rare feat for a landscaping rose.

FLOWERS   2–2½ in. wide. Vermilion red. Semidouble; 13 petals. Profuse midseason and autumn bloom, with steady bloom in between. Little or no fragrance. Blooms in large clusters.

FOLIAGE   3 ft. tall, and as wide. Bushy, vigorous. Disease resistant and winter hardy. Leaves bronzy green.

LAVENDER DREAM, *p. 116*
(Ilsink, 1984)

Winner of Germany's ADR award in 1987, Lavender Dream produces masses of lavender-pink blooms all season long. It is happiest when grown in filtered sunlight or light shade.

FLOWERS 2–2½ in. wide. Lavender-pink. Semidouble; 16 petals. Abundant midseason bloom, with excellent repeat bloom. No fragrance. Blossoms appear in wide clusters. Attractive golden yellow stamens.

FOLIAGE 4–5 ft. tall. Upright, bushy growth, well branched and compact. Disease resistant and winter hardy. Canes have very few thorns and bear light green, matte foliage.

LAVENDER LASSIE, *p. 95*
(Kordes, 1960)

Very often the name of a rose expresses what the breeder was trying to achieve rather than the reality of the rose itself. Reports from many sections of the country confirm that Lavender Lassie is really a pure, even, medium pink.

FLOWERS 3 in. wide. Medium pink; said to have lilac shadings in some regions. Semidouble; 20–30 petals. Midseason bloom with good repeat bloom. Very fragrant. Cup-shaped blossoms, in clusters.

FOLIAGE 5–7 ft. tall. Upright, vigorous, bushy. Disease resistant. Winter hardy. Canes smooth, with few thorns. Leaves abundant, large, medium green.

LINDA CAMPBELL, *p. 109*
(Moore, 1990)

The result of crossing a miniature rose and a hybrid rugosa, Linda Campbell offers bright red color and fast repeat bloom on a disease-resistant plant.

FLOWERS 3 in. wide. Bright crimson. Double; 25 petals. Good midseason bloom, with fast repeat bloom throughout the season. No fragrance. Cupped blooms occur in large clusters.

FOLIAGE   3–5 ft. tall. Upright, vigorous, bushy. Disease resistant. Winter hardy. Foliage large, dark green, semiglossy.

MAIGOLD, *p. 102*
(Kordes, 1953)

This bushy, deep yellow rose is excellent for a shrub border.

FLOWERS   4 in. wide. Deep yellow. Semidouble; 14 petals. Early to midseason bloom, not recurrent. Very fragrant. Cupped form.

FOLIAGE   5 ft. tall. Upright, vigorous, bushy. Disease resistant and winter hardy. Leaves medium green, glossy.

MARGO KOSTER, *p. 98*
(Koster, 1931)

Perhaps the most popular of the dwarf polyantha roses, Margo Koster has sported many times, and is itself a sport of Dick Koster. A climbing form is available.

FLOWERS   1–1½ in. wide. Coral. Almost single; 7–12 petals. Late-season bloom with excellent repeat bloom. Slight fragrance. Blossoms cup-shaped, in clusters.

FOLIAGE   1 ft. tall. Bushy, compact. Disease resistant. Winter hardy. Canes very smooth, with few thorns. Leaves medium gray-green, semiglossy.

MARGUERITE HILLING, *p. 90*
(Hilling, 1959)

A pink sport of Nevada, Marguerite Hilling has red canes that will enliven the gray landscape of winter in your garden.

FLOWERS   4 in. wide. Light to deep pink. Single; 5 petals. Midseason bloom with excellent repeat bloom. Little or no fragrance. Form open, saucer-shaped.

FOLIAGE   6–8 ft. tall. Upright, arching, bushy. Disease resistant. Winter hardy. Canes red, with few thorns. Leaves small, gray-green, semiglossy.

MARY ROSE, *p. 114*
(Austin, 1983)

Seldom out of bloom, this is the most profuse of the Austin English roses. There are several mutations from Mary Rose, the most notable of which is the white Winchester Cathedral.

FLOWERS   4–4½ in. wide. Rose-pink. Very double; 40-plus petals. Outstanding early bloom with excellent repeat bloom. Moderate fragrance; anise scent. Bloom form cupped.

FOLIAGE   4–6 ft. tall. Vigorous, slightly spreading, bushy, well branched. Disease resistant and winter hardy. Canes are thorny. Leaves medium green, matte.

MORDEN CENTENNIAL, *p. 114*
(Marshall, 1980)

This very hardy shrub rose was raised at, and named for, the Canadian Department of Agriculture's breeding station in Morden, Manitoba.

FLOWERS   3½–4 in. wide. Medium pink. Very double; 50 petals. Good midseason bloom with good repeat bloom. Light fragrance. Cup-shaped blooms, in clusters of up to 15.

FOLIAGE   3 ft. tall. Upright, bushy. Disease resistant and winter hardy. Slightly glossy leaves are typically composed of 7 leaflets.

MORGENROT, *p. 104*
(Kordes, 1985)

Flowering exuberantly on a compact bush, Morgenrot provides excellent color impact in the landscape and is a good rose to incorporate into the perennial border. It is one of only a few roses especially noted for attracting butterflies.

FLOWERS   2½–3 in. wide. Bright red with white eye. Single; 5 petals. Midseason bloom with excellent repeat bloom. Slight fragrance. Bloom form open, flat, with prominent yellow stamens. Blossoms occasionally show handpainted markings in cool weather.

FOLIAGE   3 ft. tall. Vigorous, bushy, compact. Disease resistant and winter hardy. Leaves light green, matte.

NEVADA, p. 83
(Dot, 1927)

This beautiful shrub rose is reportedly a *moyesii* hybrid, but many authorities have questioned this attribution. Nevada is supposedly sterile, but interested gardeners may want to try to germinate seeds from the occasional orange hips.

FLOWERS   3½–4 in. wide. White. Single; 5 petals. Midseason bloom with excellent repeat bloom. Little or no fragrance. Bloom form open, saucer-shaped, with yellow stamens. Blossoms may be tinged with pink in the fall.

FOLIAGE   6–8 ft. tall. Upright, arching, bushy. Disease resistant and winter hardy. Canes are red, with few thorns. Leaves small, gray-green, semiglossy.

OTHELLO, p. 109
(Austin, 1989)

A large rose with an admirable capacity for repeat bloom, Othello is also known by its code name, AUSlo.

FLOWERS   5–6 in. wide. Crimson, fading to purple. Very double; 50-plus petals. Midseason bloom with excellent repeat bloom. Very fragrant; fruity scent. Blooms cup-shaped, somewhat informal.

FOLIAGE   5–6 ft. tall. Vigorous, upright, bushy. Disease resistant and winter hardy. Leaves dark green, slightly glossy.

PEARL DRIFT, p. 118
(LeGrice, 1980)

One of the few descendants of *Rosa bracteata* ever released into commerce, Pearl Drift is among the final legacies of the great English rose breeder E. B. LeGrice.

FLOWERS   3–3½ in. wide. Cream, flushed pink. Semidouble; 18 petals. Midseason bloom with good repeat bloom. Slight fragrance. Blooms in clusters of 5–9.

FOLIAGE   3 ft. high by 4 ft. wide. Vigorous, bushy, spreading. Disease resistant and winter hardy. Succulent canes with small brown thorns. Dark green, glossy leaves.

PENELOPE, *p. 80*
(Pemberton, 1924)

Penelope makes an excellent hedge, and the very pale coral-pink blossoms give a white effect. The hips are quite unusual — not spectacular, but pleasing.

FLOWERS   3 in. wide. Pale coral-pink, fading to blush. Semi-double; 18–24 petals. Midseason bloom with good repeat, particularly in fall. Very fragrant. Blossoms, in clusters, become cup-shaped. Hips appear in fall; green, turning coral-pink.

FOLIAGE   5–7 ft. tall. Upright, bushy, dense. Disease resistant and winter hardy. Moderately thorny canes support medium green, dense, semiglossy leaves.

PERDITA, *p. 124*
(Austin, 1983)

An example of how rose fragrance can vary from place to place, Perdita received the Edland Fragrance Medal from England's Royal National Rose Society in 1984, but American gardeners have found it to have only a slight scent. It is an excellent shrub, in growth very similar to Dove.

FLOWERS   2½–3 in. wide. Apricot-pink and yellow. Very double; 40-plus petals. Midseason bloom with good repeat bloom. Variable fragrance. Flowers cup- to dish-shaped, in clusters.

FOLIAGE   2½–3 ft. tall and as wide. Vigorous, loose growth. Disease resistant and winter hardy. Dark green, pointed leaves like those of hybrid musk roses.

PINK GROOTENDORST, *p. 87*
(Grootendorst, 1923)

This is a color sport of the red variety F. J. Grootendorst.

FLOWERS   1½ in wide. Medium pink. Double; perhaps 35–45 petals. Profuse midseason bloom followed by good repeat bloom. No fragrance. Petals have serrated edges, like carnations. Blooms in large clusters.

FOLIAGE   5–6 ft. tall. Upright, vigorous, bushy. Disease resistant. Winter hardy. Moderately thorny canes with small, wrinkled, leathery, dark green leaves.

PINK MEIDILAND, *p. 125*
(Meilland, 1984)

The stunning pink, white-eyed blooms of this variety are perhaps the most striking of all the Meidilands. Unfortunately, blooms are seldom seen between the spring and autumn flushes.

FLOWERS   2–2½ in. wide. Deep pink with white eye. Single; 5 petals. Excellent midseason and autumn bloom. No fragrance. Blossoms in small clusters.

FOLIAGE   4 ft. tall. Upright, vigorous, somewhat stiff growth. Disease resistant and winter hardy. Leaves medium green, semiglossy.

PROSPERITY, *p. 120*
(Pemberton, 1919)

The result of a polyantha and tea rose cross, Prosperity has a different ancestry from most of the hybrid musks. But its graceful and charming blooms provide just what one would expect from the best members of this class.

FLOWERS   1–1½ in. wide. Ivory. Semidouble; 20 petals. Late-season bloom with reliable repeat bloom. Good fragrance. Rosette-shaped blooms occur in clusters.

FOLIAGE   6–8 ft. tall. Upright, vigorous, dense. Disease resistant and winter hardy. Few thorns. Leaves medium green, glossy.

RALPH'S CREEPER, *p. 105*
(Moore, 1987)

This ground cover is outstandingly effective when budded as a standard (or tree) rose.

FLOWERS   1½–2 in. wide. Vermilion with yellow eye. Semidouble; 15–18 petals. Excellent midseason bloom with good repeat bloom. Moderate fragrance; apple-blossom scent. Blooms are loose, in clusters of 10–15.

FOLIAGE   1½ ft. tall by 4–6 ft. wide. Vigorous, low, spreading. Disease resistant. May need winter protection. Leaves are small, dark green, matte.

RAUBRITTER, *p. 110*
(Kordes, 1936)

Technically a hybrid macrantha, Raubritter combines the charm of an old garden rose with the utility of a ground cover. It is a rose that will thrive in semishade.

FLOWERS   1½ in. wide. Clear pink. Double; 35 petals. Long midseason bloom, may occasionally repeat. Little fragrance. Blossoms globular, in clusters.

FOLIAGE   3 ft. tall by 7–10 ft. wide. Vigorous, sprawling. Black-spot resistant but may need protection from mildew. Extremely winter hardy. Leaves medium green, leathery, wrinkled.

ROBIN HOOD, *p. 90*
(Pemberton, 1927)

Robin Hood is widely used as a hedge rose — a purpose to which it, like many other hybrid musk roses, is well suited.

FLOWERS   ¾ in. wide. Light red. Semidouble; 18–24 petals. Midseason bloom with excellent repeat bloom. Moderate fragrance. Blooms in large clusters.

FOLIAGE   5–7 ft. tall. Upright, vigorous, bushy, dense. Disease resistant and winter hardy. Canes moderately thorny. Leaves medium green, semiglossy.

ROBUSTA, *p. 105*
(Kordes, 1979)

Robusta resents both pruning and spraying, and will do its best if left alone in a spot where it has plenty of room. Its thorny canes will make a formidable hedge.

FLOWERS   2½ in. wide. Clear medium red. Single; 5 petals. Early bloom with excellent repeat bloom. Slight fragrance. Blooms singly and in modest clusters.

FOLIAGE   6–8 ft. tall. Upright, vigorous. Disease resistant; completely free from mildew. Winter hardy. Thorny canes with dark green, glossy, leathery leaves.

ROMANZE, *p. 115*
(Tantau, 1984)

Winner of the Baden-Baden Gold Medal in 1985 and the ADR award for performance across Germany in 1986, Romanze is a tough, healthy, underrated rose. It is also known by its code name, TANezamor.

FLOWERS 3½–4 in. wide. Clear pink. Semidouble; 20 petals. Good all-season bloom. Slight fragrance. Cup-shaped blooms appear singly and in clusters of up to 7.

FOLIAGE 4–6 ft. tall. Upright, vigorous, bushy. Disease resistant and winter hardy. Leaves dark green, semiglossy.

ROSERAIE DE L'HAŸ, *p. 95*
(Cochet-Cochet, 1901)

This large, fragrant hybrid rugosa is named for a famous French rose garden.

FLOWERS 4–4½ in. wide. Dark reddish purple. Semidouble; perhaps 18–24 petals. Blooms very early in season, with occasional repeats. Very fragrant. Blossoms loosely cupped.

FOLIAGE 7–9 ft. tall. Upright, sturdy, treelike. Disease free and winter hardy. Canes thorny with gray bark. Leaves large, dark green, deeply etched (rugose).

ROSY CARPET, *p. 124*
(Ilsink, 1984)

Perhaps the ideal ground-cover rose, Rosy Carpet provides a wealth of bloom on a mound-shaped plant.

FLOWERS 1 in. wide. Deep pink. Single; 5 petals. Profuse midseason bloom with an extended period of repeat bloom in the fall. Fragrant. Blossoms have attractive golden stamens.

FOLIAGE 3 ft. tall by 4 ft. wide. Vigorous, bushy, spreading. Disease resistant and winter hardy. Many small thorns on canes with dark green, glossy leaves.

SALLY HOLMES, *p. 122*
(Holmes, 1976)

A vigorous, healthy shrub that can also be trained as a climber, Sally Holmes provides spray after spray of perfect single-petaled blooms. It won the Portland Gold Medal in 1993.

FLOWERS   3½ in. wide. Creamy white. Single; 5 petals. Excellent all-season bloom. Slight fragrance. Golden-stamened blooms appear in large clusters.

FOLIAGE   7–10 ft. tall. Vigorous, bushy, slightly sprawling. Disease resistant and winter hardy. Leaves dark green, glossy.

SARAH VAN FLEET, *p. 85*
(Van Fleet, 1926)

This is a very fragrant hybrid rugosa that will form quite a good hedge.

FLOWERS   3–3½ in. wide. Medium pink. Semidouble; 18–24 petals. Early to midseason bloom, followed by good repeat bloom. Very fragrant. Blossoms cupped, with showy yellow stamens.

FOLIAGE   6–8 ft. tall. Upright, vigorous, bushy. Disease resistant and winter hardy. Canes thorny, with dark green, leathery, deeply etched (rugose) leaves.

SCARLET MEIDILAND, *p. 107*
(Meilland, 1985)

Noted for its uniform growth habit, Scarlet Meidiland is a good choice for low-maintenance sites. A colorful display of red hips will persist well into winter.

FLOWERS   1–2 in. wide. Light cherry-pink, reverse dark carmine-pink. Semidouble; 15–25 petals. Profuse midseason bloom with intermittent repeat bloom. No fragrance. Cup-shaped blooms occur in large clusters.

FOLIAGE   3 ft. tall by 6 ft. wide. Vigorous, spreading, dense. Disease resistant and winter hardy. Leaves dark green, glossy.

SEA FOAM, *p. 81*
(Schwartz, 1964)

Sea Foam captured the Rome Gold Medal in 1963 and the American Rose Society David Fuerstenberg Prize in 1968. It makes an excellent ground cover, perfect for rough areas and for trailing down embankments.

FLOWERS   2–2½ in. wide. Light pink, fading to white. Double. Midseason bloom with excellent repeat bloom. Slight fragrance. Blossoms cupped, in clusters.

FOLIAGE   8–12 ft. long. Vigorous trailer; can be trained upright. Disease resistant and winter hardy. Moderately thorny canes with abundant, small, leathery, glossy leaves.

SPARRIESHOOP, *p. 86*
(Kordes, 1953)

A beautiful and popular rose, Sparrieshoop has fragrant single blooms.

FLOWERS   4 in. wide. Light pink. Single; 5 petals. Good midseason bloom with fair repeat bloom. Very fragrant. Blossoms open to saucer shape, with golden stamens. Blooms in clusters.

FOLIAGE   5 ft. tall. Upright, very vigorous, bushy. Disease resistant and winter hardy. Leaves medium green, leathery.

STRETCH JOHNSON, *p. 107*
(McGredy, 1988)

A rose of many names, Stretch Johnson is also known as Rock 'n' Roll and Tango. It received a gold medal from Britain's Royal National Rose Society in 1988.

FLOWERS   3 in. wide. Orange with cream and buff tones, handpainted. Semidouble; 10–14 petals. Midseason bloom with good repeat bloom. Slight fragrance. Blooms in small clusters.

FOLIAGE   4–5 ft. tall. Upright, bushy, vigorous. Disease resistant and winter hardy. Leaves medium green, semiglossy. Occasionally produces spiky nonflowering shoots late in the season.

SWEET JULIET, *p. 112*
(Austin, 1989)

This apricot English rose produces a large quantity of flowers on a compact bush. Under most conditions, Sweet Juliet is more color-fast than other apricot and yellow English roses.

FLOWERS　3–3½ in. wide. Apricot. Very double; 40-plus petals. Midseason bloom with good repeat bloom. Fragrant. Blossoms open to shallow cup shape. Blooms in tightly spaced clusters of 3–7.

FOLIAGE　3½ ft. tall. Upright, bushy, compact. Disease resistant and winter hardy. Leaves medium green, slightly glossy.

THE COUNTRYMAN, *p. 118*
(Austin, 1987)

This graceful bush has been compared to a miniature peony. The Countryman should not be confused with the other roses called Countryman, a 1978 shrub that is also pink (bred by Griffith Buck) and a yellow miniature sold in Australia.

FLOWERS　3½–4 in. wide. Deep pink. Double; 40 petals. Good midseason bloom; repeat bloom is unreliable. Very fragrant; damask scent. Blossoms open to rosette shape. Blooms singly and in clusters.

FOLIAGE　3–5 ft. tall, and as wide. Vigorous, bushy, spreading. Disease resistant and winter hardy. Canes have small thorns and narrow, medium green, matte leaves.

THE FAIRY, *p. 87*
(Bentall, 1932)

Roses — even individual cultivars — are to a degree variable, although some rose specialists feel that this variability may reflect a lack of precision in the labeling of certain plants. The Fairy is sometimes encountered as a ground-hugging trailer, and in other instances as an upright hedge.

FLOWERS　1–1½ in. wide. Medium pink. Double; 24–30 petals. Late-season bloom, followed by excellent repeat bloom. Little or no fragrance. Blossoms cupped, in clusters.

FOLIAGE   1½–2 ft. tall. Upright, bushy, compact. Disease resistant and winter hardy. Moderately thorny canes bear tiny, abundant leaves that are light to medium green and glossy.

THE REEVE, *p. 113*
(Austin, 1979)

One of the series of English roses named for characters in Chaucer's *Canterbury Tales,* The Reeve is a spreading rose ideal for training over a low wall.

FLOWERS   3–4 in. wide. Deep pink. Very double; 58 petals. Midseason bloom with good repeat bloom. Very fragrant. Blossoms are globular, in clusters of up to 5.

FOLIAGE   3–4 ft. tall. Vigorous, arching, spreading. Disease resistant and winter hardy. Canes and thorns are red, with reddish green leaves.

THE SQUIRE, *p. 106*
(Austin, 1977)

The purest red English rose, The Squire is grown and loved for its exquisitely formed bloom, despite a somewhat sparse plant.

FLOWERS   4 in. wide. Crimson. Very double; 120 petals. Good midseason bloom with fair repeat bloom. Fragrant. Blossoms open to cupped rosette shape, in clusters of 3–5.

FOLIAGE   3–4 ft. tall. Upright, sparse. Disease resistant and winter hardy. Leaves dark green, somewhat rugose.

TOPAZ JEWEL, *p. 123*
(Moore, 1987)

A rare yellow hybrid rugosa, Topaz Jewel is also known as Rustica 91 and Yellow Frau Dagmar Hastrup (though it is no relation to the original Frau Dagmar Hastrup).

FLOWERS   3½–4 in. wide. Medium yellow, fading to cream. Double; 25-plus petals. Good all-season bloom. Moderate fragrance; fruity scent. Blossoms cupped, opening wide to show golden stamens, in clusters of 5–8.

FOLIAGE   5 ft. tall, and as wide. Upright, bushy, vigorous, spreading. Disease resistant and winter hardy. Canes have long brown thorns and medium green, rugose, matte leaves.

WESTERLAND, *p. 100*
(Kordes, 1969)

Growing upright and well branched, this shrub rose makes an excellent pillar, colorfully enhanced by the bright apricot blooms.

FLOWERS   3 in. wide. Apricot blend. Double; 20 petals. Long midseason bloom. Very fragrant. Blossoms somewhat like those of hybrid teas, but not high-centered.

FOLIAGE   5–6 ft. tall. Upright, vigorous, well branched. Disease resistant and winter hardy, with moderately thorny canes. Leaves dark green, semiglossy.

WIFE OF BATH, *p. 117*
(Austin, 1969)

Suitable for even the smallest garden, this tough little rose is perhaps the most trouble-free of all of David Austin's English roses.

FLOWERS   2½–3 in. wide. Pink. Semidouble to double; 20–25 petals. Good midseason bloom with good repeat. Very fragrant; myrrh scent. Cupped blooms appear singly and in modest clusters.

FOLIAGE   2–3 ft. tall. Bushy, twiggy, compact. Disease resistant and winter hardy. Leaves small, matte, medium green.

WILLIAM BAFFIN, *p. 115*
(Svejda, 1983)

A shrub with *kordesii* ancestry that is easily trained as a climber, William Baffin is one of the hardiest of all modern roses.

FLOWERS   3–4 in. wide. Deep pink. Semidouble; 20 petals. Midseason bloom with excellent repeat bloom. No fragrance. Bloom form open, cupped. Blossoms occur in clusters of up to 30.

FOLIAGE   8–12 ft. tall. Upright, slightly arching, dense, vigorous. Disease free and very winter hardy. Glossy leaves.

WILL SCARLET, p. 98
(Hilling, 1948)

A lighter-colored sport, or mutation, of the cultivar Skyrocket, Will Scarlet has attractive hips.

FLOWERS   3 in. wide. Light red. Semidouble; 24–30 petals. Midseason bloom with good repeat bloom. Moderate fragrance. Blossoms open to become cup-shaped, in clusters.

FOLIAGE   6 ft. tall. Upright, vigorous, bushy. Disease resistant and winter hardy, with moderately thorny canes and medium to dark green leaves.

WINDRUSH, p. 122
(Austin, 1985)

A descendant of Golden Wings, with stronger, bushier growth, Windrush is a profuse bloomer that will display both blooms and hips in the fall.

FLOWERS   5 in. wide. Light yellow. Semidouble; 10–12 petals. Early bloom with excellent repeat. Fragrant; Scottish brier scent. Blooms open to become saucer-shaped, revealing striking pale yellow stamens.

FOLIAGE   4–6 ft. tall. Upright, vigorous, bushy. Disease resistant. Winter hardy. Leaves light green, matte.

Old Garden Roses

 Forming a very large class, the old garden roses have been in cultivation since before the development of the modern kinds. Many of these roses are still available today, and they are regaining the popularity that they began to lose to the hybrid perpetuals in the 19th century.

The question of which subgroups to include under the old-garden-rose heading has been much debated by rose authorities. Some feel that the old European garden roses, those in cultivation before the advent of the China and tea roses, should remain in a class by themselves. This arrangement would exclude the Bourbon roses and the hybrid perpetuals, but not the Portland roses. Other experts point out that the China and tea roses were themselves among the most ancient of garden roses, and believe they should be included within the old-garden-rose designation, along with the roses that developed from combining European and Chinese roses.

Here we recognize the following subclasses of old garden roses, distinguished chiefly by their parentage: alba, Bourbon, centifolia, China, damask, gallica, hybrid perpetual, hybrid spinosissima, moss, Noisette, Portland, and tea roses.

It is possible to assign categories based on ancestry and, when ancestry is very mixed, on flower and plant habit, but it is not possible to assign a date before which every rose was "old-fashioned" and after which, "modern." We do it for convenience, but it can only be arbitrary. The American Rose Society has settled on the date of 1867 — the introduction date of La France, one of the early hybrid teas — as the dividing line. All roses belonging to a class established before that date are designated as old garden roses; all roses belonging to a class established after that date are considered modern roses.

For purposes of exhibition, the American Rose Society recognizes only those varieties of old garden roses that were in existence prior to 1867, making many individual varieties introduced after 1867 ineligible for the higher prizes and awards, even though they may be pure to their type.

Alba Roses

Producing white and pale pink blooms, the alba roses include forms and descendants of *Rosa alba,* which is itself believed to be a natural hybrid of *R. gallica* and *R. canina.* However, this genealogy is just guesswork. Until science can analyze genetic material so as to determine ancestry, that of the albas is lost in the mists of time. Alba roses are very tall and upright. The foliage is soft and downy, and the canes are rather thorny. Like all old garden roses, albas are extremely fragrant. In every case they are once-blooming.

Bourbon Roses

A natural hybrid, *Rosa borboniana* was discovered on the Isle of Bourbon (now Reunion Island), where farmers hedged their fields with China and damask roses — its parents. Seeds and plants of the new rose were sent back to France, where new varieties were soon developed and Bourbon roses became popular garden flowers. Taller and more vigorous than either parent, and with a much larger bloom, the moderately hardy Bourbons are much more shapely than China roses and more recurrent than the damasks.

Centifolia Roses

Believed to have been developed in Holland during the 17th and 18th centuries, and found also in the Provence region of France, the centifolia (*Rosa centifolia*) is considered to be the youngest of the true old garden roses. The varieties and hybrids were popular garden roses in the late 18th and early 19th centuries.

Centifolia roses have very full-petaled double flowers; they are once-blooming. The large outer petals enclose many tightly packed inner petals, often with a button center, often quartered. The perfume is intense.

The very thorny, long, sparsely foliaged canes spring up in all directions; very few centifolia varieties grow into a full, dense bush.

China and Tea Roses

European explorers of the late 1700s and early 1800s collected some very important China roses and tea-scented China roses. Unlike European roses, Chinas and teas were capable of dependable repeat flowering.

The original China roses were mostly dwarf bushes. The blooms, which are rather loosely cup-shaped, tend to darken in the sun instead of fading, and they shatter cleanly when fully expanded and aged. (Thus the early Chinas came to be known as the aristocrats of the roses, because they knew how to die gracefully.)

Chinas bloom almost continually during the growing season, and bear very smooth stems and leaves. They are not very winter hardy, but being fairly small plants, they may be grown in pots indoors in the winter.

The tea roses, whether dwarf bushes or rampant climbers, have loosely cupped blooms in delicate shades and blends of white, pink, and pale yellow. They are very smooth, with glossy leaves and few real thorns. Like Chinas, they bloom nearly all season long. The teas are the roses that, crossed with the hybrid perpetuals, gave us our reliably repeat-flowering hybrid teas.

Damask Roses

Hybrids of *Rosa damascena,* the damask roses — along with the gallicas — are among the most ancient of garden roses. Known to the Romans, the damasks were pruned and grown in heated houses so that they would bloom out of season. Grown throughout the Roman Empire, they would have died out in medieval times had it not been for the hundreds of monasteries across Europe, where roses and many other flowers were grown for medicinal purposes and thus preserved.

Damasks require careful cultivation. They are mostly very thorny shrubs, with blooms in clusters of three or five; some varieties are repeat bloomers. The cup-shaped, intensely fragrant flowers sometimes cannot open fully because of the tight clusters.

Gallica Roses

Like the damasks, the gallica roses were cultivated by the Romans, who took them to the farthest reaches of their empire. After the fall of Rome, gallica roses became established wherever they had been planted — a process that continues today.

Rosa gallica crossbred readily and also sported prolifically. Varieties appeared in deep shades of pink, sometimes striped or mottled with lighter pink, sometimes shading into lavender and violet; some of the deepest of purples are also found among the gallicas. All these shades of rich color are enhanced by showy yellow or golden-yellow stamens.

Tidy, neat, upright roses that hold their flowers poised aloft, gallicas are fragrant—remarkably more so when the petals are dried. Gallicas are once-blooming and produce attractive hips later in the season.

Hybrid Perpetuals

The forerunners of our modern hybrid teas, the hybrid perpetuals are of mixed ancestry, descended mainly from teas, Bourbons, and Portlands. They were the popular garden rose from 1840 to 1880, but were cultivated before that time and continued to be developed long afterward; many varieties continued to be widely grown into the 1920s.

The hybrid perpetuals can be divided into three groups. The first and earliest varieties strongly resemble the old-garden-rose form, with tightly packed central petals surrounded by larger outer guard petals, sometimes quartered, with a button center. The second stage gave rise to roses with very full, globular blooms; some of the largest blooms ever developed belong to this group. In the third stage of development, some hybrid perpetuals began to take on the characteristics of the modern hybrid tea and, while usually fuller than today's typical hybrid tea, resemble it in every other way, having the long central petals that give it its distinctive form.

Hybrid Spinosissimas

Also known as Scotch, burnet, and pimpinellifolia roses, the hybrid spinosissimas are varieties of *R. spinosissima*. Most roses of this lineage are shrub roses, but some of the older varieties are ancient and thus classed as old garden roses.

The Scotch roses were ferny, low-growing shrubs with surprisingly well-formed blooms. The most notable variety, and the only one that currently produces a good repeat bloom, is Stanwell Perpetual, which was introduced into commerce in 1838 by Lee. This rose produces a large, full, beautifully formed bloom on a ferny mound of foliage. No long straight stems here, but a delightful fragrance.

Moss Roses

These roses are a single group derived from two sources: those that sported from the centifolias and those that sported from the damask perpetuals. It is easy to tell the difference between the roses in these two categories, because the former have heavy green moss on calyx and stems, while the latter have rather sparse, brownish moss, and bloom a second time in the fall.

Moss roses were very popular during Victorian times. The mossy buds yield a pine scent when touched, further enhancing the pleasure of the intensely fragrant, fully double bloom with its tightly packed petals. The mossy side buds, with their long, fringed sepals, make a finished picture surrounding the open bloom.

Noisette Roses

Early in the 1800s, a wealthy American planter and gardening enthusiast by the name of Champneys developed a repeat-blooming climber from a cross between China and musk roses. This was Champneys' Pink Cluster. Champneys' friend, a nurseryman named Noisette, sent it to his brother in France, who developed many more varieties; these became known as Noisette roses. Most Noisettes were developed in the first half of the 19th century. They flourished in warm climates but lacked winter hardiness, so they never became popular except in those areas best suited to them.

Portland Roses

Sometimes called damask perpetuals, the Portland roses are descended from the autumn damask, gallica, and China roses. They represent the direction nurserymen were taking in the early 19th century to develop repeat-blooming roses. This effort was abandoned when Chinas and tea-scented Chinas, dependable repeat bloomers, became widely available.

The Portland roses reached their peak of popularity in the third quarter of the 19th century. Today, the varieties are few, but those Portlands that have survived show very good repeat blooming characteristics. They are neat, rounded bushes, with the smooth stems and foliage granted by their China ancestry. The fully double blooms have short stems, so they nestle among their leaves. They are very fragrant, and when fully expanded the outer petals curl in on themselves, creating fluffy balls.

ALFRED DE DALMAS, p. 137
(Portemer, 1855)

Like other perpetual damask mosses, Alfred de Dalmas has a repeat bloom in the fall.

FLOWERS   2½–3 in. wide. Light blush pink, fading to white. Double; 55–65 petals. Midseason bloom with fair repeat bloom. Fragrant. Cupped blossom form. Sparse, brownish moss on calyx and stems. Blooms in clusters.

FOLIAGE   2½–3 ft. tall. Upright, bushy, spreading. Disease resistant and winter hardy. Canes very bristly, with rough gray-green leaves.

AMERICAN BEAUTY, *p. 161*
(Ledechaux, 1875)

This famous greenhouse rose is named Madame Ferdinand Jamain in Europe. A later, or third-stage, example of hybrid perpetual development, it is identical in many important characteristics to the hybrid teas of today.

FLOWERS   5–6 in. wide. Deep pink. Double; 50 petals. Midseason bloom with fair repeat bloom in the fall. Very fragrant. Bloom form full, globular, tending toward the classic high center of the hybrid teas.

FOLIAGE   5–6 ft. tall. Vigorous, upright. Disease resistant and winter hardy. Canes fairly smooth, with few thorns. Leaves medium to dark green, semiglossy.

ARCHDUKE CHARLES, *p. 152*
(Laffay, 1840)

As with China roses, the color of Archduke Charles intensifies, rather than fades, in sunlight.

FLOWERS   2½–3 in. wide. Pink blended with white, becoming medium red. Double; perhaps 35–40 petals. Good all-season bloom. Blossoms rather loose, informally shaped.

FOLIAGE   2–3 ft. tall. Moderately vigorous, bushy. Disease resistant, but tender. Smooth reddish canes bear a few large red thorns. Leaves smooth, red when young; rather sparse and glossy.

BARONESS ROTHSCHILD, *p. 149*
(Pernet Père, 1868)

Also known as Baronne Adolphe de Rothschild, this rose is a sport of Souvenir de la Reine d'Angleterre.

FLOWERS   5½–6 in. wide. Light pink. Double; 40 petals. Profuse midseason bloom with fair repeat bloom in fall. Very fragrant. Bloom form very full, globular.

FOLIAGE   4–6 ft. tall. Upright, vigorous, well branched. Disease resistant and winter hardy. Canes quite smooth with few thorns. Leaves light to medium green, semiglossy.

BARON GIROD DE L'AIN, *p. 167*
(Reverchon, 1897)

At some seasons the white deckle edging of Baron Girod de l'Ain is hardly noticeable; at others it is quite marked. A distinctly beautiful rose either way, it is a sport of Eugène Fürst.

FLOWERS   4 in. wide. Medium red, tipped white. Double; 35–40 petals. Good midseason bloom with fair repeat bloom in the fall. Fragrant. Blossom form cupped; when fully expanded, outer row of petals assumes a saucer shape, while central petals remain cupped.

FOLIAGE   4–5 ft. tall. Upright, vigorous, well branched. Disease resistant and winter hardy. Canes moderately thorny. Leaves medium to dark green, semiglossy.

BARONNE PRÉVOST, *p. 159*
(Despres, 1842)

This pink rose is an early hybrid perpetual of the old-garden-rose type, representing the first stage of development of the class. The larger outer petals enclose many tightly packed, shorter central petals.

FLOWERS   3½–4 in. wide. Medium pink. Fully double; perhaps 100 petals. Good midseason bloom with good repeat bloom in the fall. Fragrant. Old-garden-rose bloom form, full and quartered.

FOLIAGE   4–6 ft. tall. Upright, vigorous, bushy. Disease resistant and winter hardy. Canes very thorny, with rough dark green leaves.

BELLE AMOUR, *p. 142*
(Ancient)

Said to have been discovered at a convent at Elboeuf in Germany, Belle Amour is believed to be a cross between an alba and a damask rose.

FLOWERS   3½ in. wide. Light pink. Semidouble; 20–30 petals. Profuse early-season bloom. Intensely fragrant; spicy scent mixed with a faint bitterness, said to resemble myrrh. Very symmetrical, camellia-like form, opening to show bright yellow stamens. Round red hips appear later in the season.

FOLIAGE   5–6 ft. tall. Upright, vigorous, bushy. Disease free and winter hardy. Canes moderately thorny. Leaves rough, dull, blue-green.

BELLE DE CRÈCY, p. 165
(Unknown; 1848)

Named for Madame de Pompadour, this rose is said to have been grown in her garden at her estate at Crècy. The violet tones develop very quickly, so blooms of pink and shades of mauve occur in fresh condition on the bush at the same time.

FLOWERS   2½–3 in. wide. Pink, turning mauve. Very double; perhaps 200 petals. Long midseason bloom, not recurrent. Very fragrant. Very full, evenly petaled bloom with green pip at center; reflexes into a ball on full expansion.

FOLIAGE   3½–4½ ft. tall. Upright, vigorous, rounded, and compact. Disease resistant and winter hardy. Canes bristly but not thorny, with rough, dull, medium to dark green leaves.

BELLE ISIS, p. 143
(Parmentier, 1845)

All the gallica roses developed in the 19th century must be considered late or "modern" developments in a class that goes back to Roman times and beyond — undoubtedly into prehistory.

FLOWERS   2½–3 in. wide. Light pink. Double; perhaps 45–55 petals. Midseason bloom, not recurrent. Fragrant. Blossom cupped, well filled with tightly packed petals.

FOLIAGE   2½–3 ft. tall. Compact, rounded, bushy. Disease resistant and winter hardy. Canes bristly but not thorny, with small gray-green leaves.

BLUSH NOISETTE, p. 135
(Noisette, 1817)

This tall, pale Noisette is a blush to white seedling of Champneys' Pink Cluster.

FLOWERS   2 in. wide. Blush white. Double; 24 petals. Midseason bloom with excellent repeat bloom. Very fragrant. Cupped form, blooming in clusters.

FOLIAGE 8–12 ft. tall. Upright, vigorous, arching. Disease resistant, but tender. Canes very smooth with few thorns. Leaves light green, glossy.

BOULE DE NEIGE, p. 133
(Lacharme, 1867)

This Bourbon rose is aptly named — "boule de neige" is French for "snowball." When the bloom is fully expanded, the outer petals curl in, giving the impression of a great white ball.

FLOWERS 2½–3½ in. wide. Pink buds open to creamy white blooms. Double; perhaps 100 petals. Long midseason bloom with good repeat bloom. Fragrant. Fully expanded blooms reflex into a ball.

FOLIAGE 4–5 ft. tall. Upright, slender growth. Disease resistant and winter hardy, with moderately thorny canes and dark green, leathery leaves.

CAMAIEUX, p. 173
(Unknown; 1830)

The foliage of Camaieux, like that of other gallicas, is susceptible to mildew in some areas, especially in the South. In other regions, however, the problem is minimal or even absent.

FLOWERS 3–3½ in. wide. Blush with even deep pink stripes; fading to white and mauve. Double; perhaps 65 petals. Fragrant. Blooms early to midseason; no repeat. Very evenly petaled, full, cupped, camellia-like blossoms. Hips appear later in season.

FOLIAGE 3–3½ ft. tall. Upright, rounded, compact. Disease resistant, but prone to mildew in South. Winter hardy. Bristly canes, with few thorns, bear medium green leaves.

CARDINAL DE RICHELIEU, p. 163
(Laffay, 1840)

The blooms of this rose are deepest in color of all gallica roses. On an overcast day, very deep midnight blue tones are prevalent; on sunny days the flower is a rich purple. Some authorities point to a possible China rose influence in this variety.

FLOWERS　2½–3 in. wide. Purple with white at base. Double; perhaps 35–45 petals. Midseason bloom, not recurrent. Fragrant. Loosely cupped form.

FOLIAGE　2½–3 ft. tall. Upright, compact. Disease resistant and winter hardy. Canes moderately thorny with small, dark green, semiglossy leaves.

CELESTIAL, *p. 147*
(Ancient)

Also called Celeste. Like other albas, the pale blossoms of this rose have an intense, sweet fragrance.

FLOWERS　3½ in. wide. Light blush pink. Semidouble; 20–25 petals. Early blooming, not recurrent. Very sweetly fragrant. Evenly petaled, camellia-like, cupped form, showing yellow stamens.

FOLIAGE　4½–5 ft. tall and as wide. Upright, vigorous, bushy. Disease free and winter hardy. Canes quite smooth for an alba, with few thorns. Leaves rough, dull, grayish blue-green.

CELINE FORESTIER, *p. 129*
(Trouillard, 1842)

This cultivar was a later development of the Noisette roses, bringing yellow into the class.

FLOWERS　2–2½ in. wide. Light yellow. Double; 24 petals. Midseason bloom with excellent repeat bloom. Very fragrant. Cupped blossoms occur in clusters.

FOLIAGE　10–15 ft. tall. Upright, vigorous, arching. Disease resistant but tender. Canes fairly smooth with few thorns. Leaves medium green, semiglossy.

CELSIANA, *p. 148*
(Before 1750)

A neat, upright damask, Celsiana is perfect for the beginner. Some people consider it ideal for small gardens as well, although others contend that it is too vigorous for a limited space.

FLOWERS 3½–4 in. wide. Light pink. Semidouble; 12–18 petals. Long midseason bloom, not recurrent. Intensely fragrant. Bloom opens to wide cupped form, showing golden stamens. A few long, tubular red hips later in the season.

FOLIAGE 3½–4 ft. tall. Upright, vigorous, forming an open clump. Disease free and winter hardy. Moderately thorny canes bear soft, dull, light green leaves.

CHAMPNEYS' PINK CLUSTER, *p. 134*
(Champneys; date uncertain)

The forerunner of the Noisette class, Champneys' Pink Cluster was an American invention, the result of crossing China and musk roses.

FLOWERS 2 in. wide. Medium pink. Double; 24 petals. Midseason bloom with excellent repeat bloom. Very fragrant. Cupped form, blooming in clusters.

FOLIAGE 8–12 ft. tall. Upright, vigorous, arching. Disease resistant; tender. Canes very smooth with few thorns. Leaves light green, glossy.

CHARLES DE MILLS, *p. 171*
(Unknown; probably 19th century)

By reputation a magenta rose, Charles de Mills has been known to occur in shades of maroon, crimson, purple, wine, and violet. Although no date of origin has been turned up, experts believe that this is a 19th-century gallica.

FLOWERS 3–3½ in. wide. Magenta. Very double; perhaps 200 petals. Midseason bloom, not recurrent. Fragrant. Very full, very evenly petaled bloom with swirled petals; flat-topped before expansion, as if sliced off.

FOLIAGE 4½–5 ft. tall. Upright, vigorous, bushy, compact. Disease resistant and winter hardy. Moderately bristly canes have few thorns. Leaves rough, medium green.

CHLORIS, *p. 140*
(Ancient)

As with all albas, the size of the blossoms of this rose will increase with judicious pruning and enriched soil. But the abundance of flowers will not decrease with neglect.

FLOWERS   3½ in. wide. Soft light pink. Very double; perhaps more than 200 petals. Early blooming, not recurrent. Intense, sweet fragrance. Very full blossom with button center.

FOLIAGE   5–6 ft. tall. Upright, vigorous, about two-thirds as wide as tall. Disease free and winter hardy. Canes very smooth with few thorns. Leaves soft, medium green, with a less pronounced bluish tint than is usual with albas.

COMMANDANT BEAUREPAIRE, *p. 173*
(Moreau-Robert, 1874)

This spectacular striped rose is unusual because its white, blush, light pink, and scarlet stripes and splashes appear against a deep pink ground.

FLOWERS   3–3½ in. wide. Pink striped with red and white. Double; perhaps 35–45 petals. Blooms in midseason with sparse repeat bloom. Fragrant.

FOLIAGE   4–5 ft. tall. Upright, vigorous. Disease resistant and winter hardy. Canes very smooth with few thorns; leaves long, smooth, light green.

COMMON MOSS, *p. 148*
(Unknown; 1696)

This famous centifolia moss is also known as Communis, *Rosa centifolia muscosa,* and Old Pink Moss.

FLOWERS   3 in. wide. Light to medium pink. Double; perhaps 200 petals. Midseason bloom, not recurrent. Very fragrant. Very full bloom with tightly packed petals; usually quartered, with a button center. Heavy moss on calyx, stem, and long, fringed sepals. The green moss is sticky and pine-scented.

FOLIAGE   5–7 ft. tall. Upright, vigorous, arching, open growth. Disease resistant and winter hardy. Canes very bristly and thorny. Leaves rough, dark green, rather sparse.

COMPLICATA, *p. 161*
(Unknown)

A gallica hybrid of uncertain antecedents, Complicata may be the progeny of *Rosa canina* or *R. macrantha.*

FLOWERS   4–4½ in. wide. Medium pink with white at base. Single; 5 petals. Midseason bloom, not recurrent. Fragrant. Bloom opens flat, showing golden stamens.

FOLIAGE   5 ft. tall and as wide. Dense, vigorous, arching. Disease resistant and winter hardy. Canes fairly smooth with few thorns. Leaves large, soft, medium green.

COMTE DE CHAMBORD, *p. 151*
(Moreau-Robert, 1860)

Comte de Chambord is a Portland, or damask perpetual, rose. It has very full mauve-tinted blossoms.

FLOWERS   3 in. wide. Medium pink with mauve tints. Very double; perhaps 200 petals. Midseason bloom followed by good repeat bloom. Very fragrant. Full outer petals enclose many central petals; bloom sometimes quartered, reflexing when fully expanded.

FOLIAGE   3½–4 ft. high. Upright, rounded, compact. Disease resistant and winter hardy. Canes moderately thorny. Leaves medium green, semiglossy.

CRESTED MOSS, *p. 157*
(Vibert, 1827)

Also known as Chapeau de Napoléon and *Rosa centifolia cristata,* this fringed bloom is not a true moss rose but a parallel centifolia sport. It is not really mossy; rather, a fringe occurs just on the edges of the sepals, giving the buds the appearance of a three-cornered hat.

FLOWERS   3–3½ in. wide. Medium pink. Very double; perhaps 200 petals. Midseason bloom, not recurrent. Very fragrant. Blossoms very full and globular.

FOLIAGE   5–7 ft. tall. Upright, vigorous, arching canes, very open plant habit. Disease resistant and winter hardy. Canes very bristly and thorny. Leaves rough, dull, medium green.

DUCHESSE DE BRABANT, *p. 144*
(Bernède, 1857)

This tea rose once achieved an interesting distinction — it was well known as Teddy Roosevelt's favorite rose.

FLOWERS　4–5 in. wide. Blend of light pink through deep pink. Double; 45 petals. Early to midseason bloom with excellent repeat bloom. Very fragrant. Cupped blossom, well filled with petals.

FOLIAGE　3–5 ft. tall. Upright, vigorous, bushy. Disease resistant. Tender, but closer to borderline hardy than most other tea roses. Canes moderately thorny. Leaves medium to dark green, glossy.

DUCHESSE DE MONTEBELLO, *p. 138*
(Laffay, before 1829)

The lax growth of this rose is unusual in a gallica, and it suggests that Duchesse de Montebello may be a hybrid with another species. In addition, it has longer canes than most other varieties. Careful placement in the garden is suggested.

FLOWERS　2½–3 in. wide. Light blush pink. Double; perhaps 65 petals. Mid- to late-season bloom, not recurrent. Fragrant. Blossoms, full and globular, occur in loose clusters.

FOLIAGE　5 ft. tall. Spreading and rather lax; can be trained upright or grown in with other shrubs. Disease resistant and winter hardy. Canes have few thorns. Leaves rough, gray-green.

EMPRESS JOSEPHINE, *p. 153*
(Before 1583)

Also known as the Frankfort Rose, Empress Josephine is believed to be a cross between *Rosa cinnamomea* and *R. gallica*. It goes well with other gallica roses in the garden.

FLOWERS　3–3½ in. wide. Light to medium pink. Semidouble; perhaps 24–30 petals. Midseason bloom, not recurrent. Slight fragrance. Rather loose form; flowers have a papery quality. Hips, shaped like a top or inverted cone, appear later.

FOLIAGE　3–4 ft. tall. Upright, compact. Disease resistant and winter hardy. Smooth, almost thornless canes bear narrow gray-green leaves.

FANTIN-LATOUR, *p. 150*
(Hybridizer and date unknown)

It is obvious even to the beginning student of the old roses that this beautiful rose does not really fit into the centifolia class, to which it has been assigned. Research will one day discover its correct identity.

FLOWERS   3–3½ in. wide. Pale blush. Double; perhaps 200 petals. Profuse midseason bloom, not recurrent. Very fragrant. The full, rather flat bloom has a good button center.

FOLIAGE   5–6 ft. tall. Upright, vigorous, well branched. Disease resistant and winter hardy. Canes have few thorns. Leaves smooth, medium green, semiglossy.

FÉLICITÉ ET PERPÉTUE, p. 135
(Jacques, 1827)

This hybrid sempervirens climber is best suited to mild climates, where it is almost evergreen.

FLOWERS   1½ in. wide. White. Double; perhaps 65 petals. Long late-season bloom, not recurrent. Fragrant. Full, globular blooms in large clusters.

FOLIAGE   20 ft. tall. Very vigorous and almost evergreen. Disease free; tender. Leaves small, abundant, medium green, glossy.

FERDINAND PICHARD, p. 172
(Tanne, 1921)

This hybrid perpetual shows great similarity to the Bourbon rose Commandant Beaurepaire, although there is no record of parentage linking the earlier rose to this one.

FLOWERS   3–3½ in. wide. Red and white striped. Double; 25 petals. Good midseason bloom followed by fair repeat bloom. Fragrant. Blossom form cupped.

FOLIAGE   4–5 ft. tall. Upright, moderately vigorous, compact. Disease resistant and winter hardy. Canes fairly smooth, with few thorns. Long leaves, light to medium green, and soft.

FRAU KARL DRUSCHKI, p. 131
(Lambert, 1901)

This white hybrid perpetual is also called Reine des Neiges, Snow Queen, and White American Beauty. Representative of the third, or final, stage of development in the class, it is identical in many ways to hybrid teas.

FLOWERS   4–4½ in. wide. White. Double; 35 petals. Midseason bloom with good repeat in the fall. Little or no fragrance. Blossoms have classic hybrid tea shape.

FOLIAGE   5–7 ft. tall. Upright, vigorous, well branched. Disease resistant and winter hardy. Canes fairly smooth with few thorns. Leaves soft, medium green.

GÉNÉRAL KLÉBER, *p. 138*
(Robert, 1856)

This centifolia moss rose has a praiseworthy clear pink bloom. Its dense, pleasing habit of growth is unusual — most moss roses, and most centifolias, have rangy, sparse, gaunt canes.

FLOWERS   2½–3 in. wide. Medium pink. Double; perhaps 100 petals. Blooms at midseason or later; does not recur. Very fragrant. Blossom form full, quartered, with a button center. Buds mossy.

FOLIAGE   5 ft. tall. Upright, vigorous, bushy. Disease resistant and winter hardy. Canes thorny. Leaves rough, dull, light to medium green.

GEORG ARENDS, *p. 145*
(Hinner, 1910)

A later, or third-stage, hybrid perpetual rose, Georg Arends comes very close to fitting in the hybrid tea class.

FLOWERS   4–4½ in. wide. Light to medium pink. Double; 25 petals. Midseason bloom with good repeat bloom in the fall. Very fragrant. Classic hybrid tea form, with petals unfurling evenly from a high center.

FOLIAGE   4–5 ft. tall. Upright, vigorous, well branched. Disease resistant and winter hardy. Fairly smooth canes, with few thorns, bear medium green, semiglossy leaves.

GLOIRE DE DIJON, *p. 129*
(Jocotot, 1853)

A good pillar rose, Gloire de Dijon needs the protection of a wall in borderline climates. The canes become leggy at base, a fault you can obscure with other plantings.

FLOWERS   4 in. wide. Yellow with orange at center, sometimes shaded with pink. Double; 45–55 petals. Early-season bloom with good repeat bloom. Fragrant. Very full hybrid-tea-type bloom with occasional quartering.

FOLIAGE   10–12 ft. tall. Upright, vigorous, arching. Disease resistant; tender. Canes moderately thorny, with medium green, glossy leaves.

GLOIRE DE FRANCE, *p. 146*
(1819)

Gallica roses are well suited to the small garden, offering a wide variety of colors and shapes and blooming over a six-week period at the beginning of summer.

FLOWERS   2½–3 in. wide. Medium pink. Double; perhaps 200 petals. Midseason bloom, not recurrent. Fragrant. Blossom pompon-shaped; reflexes into a ball upon full expansion.

FOLIAGE   2–2½ ft. tall. Upright, bushy, spreading. Disease resistant and winter hardy. Canes bristly but not thorny, with rough gray-green leaves.

GLOIRE DE GUILAN, *p. 140*
(Hilling, 1949)

This exotic rose was first discovered by Miss Nancy Lindsay in the Caspian provinces of Persia.

FLOWERS   3 in. wide. Light pink. Double; perhaps 45–55 petals. Profuse early to midseason bloom, not recurrent. Intensely fragrant. Bloom form full, globular, with quartered center.

FOLIAGE   3–5 ft. tall. Vigorous, sprawling. Disease free and winter hardy. Canes moderately thorny, with soft, dull light green leaves.

GLOIRE DES MOUSSEUSES, *p. 141*
(Laffay, 1852)

This centifolia moss has very large blooms for its class. Its name is alternately spelled Mousseaux and Mousseux.

FLOWERS   3 in. wide. Light to medium pink with a faint lavender tint. Very double; perhaps 200 petals. Midseason bloom, not recurrent. Very fragrant. Bloom form very full, quartered, with a button center. Buds and stems very mossy.

FOLIAGE   2½–3 ft. tall. Upright, moderately vigorous, compact. Disease resistant and winter hardy. Canes very thorny; leaves soft, dull, light green.

GLOIRE DES ROSOMANES, p. 168
(Vibert, 1825)

Also called Ragged Robin, this red China rose is sometimes used as an understock.

FLOWERS   3 in. wide. Medium red. Double; perhaps 25–30 petals. Good all-season bloom. Little or no fragrance. Blossom form rather loose, cupped.

FOLIAGE   3½–4½ ft. tall. Upright, vigorous, bushy. Disease resistant; moderately hardy. Fairly smooth canes, with few thorns, bear medium to dark green, semiglossy leaves.

GRÜSS AN TEPLITZ, p. 169
(Geschwind, 1897)

Of mixed parentage, this rose has been classed several ways. But its growth habit and style of bloom place it appropriately with the Bourbons.

FLOWERS   3–3½ in. wide. Medium red. Double; 34–40 petals. Profuse midseason bloom followed by good repeat bloom. Strong, spicy fragrance. Blossom cupped, well filled with petals.

FOLIAGE   5–6 ft. tall. Upright, vigorous, bushy. Disease resistant; winter hardy, except in very severe winter climates. Leaves dark green, semiglossy.

HENRI MARTIN, p. 170
(Laffay, 1863)

Like the other moss roses that have sported from centifolias, Henri Martin is not a repeat bloomer, and it has heavy green moss on the calyx and sepals.

FLOWERS   2½ in. wide. Dark red. Double; perhaps 65–75 petals. Mid- to late-season bloom, not recurrent. Fragrant. Blossom globular, well filled with petals. Very well mossed.

FOLIAGE   5 ft. tall. Upright, vigorous, bushy. Disease resistant and winter hardy. Canes thorny. Leaves medium to dark green, rough, abundant.

HENRY NEVARD, *p. 169*
(Cant, 1924)

Henry Nevard represents the third stage of hybrid perpetual development; it is very close in many ways to the hybrid tea class.

FLOWERS   4–4½ in. wide. Dark red. Double; 30 petals. Good midseason bloom with good repeat bloom in the fall. Very fragrant. Blossom cupped, well filled with petals.

FOLIAGE   4–5 ft. tall. Upright, vigorous, bushy. Disease resistant and winter hardy. Very thorny canes bear dark green, semiglossy leaves.

HERMOSA, *p. 154*
(Marcheseau, 1840)

Widely planted at one time, Hermosa is a China rose that was formerly classed with the Bourbons.

FLOWERS   3 in. wide. Light pink. Double; 35 petals. Good all-season bloom. Fragrant. Form high-centered, rather globular.

FOLIAGE   3–4 ft. tall. Upright, moderately vigorous, and bushy. Disease resistant, but not winter hardy. Canes very smooth, with few thorns. Leaves blue-green to medium green, semiglossy.

ISPAHAN, *p. 142*
(Before 1832)

Also named Pompon des Princes. Ispahan is classed as a damask, although some experts feel that it may have other parentage in its background as well.

FLOWERS   2½–3 in. wide. Medium pink. Double; perhaps 24–30 petals. Long midseason bloom, not recurrent. Very fragrant. Bloom form loosely cupped.

FOLIAGE   3–4 ft. tall. Upright, moderately vigorous, bushy. Disease free and winter hardy. Canes thorny. Leaves small, medium green, semiglossy.

JOHN HOPPER, *p. 170*
(Ward, 1862)

This hybrid perpetual is one of the rare examples of the early development of that class.

FLOWERS   4 in. wide. Medium pink with deeper center and lavender edges. Very double; 70 petals. Good midseason bloom with occasional repeat bloom in the fall. Very fragrant. Larger outer petals enclosing many tightly packed central petals; center usually muddled.

FOLIAGE   5–7 ft. tall. Upright, vigorous, bushy. Disease resistant and winter hardy. Canes very thorny; leaves medium green, semiglossy.

KÖNIGIN VON DÄNEMARK, *p. 154*
(1826)

A distinctive alba rose. Most blooms have a quartered appearance, with 3, 4, or 5 divisions, and show a good button center.

FLOWERS   3½ in. wide. Light pink, with a deeper pink center. Very double; perhaps 200 petals. Early bloom, not recurrent. Intense, sweet fragrance. Quartered blossom has button center. Upon full expansion, outer petals reflex and fade to nearly white.

FOLIAGE   6 ft. tall. Upright, treelike habit, more slender and open than more typical albas. Disease free and winter hardy. Canes very thorny, with rough, dull blue-green leaves, darker than those of most albas.

LADY HILLINGDON, *p. 128*
(Lowe & Shawyer, 1910)

The bush form of Lady Hillingdon is not very vigorous, but the climbing form is an excellent rose for pillar or trellis.

FLOWERS 3½ in. wide. Apricot-yellow. Semidouble; 18–24 petals. Early-season bloom with good repeat bloom. Fragrant. Blossom form rather loose, but classic hybrid tea shape.

FOLIAGE 2½–3 ft. tall. Upright, bushy, not very vigorous; the vigorous climbing form reaches 15 ft. Disease resistant but not winter hardy. Canes very smooth with few thorns. Leaves dark green, glossy.

LA NOBLESSE, *p. 156*
(1856)

A typical centifolia, or Provence, rose, La Noblesse has gaunt, thorny canes that are often a problem to manage. Using a low trellis, pegging down, or close planting (treating 3 plants as 1) may solve the problem in some garden situations.

FLOWERS 3–3½ in. wide. Light pink. Very double; perhaps 200 petals. Profuse mid- to late-season growth, not recurrent. Extremely fragrant. The very full bloom, usually muddled or quartered, has large outer petals surrounding many shorter petals.

FOLIAGE 5 ft. tall. Upright, arching, loose habit. Disease free and winter hardy. Canes very thorny. Leaves rough, dull, medium to dark green.

LA REINE VICTORIA, *p. 155*
(Schwartz, 1872)

This profuse bloomer has overlapping shell-shaped petals. It makes a nice garden grouping with Madame Pierre Oger and Louise Odier.

FLOWERS 3–3½ in. wide. Medium pink. Double; perhaps 35 petals. Abundant midseason bloom with good repeat bloom in the fall. Very fragrant. Bloom cup-shaped.

FOLIAGE 4½–5½ ft. tall. Upright, slender growth. Disease resistant and winter hardy. Canes quite smooth, with few thorns. Leaves soft, dull, medium green.

LA VILLE DE BRUXELLES, *p. 151*
(Vibert, 1849)

The weight of this rose's large, heavy blooms makes them nod down into the foliage. Otherwise, this is a fine variety.

FLOWERS   3½–4 in. wide. Medium to deep pink. Double; perhaps 45–55 petals. Abundant midseason bloom, not recurrent. Very fragrant. Very full, quartered bloom with button center.

FOLIAGE   5 ft. tall. Upright, vigorous, bushy. Disease free and winter hardy. Canes moderately thorny. Leaves abundant, light green, semiglossy.

LEDA, p. 175
(Before 1827)

Also called the Painted Damask, Leda is difficult to manage because of its lax habit. It is nonetheless worth the effort of training to a low trellis or other support.

FLOWERS   2½–3 in. wide. White with red edge. Double; perhaps 200 petals. Midseason bloom, not recurrent. Fragrant. Fat red buds open to very full white blooms with button centers.

FOLIAGE   2½–3 ft. tall if trained upright. Lax, trailing. Disease free and winter hardy. Thorny canes bear dark gray-green leaves.

LITTLE GEM, p. 157
(Paul, 1880)

A pretty little pompon rose, Little Gem has alternately been described as being heavily or sparsely mossed. Most reports, however, indicate that the moss is not abundant.

FLOWERS   2 in wide. Medium red. Double; perhaps 55–65 petals. Midseason bloom; no repeat. Fragrant. Bloom has pompon form.

FOLIAGE   4 ft. tall. Upright, compact. Disease resistant and winter hardy. Canes thorny. Leaves small, abundant, medium green.

LOUISE ODIER, p. 152
(Margottin, 1851)

Considering its petal count, Louise Odier has very full blossoms, but the rather slender, upright bush is not typical of the big, blowsy Bourbons. It makes a good trio with La Reine Victoria and Madame Pierre Oger.

FLOWERS   3½ in. wide. Medium pink. Double; 35–45 petals. Abundant midseason bloom followed by good repeat bloom. Very fragrant. Classic old rose form, sometimes quartered.

FOLIAGE   4½–5½ ft. tall. Upright, slender. Disease resistant and winter hardy. Canes smooth with few thorns. Leaves light to medium green.

LOUIS GIMARD, *p. 145*
(Perner Père, 1877)

Like other centifolia mosses, Louis Gimard has abundant green, pine-scented moss on its calyx and sepals.

FLOWERS   3–3½ in. wide. Mauve pink. Double; 65–75 petals. Midseason bloom, not recurrent. Very fragrant. Bloom very full with muddled center. Buds well mossed.

FOLIAGE   4–5 ft. tall. Upright, vigorous, bushy. Disease resistant and winter hardy. Canes very thorny. Leaves rough, medium green.

MABEL MORRISON, *p. 134*
(Broughton, 1878)

This hybrid perpetual has been compared to the Portlands because the bloom is closely surrounded with foliage.

FLOWERS   3½–4 in. wide. White. Double; 30 petals. Good midseason bloom with good repeat in the fall. Fragrant. Blossom cupped. Fall blooms sometimes splashed with pink.

FOLIAGE   4–4½ ft. tall. Upright, vigorous, well branched. Disease resistant and winter hardy. Canes moderately thorny. Leaves medium to dark green, semiglossy.

MADAME ALFRED CARRIÈRE, *p. 130*
(Schwartz, 1879)

A wall may offer enough protection to enable this beauty to be grown in borderline winter conditions.

FLOWERS   2½–3 in. wide. White. Double; 35 petals. Midseason bloom with excellent repeat bloom. Fragrant. Evenly petaled, gardenia-shaped blossoms, in clusters.

FOLIAGE   10–15 ft. tall. Upright, vigorous, arching. Disease resistant. Borderline hardy. Moderately thorny canes bear medium green, semiglossy leaves.

MADAME DE LA ROCHE-LAMBERT, *p. 158*
(Robert, 1851)

This centifolia moss has large outer petals enclosing many tightly packed smaller petals.

FLOWERS   3 in wide. Medium pink with purple shadings. Double; 65–75 petals. Midseason bloom, not recurrent. Very fragrant. Very full bloom form, usually with a button center. Buds well mossed.

FOLIAGE   4–5 ft. tall. Upright, arching growth. Disease resistant and winter hardy. Canes very thorny. Leaves rough, dull, light to medium green.

MADAME HARDY, *p. 132*
(Hardy, 1832)

Considered to represent the very finest development of its particular style of floral art, Madame Hardy is perhaps the most popular white rose of its type.

FLOWERS   3–3½ in. wide. White. Very double; perhaps 200 petals. Midseason bloom, not recurrent. Fragrant. Very full, evenly petaled blossoms with a green pip in the center.

FOLIAGE   5–5½ ft. tall. Upright, vigorous, bushy. Disease free and winter hardy. Canes moderately thorny. Leaves gray-green, rough, abundant.

MADAME ISAAC PEREIRE, *p. 158*
(Garçon, 1881)

This is a typical Bourbon rose, big and billowy. It is famous for its intense fragrance. It has a lighter pink sport, Madame Ernst Calvat.

FLOWERS 3½–4 in. wide. Deep pink. Double; perhaps 45–55 petals. Profuse midseason bloom followed by fair repeat bloom. Intensely fragrant. Large, full, globular blossoms usually quartered, sometimes muddled.

FOLIAGE 5–6 ft. tall. Upright and well branched; vigorous, bushy, and spreading. Disease resistant and winter hardy, with moderately thorny canes. Leaves dark green, semiglossy.

MADAME LAURIOL DE BARNY, p. 156
(Trouillard, 1868)

Madame Lauriol de Barny is considered by some authorities to be one of the finest of the Bourbon roses.

FLOWERS 3½–4 in. wide. Light pink. Very double; 45–55 petals. Fruity fragrance. Abundant midseason bloom; followed occasionally by repeat bloom. Flower form full, globular, sometimes quartered.

FOLIAGE 5–6 ft. tall. Upright, vigorous, bushy. Disease resistant and winter hardy. Moderately thorny canes bear large, dull medium green leaves.

MADAME LEGRAS DE ST. GERMAIN, p. 130
(1846)

Thought to be an alba crossed with a damask, Madame Legras de St. Germain has delicate blooms. It is tougher than it looks, however, and not easily spoiled by rain.

FLOWERS 3½ in. wide. White with lemon yellow center. Very double; perhaps 200 petals. Early blooming, not recurrent. Very sweet fragrance. Upon full expansion, tightly packed petals reflex into a ball.

FOLIAGE 6–7 ft. tall. Upright, treelike habit. Disease free and winter hardy. Canes very smooth, almost thornless. Leaves light to medium green.

MADAME LOUIS LÉVÊQUE, p. 147
(Lévêque, 1898)

Monsieur Louis Lévêque must have loved his wife very much, for he named three roses for her: a tea rose, a hybrid perpetual, and this one, a perpetual damask moss.

FLOWERS 3–3½ in. wide. Light pink. Double; perhaps 100 petals. Midseason bloom; well-established plants will repeat bloom in the fall. Very fragrant. Very full, globular form. Sparsely mossed.

FOLIAGE 4–5 ft. tall. Upright, arching. Disease resistant and winter hardy. Canes very thorny. Leaves dull, rough, medium green.

MADAME PIERRE OGER, p. 144
(Oger, 1878)

A color sport of La Reine Victoria, to which it is similar in every other way. Blooms are very pale at first, particularly in overcast weather, but the color deepens wherever touched by sunlight.

FLOWERS 3–3½ in. wide. Pale blush, deepening in the sun. Double; perhaps 35 petals. Abundant midseason bloom, good repeat bloom in the fall. Very fragrant. Bloom cupped.

FOLIAGE 4½–5½ ft. tall. Upright, slender growth. Disease resistant. Winter hardy. Canes very smooth with few thorns. Leaves soft, dull, medium green.

MADAME PLANTIER, p. 133
(Plantier, 1835)

Thought to be a hybrid between the albas and the musks, Madame Plantier will grow upward and then billow out, especially if given some training. It can be trained onto a trellis or into a small tree, where its canes will grow longer.

FLOWERS 2½–3 in. wide. White. Very double; perhaps over 200 petals. Profuse midseason bloom, not recurrent. Very fragrant. Very full blooms in clusters. Good button eye. Fully expanded bloom reflexes into a ball.

FOLIAGE 5–6 ft. tall. Upright, vigorous, dense, bushy. Disease free and winter hardy. Very smooth canes have few thorns. Leaves smooth, long, medium green.

MAIDEN'S BLUSH, p. 139
(Before 1600)

Perhaps this rose's long history accounts for the many names it has been given: Great Maiden's Blush, La Virginale, La Séduisante, Incarnata, and Cuisse de Nymphe; when deeper color develops, the rose is sometimes called Cuisse de Nymphe Emué. There is also a Small Maiden's Blush, which is exactly the same except for the size of the bush.

FLOWERS   2½–3 in. wide. Light blush pink. Very double; perhaps over 200 petals. Extremely profuse early to midseason bloom, not recurrent. Very fragrant. Very full blooms have muddled centers, but occasionally blooms develop a good button center under good cultivation.

FOLIAGE   5–6 ft. tall. Upright; treelike at first, then arching out. Disease free and winter hardy. Canes bristly and thorny. Leaves rough, dull, blue-green.

MAMAN COCHET, *p. 153*
(Cochet, 1893)

One of the most popular of the tea roses, this pink-and-yellow rose has a climbing form and a white sport, White Maman Cochet.

FLOWERS   3½–4 in. wide. Light pink with deeper center; base of petals yellow. Double; 35–45 petals. Midseason bloom with excellent repeat bloom. Fragrant. Classic hybrid tea form with petals unfurling evenly from a high center.

FOLIAGE   3–3½ ft. tall. Upright, vigorous, bushy. Disease resistant. Not winter hardy. Fairly smooth canes have few thorns. Leaves medium to dark green, glossy.

MARCHIONESS OF LONDONDERRY, *p. 141*
(Dickson, 1893)

This hybrid perpetual, with its full, globular blossoms, represents the middle stage of development in this class more than it does the third stage.

FLOWERS   4½–5 in. wide. Very light pink. Double; 50 petals. Profuse midseason bloom, with occasional repeat in the fall. Very fragrant. Blossoms full, globular.

FOLIAGE   5–7 ft. tall. Upright, vigorous, arching. Disease resistant and winter hardy. Canes fairly smooth, with few thorns. Leaves medium green, semiglossy.

MARÉCHAL DAVOUST, *p. 155*
(Robert, 1853)

In spite of the influx of hybrid perpetuals during the Victorian era, moss roses such as this one retained their popularity.

FLOWERS   3 in. wide. Deep pink with lighter pink reverse. Double; perhaps 100 petals. Midseason bloom, not recurrent. Very fragrant. Very full form, sometimes quartered, with button eye and green pip in center. Sparsely mossed.

FOLIAGE   5 ft. tall. Upright, vigorous, bushy. Disease resistant and winter hardy. Thorny canes bear soft, dull medium green leaves.

MARY WASHINGTON, *p. 136*
(Ross, 1891)

Mary Washington is currently believed to be a Noisette, although it has sometimes been classed with the hybrid musks.

FLOWERS   2½ in. wide. White tinged with pink, fading to white. Double; 24 petals. Midseason bloom with good repeat. Fragrant. Cupped blossoms occur in clusters.

FOLIAGE   8–12 ft. tall. Very vigorous, upright, and well branched. Disease resistant. Not winter hardy without protection. Canes very smooth with few thorns. Leaves medium green, semiglossy.

MAXIMA, *p. 131*
(Ancient)

This fragrant rose is also known as the Great Double White and the Jacobite Rose. It has been in cultivation for so long that its date of introduction is unknown.

FLOWERS   2½–3 in. wide. White. Very double; perhaps over 200 petals. Profuse early to midseason bloom, not recurrent. Very fragrant. Very full blossoms have muddled centers.

FOLIAGE   6–8 ft. tall. Upright, treelike. Disease free and winter hardy. Canes moderately thorny; leaves rough, dull, bluegreen.

NUITS DE YOUNG, *p. 167*
(Laffay, 1845)

This rose was named for the 18th-century English poet Edward Young. His 9-volume poem, *The Complaint; or, Night-Thoughts on Life, Death, and Immortality* — commonly referred to as *Night Thoughts* — gave rise to the "graveyard school" of poetry.

FLOWERS   2½ in. wide. Maroon with purple. Double; perhaps 50 petals. Midseason bloom, not recurrent. Very fragrant. Blossom not very full for a moss rose, but well packed with petals and a few golden stamens in the center. Sparsely mossed.

FOLIAGE   5 ft. tall. Arching, somewhat open. Disease resistant and winter hardy. Canes very thorny. Leaves small, dark green, sparse.

OLD BLUSH, *p. 149*
(1752)

This tender pink rose is believed to be the same as Parsons' Pink China Rose.

FLOWERS   3 in. wide. Medium pink. Double; perhaps 24–30 petals. Good all-season bloom. Little or no fragrance. Bloom form loose, cupped.

FOLIAGE   3–4 ft. tall. Upright, moderately vigorous, bushy. Disease resistant. Not winter hardy. Canes smooth, with few thorns. Leaves smooth, medium green, glossy.

PAUL NEYRON, *p. 163*
(Levet, 1869)

Paul Neyron is a middle stage hybrid perpetual. Its size is often exaggerated, but a fully expanded bloom can reach 6 or 7 inches on occasion.

FLOWERS   4½–5½ in. wide. Medium to lavender-pink or deep pink. Very double; 65–75 petals. Midseason bloom with fair repeat in the fall. Fragrant. Blossom globular to cupped, well filled with tightly packed petals; sometimes quartered but usually layered in rows; muddled when fully expanded.

FOLIAGE   5–6 ft. tall. Upright, vigorous, arching. Disease resistant and winter hardy. Canes fairly smooth, few thorns. Leaves medium green, semiglossy.

PETITE DE HOLLANDE, *p. 150*
(Hybridizer and date uncertain)

This small centifolia is considered to be the best of the Provence roses for smaller gardens.

FLOWERS   2–2½ in. wide. Medium pink. Double; perhaps 45–55 petals. Long midseason bloom, not recurrent. Very fragrant. Very full, globular blossoms.

FOLIAGE   3½–4 ft. tall. Upright, vigorous, bushy. Disease resistant and winter hardy. Canes very thorny. Leaves small, medium green.

REINE DES VIOLETTES, *p. 163*
(Millet-Malet, 1860)

The Queen of the Violets. This hybrid perpetual has been likened to the Bourbons. The color is a changing blend of lavender, sometimes very much on the blue side of the mauve tones. The foliage is reported to have a pepperlike fragrance, but this is usually difficult to detect.

FLOWERS   3 in. wide. Mauve. Very double; 75 petals. Profuse midseason bloom with occasional sparse repeat bloom in the fall. Very fragrant. Bloom form cupped, muddled.

FOLIAGE   5–6 ft. tall and as wide. Upright, vigorous, bushy, and rounded. Disease resistant and winter hardy. Canes very smooth, with few thorns. Leaves abundant, soft, medium green.

ROGER LAMBELIN, *p. 166*
(Schwartz, 1890)

A sport of Fisher Holmes, Roger Lambelin requires good cultivation and frequent repropagation. At one time there was a sport called Striped Roger Lambelin; interested gardeners may want to watch for its reappearance.

FLOWERS   2½–3 in. wide. Maroon, edged in white. Double; 30 petals. Midseason bloom with fair repeat bloom in the fall. Blossom irregular, raggedy-looking.

FOLIAGE   2–2½ ft. tall. Upright; not vigorous. Disease resistant and winter hardy. Canes moderately thorny. Leaves rough, dark green.

ROSA CENTIFOLIA VARIEGATA, p. 174
(1845)

This garden variety should not have been given a species name. The common names for it, however — Cottage Maid and Village Maid — have also been used for other varieties, which makes for much confusion. In a few remote references it is called Striped Centifolia, which is the only common name that is appropriate.

FLOWERS   3–3½ in. wide. White with very delicate pink striping or penciling. Double; perhaps 200 petals. Abundant midseason bloom, not recurrent. Very fragrant. Large, very full outer petals enclose many tightly packed shorter petals. Often muddled, sometimes quartered, with a button center.

FOLIAGE   5 ft. tall and as wide. Upright and vigorous; dense and bushy, unlike most in its class. Disease resistant and winter hardy. Canes very thorny. Leaves dull, medium to dark green.

ROSA GALLICA OFFICINALIS, p. 160
(Ancient)

This is probably the most famous rose of all time. Known also as the Apothecary Rose, it was tremendously popular for several centuries as the mainstay of a flourishing industry. In dried and candied form, it was fashioned into preserves and syrups as well as powders, and it was believed to cure many and diverse ailments.

FLOWERS   3–3½ in. wide. Medium to deep pink. Semidouble; 12–18 petals. Midseason bloom, not recurrent. Fragrant (much more so when petals are dried). Cupped blossoms open to reveal golden stamens. Attractive round red hips later in season.

FOLIAGE   3–3½ ft. tall. Upright, rounded, compact. Disease resistant and winter hardy. Canes have bristles but few thorns. Leaves medium-size, rough, medium green.

ROSA MUNDI, p. 172
(Before 1581)

The striped sport of *Rosa gallica officinalis,* sometimes called *R. gallica vericolor,* this is the earliest striped rose and the most striking of them all. No two blooms that open on the bush are striped and splashed in exactly the same way.

FLOWERS   3–3½ in. wide. Medium to deep pink, striped with blush or white. Semidouble; 18–24 petals. Midseason bloom, not recurrent. Fragrant. Cupped bloom opens to show golden stamens. Round red hips appear later in season.

FOLIAGE   3–3½ ft. tall. Upright, rounded, compact. Disease resistant and winter hardy. Canes have bristles but few thorns. Medium-size, rough medium green leaves.

ROSE DE RESCHT, *p. 168*
(Hybridizer and date uncertain)

This rose was reportedly brought from Persia by Miss Nancy Lindsay, who is also credited with the discovery of Gloire de Guilan. Rose de Rescht is very much like Rose du Roi, except in color.

FLOWERS   2–2½ in. wide. Deep pink with mauve shadings. Double; perhaps 100 petals. Midseason bloom and good repeat bloom. Very fragrant. Blossoms very full, rather raggedy-looking.

FOLIAGE   2½–3½ ft. tall. Upright, vigorous, compact. Disease resistant and winter hardy. Canes moderately thorny. Leaves medium green, semiglossy.

ROSE DES PEINTRES, *p. 143*
(1596)

Given a species name, *Rosa centifolia,* in error, Rose des Peintres has infertile flowers. Many of the varieties associated with it are sports. Also called the Provence Rose.

FLOWERS   3–3½ in. wide. Medium pink. Double; perhaps 200 petals. Profuse midseason bloom, not recurrent. Very fragrant. Very full blooms typically have large outer petals enclosing many shorter petals, often with a button center.

FOLIAGE   5–6 ft. tall. Upright and vigorous, with arching, open growth. Disease free and winter hardy. Canes very thorny. Leaves rough, medium to dark green.

ROSE DU ROI, *p. 164*
(Lelieur, 1815)

This red-and-purple rose was a sensation in its day. The deepest shadings occur on the outer petals and the top surface.

FLOWERS   2½ in. wide. Medium red with purple shadings. Double; perhaps 100 petals. Midseason bloom with good repeat bloom. Very fragrant. Large outer petals with shorter central petals.

FOLIAGE   3–4 ft. tall. Upright, vigorous, compact. Disease resistant and winter hardy. Canes moderately thorny. Leaves medium green, semiglossy.

ROSETTE DELIZY, p. 128
(Nabonnand, 1922)

A little larger and more vigorous than most tea roses, Rosette Delizy may be borderline winter hardy in protected positions. It was one of the last teas to be introduced.

FLOWERS   3½–4 in. wide. Yellow with apricot reverse; outer petals deep pink. Double; 45–55 petals. Midseason bloom with good repeat. Spicy fragrance. Full, classic hybrid tea form.

FOLIAGE   3½–4 ft. tall. Upright, vigorous, bushy. Disease resistant. Not winter hardy. Canes smooth, with few thorns. Leaves dark green, glossy.

SALET, p. 146
(Lacharme, 1854)

Like other perpetual damask mosses, Salet is sparsely mossed on its calyx and sepals.

FLOWERS   2½–3 in. wide. Medium pink. Double; perhaps 55–65 petals. Midseason bloom with fair repeat bloom in the fall when well established; repeats reliably in the South. Fragrant. Full, globular form.

FOLIAGE   4–5 ft. tall. Upright, vigorous, arching. Disease resistant and winter hardy. Canes very thorny. Leaves rough, dull, medium green.

SOMBREUIL, p. 132
(Robert, 1850)

A climbing tea rose, Sombreuil is worth trying in protected positions in northern gardens.

FLOWERS   3½–4 in. wide. Creamy white. Very double; perhaps 100 petals. Early to midseason bloom with good repeat. Fragrant. Blossom cupped, full, often quartered.

FOLIAGE   12–15 ft. tall. Upright, vigorous. Disease resistant. Borderline winter hardy. Canes moderately thorny. Leaves medium green, leathery, semiglossy.

SOUVENIR DE LA MALMAISON, p. 137
(Beluse, 1843)

The Empress Josephine, first wife of Napoleon Bonaparte, maintained a fabulous rose garden at Malmaison, her residence just outside Paris. Named in honor of the garden, this is an unforgettable rose, but unfortunately a very sparse bloomer. A climbing form is available.

FLOWERS   4½–5 in. wide. Light pink. Very double; perhaps 65–75 petals. Sparse bloom, midseason or late season, with sparse repeat in the fall. Strong spicy fragrance. Large, full blooms are usually well quartered.

FOLIAGE   2 ft. tall; climbing form reaches 6–8 ft. Compact. Vigorous, but bush form is a small plant. Climbing form suitable for a low trellis or pillar. Canes moderately thorny; leaves medium green, semiglossy.

STANWELL PERPETUAL, p. 136
(Lee, 1838)

Believed to be a cross between *Rosa damascena semperflorens* and *Rosa spinosissima*, this is the only spinosissima hybrid that is a reliable repeat bloomer. However, to repeat, the plant must be well established in the garden. The plant is an attractive, ferny bush.

FLOWERS   3–3½ in. wide. Light pink, fading to white. Double; perhaps 45–55 petals. Fragrant. Early to midseason bloom, with reliable repeat. Loose, muddled form gives an even appearance. Blooms appear singly on very short stems.

FOLIAGE   3–5 ft. tall and as wide. Vigorous, spreading. Disease resistant and winter hardy. Canes very thorny. Leaves small, dull, blue-green to deep green.

STRIPED MOSS, *p. 174*
(Verdier, 1888)

Also called Oeillet Panachée. This variety shows greater relationship to the perpetual damask mosses than to the centifolias, although it does not repeat bloom in the fall.

FLOWERS 1½–2 in. wide. Red and white striped in cool, overcast weather, pink and white striped in full sunlight. Double; perhaps 45–65 petals. Fragrant. Midseason bloom, not recurrent. Cupped form with tightly packed petals. Not very mossy.

FOLIAGE 5–6 ft. tall. Upright, vigorous, bushy. Disease resistant and winter hardy. Canes very thorny. Leaves small, rough, dark green.

THE BISHOP, *p. 164*
(Hybridizer and date uncertain)

The slender habit of The Bishop is not typical of centifolias. At one time, members of this class were the most popular garden roses, which may explain why some roses that might fit better elsewhere were given this classification.

FLOWERS 2½–3 in. wide. Cerise-magenta, quickly fading to slate-blue. Very double; perhaps 200 petals. Early to midseason bloom, not recurrent. Fragrant. Full, rosette form.

FOLIAGE 4–5 ft. tall. Upright, slender growth. Moderately vigorous. Disease resistant and winter hardy. Canes moderately thorny. Neat, medium-size leaves are medium green and semi-glossy.

TOUR DE MALAKOFF, *p. 163*
(Soupert & Notting, 1856)

As this bloom ages, the blue and violet tones take predominance over the pink tones.

FLOWERS 3–3½ in. wide. Mauve. Double; perhaps 45–55 petals. Midseason bloom, not recurrent. Very fragrant. Full, rather loose and raggedy bloom form.

FOLIAGE 6–7 ft. tall. Upright, vigorous, sprawling. Disease free and winter hardy. Very thorny canes bear large, rough, medium to dark green leaves.

TUSCANY, *p. 166*
(1596)

Tuscany is also known as the Old Velvet Rose, for the color and texture of its purple-petaled blossoms.

FLOWERS   3–3½ in. wide. Purple. Semidouble; 18–24 petals. Midseason bloom, not recurrent. Very fragrant. Rather loose, cupped bloom form, showing bright golden stamens.

FOLIAGE   3–4 ft. tall. Upright, rounded, compact. Disease resistant and winter hardy. Canes have bristles but few thorns. Leaves rough, medium to dark green.

TUSCANY SUPERB, *p. 165*
(Hybridizer and date uncertain)

This is a slightly larger bloom than Tuscany, but its more numerous petals partly obscure the contrasting yellow stamens.

FLOWERS   3½–4 in. wide. Purple. Double; 24–30 petals. Midseason bloom, not recurrent. Very fragrant. Bloom cupped, well filled with petals.

FOLIAGE   3–4 ft. tall. Upright, rounded, compact. Disease resistant and winter hardy. Canes have bristles, few thorns. Leaves rough, medium to dark green.

ULRICH BRUNNER FILS, *p. 159*
(Levet, 1881)

Also known simply as Ulrich Brunner. This rose has been widely distributed under another name, so rose enthusiasts might look carefully at the plants in their gardens to see if Ulrich Brunner Fils is among them.

FLOWERS   3½–4 in. wide. Deep pink or medium red. Double; 30 petals. Midseason bloom with occasional repeat bloom in the fall. Very fragrant. Classic hybrid tea form, but not particularly high-centered.

FOLIAGE   5–7 ft. tall. Upright, vigorous, bushy. Disease resistant and winter hardy. Fairly smooth canes with few thorns. Leaves soft, light to medium green.

VARIEGATA DI BOLOGNA, p. 175
(Bonfiglioli, 1909)

In some climates, this Bourbon is reported to have wine-red or even purple stripes.

FLOWERS   3½–4 in. wide. Red and white striped. Double; perhaps 45–55 petals. Midseason bloom, not recurrent. Fragrant. Very evenly petaled bloom, almost ball-shaped when fully expanded.

FOLIAGE   5–7 ft. tall. Upright, slender growth, suitable for trellis or pillar. Disease resistant and winter hardy. Canes very smooth, with few thorns. Leaves light green, semiglossy.

WILLIAM LOBB, p. 171
(Laffay, 1855)

A centifolia moss. The very mossy buds have a strong pine scent when touched.

FLOWERS   3 in. wide. Deep mauve. Double; 65–75 petals. Midseason bloom, not recurrent. Very fragrant. Full blossoms, usually muddled (rarely quartered); larger outer petals enclose many shorter central petals.

FOLIAGE   4–5 ft. tall. Vigorous, upright, arching, open. Disease resistant and winter hardy. Canes bristly and thorny. Leaves soft, medium green.

YORK AND LANCASTER, p. 138
(1551)

Also called *Rosa damascena versicolor*. This festive rose has some pink petals and some white ones mixed irregularly in blooms that may be all pink or all white, or roughly half-and-half. York and Lancaster is named for the rival houses of 15th-century England; the emblem of York was a white rose, that of Lancaster a red rose. The periodic battles of these rivals for the English throne came to be known as the Wars of the Roses.

FLOWERS   2½–3 in. wide. Particolored pink and white. Double; 24–30 petals. Midseason bloom, not recurrent. Fragrant. Loosely cup-shaped.

FOLIAGE   3–4 ft. tall. Bushy but not very vigorous. Needs good cultivation and frequent repropagation to keep it going. Disease free and winter hardy. Canes very bristly and thorny. Leaves rough, gray-green.

ZÉPHIRINE DROUHIN, *p. 160*
(Bizot, 1868)

An excellent low to medium climber, this pink Bourbon is recommended for areas near walkways because of its fragrance and because it is almost thornless.

FLOWERS   3½–4 in. wide. Medium pink. Semidouble; perhaps 20–24 petals. Good all-season bloom. Very fragrant. Loose, cupped form.

FOLIAGE   8–12 ft. tall. Upright, vigorous, well branched. Disease resistant and winter hardy. Canes very smooth, almost thornless. Leaves medium green, semiglossy.

Floribundas

Early in the 20th century, in an attempt to bring larger flowers and repeat flowering to winter-hardy roses, the polyantha roses were crossed with the hybrid teas. Working in Denmark in the 1920s, D. T. Poulsen was the first to breed floribundas intentionally, although some experts, reaching back to find the "first" floribunda, have settled on Grüss an Aachen (1909) as the earliest example of the class.

A Hardy New Breed

Whatever their strict origins, the roses that resulted from this experimentation were hardy plants with open cupped or saucer-shaped flowers. Known at the time as hybrid polyanthas, they made wonderful additions to any garden, almost continually in bloom with gay, colorful, outreaching clusters of flowers.

Development Within the Class

By the 1940s, it had become evident that the term "hybrid polyantha" was not suitable. By this time in their development, through continual successful breeding, floribundas had become established as larger, shrubbier plants than the dwarf polyanthas. So the name floribunda was adopted; the term captures the most exciting feature of the class — the prolific blooms that these roses put forth, year after year.

One early and very interesting variety in the class is Betty Prior, which has abundant clusters of single (five-petaled) blossoms. When in bloom, it has the look of a flowering dogwood tree.

The trend toward high-centered blooms

Toward the second half of this century, breeders began experimenting to develop a floribunda with a formal, high-centered bloom, like that of a hybrid tea. In the 1950s, Gene Boerner developed two varieties, Fashion and Vogue, which are highly acclaimed floribundas with a high-centered, hybrid-tea-type bloom.

Prizes and awards

In addition to Fashion and Vogue, many other floribundas have claimed top awards in the rose world. Frensham, introduced in 1946, Little Darling (1956), Angel Face (1969), Margaret Merril (1977), and Dicky (1984) have all won prizes through the years. But the most popular floribunda of all time is the dark crimson Europeana, which remains a favorite in its color range and class.

Floribundas Today

Today, floribundas come in an enormously wide range of colors; most varieties bear well-formed flowers in small to large clusters. Floribundas are slightly hardier and more disease resistant than the hybrid teas.

Exceptional landscape value

Adaptable to numerous garden settings, floribundas thrive in combination with other roses. Because they come in such a wide array of colors, they are very popular for use as borders. Floribundas will also make fine hedges, planted fairly close in two staggered rows.

Culture

Because most floribundas are quite hardy, they can be grown in a range of locales. Most varieties in this class are resistant to disease, although a few require protection from mildew in cool, wet environments. In the garden, you can treat them as you would hybrid teas, although they require a little less attention throughout the growing season. You should, of course, be careful to maintain them neatly, pruning when necessary and removing spent blooms and twigs.

The Future of Floribundas

The experimentation begun earlier in this century goes on today; the hybrid tea and floribunda classes are merging, and the creation of the grandiflora class is only one indication of this trend. The firm of Jackson & Perkins has established the so-called flora-tea rose; some of the roses introduced under this heading are sold as floribundas in the United States and as hybrid teas abroad. Inspired by the problems that this merger entails, the World Federation of Rose Societies is attempting to provide a new classification system, which would create new classes based on the distinction between large-flowered and cluster-flowered roses.

Working first in Northern Ireland and then in New Zealand, Sam McGredy IV has developed "handpainted" floribundas featuring dramatic red, cerise, pink, and orange markings against paler backgrounds. All handpainted roses vary with the weather, displaying their best colors in spring and fall.

ANABELL, *p. 193*
(Kordes, 1972)

An uncommon example of a florist's rose that is as productive in the home garden as it is in a greenhouse, Anabell has classically shaped blooms that appear in large, perfectly proportioned sprays.

FLOWERS   3–3½ in. wide. Salmon-orange with silver undertones. Double; 30 petals. Good midseason bloom with good repeat bloom. Fragrant. High-centered hybrid tea form, blooming in large sprays.

FOLIAGE   2½–3 ft. tall. Compact, bushy, vigorous. Disease resistant and winter hardy. Thorny canes, with small, medium green, semiglossy leaves.

ANGEL FACE, *p. 185*
(Swim & Weeks, 1969)

The mauve Angel Face was an All-America Rose Selection in 1969 and winner of the American Rose Society John Cook Medal in 1971. There is a climbing form.

FLOWERS   3½–4 in. wide. Deep mauve. Double; 35–40 petals. Midseason bloom followed by good repeat bloom. Very fragrant. Formal, high-centered blossom opens to become cupped; petals ruffled; showy yellow stamens. Blooms singly and in small clusters.

FOLIAGE   2½–3 ft. tall. Bushy, spreading, vigorous. Disease resistant and winter hardy. Dark green, leathery, semiglossy leaves borne on moderately thorny canes.

BETTY PRIOR, *p. 188*
(Prior, 1935)

The abundant single flowers of Betty Prior have an overall effect that has been likened to that of flowering dogwood.

FLOWERS   3–3½ in. wide. Medium to deep pink. Single; 5 petals. Abundant midseason bloom with excellent repeat. Fragrant. Blossom cupped, opening to become saucer-shaped. Blooms in clusters.

FOLIAGE   5–7 ft. tall. Upright, vigorous, bushy. Disease resistant and winter hardy. Canes moderately thorny. Leaves medium green, semiglossy.

CHERISH, p. 199
(Warriner, 1980)

Part of the 1980 All-America Rose Selection trio of Love, Honor, and Cherish, this floribunda boasts blooms of hybrid tea quality on a compact bush.

FLOWERS   3–4 in. wide. Coral-pink. Double; 28 petals. Good midseason bloom with repeat bloom in regular cycles. Fragrant; spicy scent. Blooms have high-centered form and appear singly and in small clusters.

FOLIAGE   3–3½ ft. tall. Vigorous, bushy, spreading. Disease resistant. May require protection where winters are severe. Leaves dark green, semiglossy.

CIRCUS, p. 189
(Swim, 1956)

An All-America Rose Selection for 1956, Circus is one of the multicolored roses that develop their changing colors with exposure to sunlight. There is a climbing form.

FLOWERS   3 in. wide. Yellow, changing to coral, pink, and red in sunlight. Double; 45–58 petals. Midseason bloom with good repeat bloom. Spicy fragrance. High-centered form becomes cupped, with gold stamens.

FOLIAGE   2½–3 ft. tall. Bushy, spreading. Disease resistant, but needs protection from black spot. Winter hardy. Canes moderately thorny. Leaves medium green, leathery, semiglossy.

CLASS ACT, p. 181
(Warriner, 1989)

Also known as First Class and White Magic, Class Act received both an All-America Rose Selection award and the Portland Gold Medal in 1989.

FLOWERS 3–3½ in. wide. White. Semidouble; 20 petals. Good midseason bloom with good repeat bloom. Slight fragrance; fruity scent. Blooms have loosely arranged petals and open flat, in clusters of 3–6.

FOLIAGE 3–4 ft. tall. Bushy, medium growth. Disease resistant. Winter hardy. Canes have long, narrow thorns. Leaves dark green, semiglossy.

DICKY, *p. 187*
(Dickson, 1984)

Also known as Anisely Dickson and Münchner Kindl, Dicky received Britain's Royal National Rose Society's top award, the President's International Trophy, in 1984. This variety epitomizes the excellent growth and bloom habits of floribundas developed in the 1980s.

FLOWERS 3–3½ in. wide. Reddish salmon-pink, reverse paler. Double; 35 petals. Excellent midseason bloom with excellent repeat bloom when grown in full sun. Slight fragrance. Blooms have petals unfurling evenly from a high center. Blooms singly and in large clusters.

FOLIAGE 3–3½ ft. tall. Upright, vigorous, bushy. Disease resistant. Winter hardy. Canes have few thorns. Leaves medium green, glossy.

DUSKY MAIDEN, *p. 196*
(LeGrice, 1947)

The Royal National Rose Society Gold Medal winner in 1948, this extremely floriferous rose is one of the outstanding "Maid" series of floribundas created by E. B. LeGrice.

FLOWERS 3–3½ in. wide. Deep crimson. Single; 5–7 petals. Abundant midseason bloom with excellent repeat bloom. Fragrant. Blooms open to become saucer-shaped, with bright golden stamens. Blooms in small clusters.

FOLIAGE 2–3 ft. tall. Upright, well branched, vigorous. Disease resistant and winter hardy. Canes fairly smooth, with few thorns. Leaves dark green, large, glossy.

ESCAPADE, *p. 184*
(Harkness, 1967)

This prolific bloomer is not a true single—its blossoms have 12 petals—but it has much the same garden effect as a single rose.

FLOWERS   3 in. wide. Pink with a white center. Semidouble; 12 petals. Good midseason bloom with excellent repeat bloom. Fragrant. Blossoms open to become saucer-shaped. Blooms in clusters.

FOLIAGE   2½–3 ft. tall. Upright, well branched, spreading. Disease resistant and winter hardy. Canes moderately thorny. Leaves light to medium green, glossy.

EUROPEANA, *p. 195*
(DeRuiter, 1968)

This dark crimson floribunda was an All-America Rose Selection for 1968 and winner of The Hague Gold Medal in 1962. It remains the most popular exhibition rose of its type and color range.

FLOWERS   3 in. wide. Dark crimson. Semidouble; 15–20 petals. Abundant midseason bloom, good repeat bloom. Cupped form blooming in large clusters. Very slight fragrance.

FOLIAGE   2½–3 ft. tall. Upright and vigorous; bushy and spreading. Disease resistant. Winter hardy. Canes moderately thorny. Young leaves red, maturing to dark green; leathery, glossy.

EVENING STAR, *p. 182*
(Warriner, 1974)

Sold as a hybrid tea in Europe, this pure white rose is one of the "flora-tea" series introduced by Jackson & Perkins.

FLOWERS   4–4½ in. wide. Pure white. Double; 35 petals. Midseason bloom with fair repeat bloom. Slightly fragrant. Formal, high-centered, hybrid-tea-type bloom. Blooms singly and in small clusters.

FOLIAGE   3–3½ ft. tall. Upright, vigorous, bushy. Disease resistant. Very tender. Leaves dark green, large, leathery.

EYE PAINT, p. 194
(McGredy, 1975)

The multicolored Eye Paint, with its bushy habit of growth, performs like a shrub rose and makes a good hedge.

FLOWERS   2½ in. wide. Red with white center and golden stamens. Single; 5–7 petals. Midseason bloom with good repeat bloom. Slightly fragrant. Blossom form open, flat; in clusters.

FOLIAGE   3–4 ft. tall. Upright, vigorous, bushy, spreading. Disease resistant, but needs protection from black spot. Winter hardy. Canes rather thorny, with small, abundant dark green leaves.

FASHION, p. 189
(Boerner, 1950)

Fashion is a highly acclaimed floribunda. In addition to being an All-America Rose Selection for 1950, it claimed the Royal National Rose Society Gold Medal in 1948, the Bagatelle Gold Medal in 1949, the Portland Gold Medal in 1949, and the American Rose Society Gold Medal in 1954.

FLOWERS   3–3½ in. wide. Coral-pink. Double; 21–24 petals. Midseason bloom with excellent repeat. Slight fragrance. Hybrid-tea-type form. Blooms singly and in small clusters.

FOLIAGE   3½–4½ ft. tall. Upright, vigorous, bushy. Disease resistant and winter hardy. Canes moderately thorny, with medium green, semiglossy leaves.

FIRST EDITION, p. 188
(Delbard, 1977)

This bright floribunda was an All-America Rose Selection for the year of its introduction.

FLOWERS   2½–3 in. wide. Coral-orange. Double; 28 petals. Good midseason bloom with fair repeat bloom. Slight fragrance. Hybrid-tea-type form. Blooms singly and in clusters.

FOLIAGE   3½–4 ft. tall. Upright, vigorous, well branched. Disease resistant. Not winter hardy without protection. Canes moderately thorny. Leaves large, light green, glossy.

FRAGRANT DELIGHT, *p. 198*
(Wisbech, 1978)

This coppery orange-salmon floribunda was the winner in 1988 of England's James Mason Gold Medal, for "the rose which has given the most pleasure over the past ten years."

FLOWERS   3 in. wide. Orange-salmon, reverse copper. Double; 22 petals. Good midseason bloom with good repeat bloom. Very fragrant. Flower form cupped, ruffled; blooms in clusters.

FOLIAGE   3½–4 ft. tall. Upright, vigorous, somewhat narrow growth. Disease resistant. May require winter protection. Canes moderately thorny. Leaves reddish green, glossy.

FRENCH LACE, *p. 180*
(Warriner, 1980)

An All-America Rose Selection in 1982, French Lace is a hybrid-tea-type floribunda variety.

FLOWERS   3½–4 in. wide. White. Double; 35 petals. Good midseason bloom with good repeat bloom. Moderate fragrance. Bloom form classic hybrid tea type, with petals unfurling evenly from a high center.

FOLIAGE   3–3½ ft. tall. Upright, bushy, well branched. Disease resistant and winter hardy. Canes moderately thorny. Leaves medium green, semiglossy.

FRENSHAM, *p. 194*
(Norman, 1946)

Winner of the Royal National Gold Medal in 1943 and the American Rose Society Gold Medal in 1955, Frensham is a classic floribunda variety.

FLOWERS   3 in. wide. Dark red. Semidouble; 15 petals. Excellent midseason bloom with good repeat bloom. Slight fragrance. Bloom form cupped to saucer-shaped, in clusters.

FOLIAGE   2½–3 ft. tall. Vigorous, bushy, spreading. Disease resistant and winter hardy. Canes moderately thorny. Leaves dark green, semiglossy.

GENE BOERNER, *p. 185*
(Boerner, 1969)

An All-America Rose Selection for 1969. This flower's namesake is the hybridizer who has done more than any other in this country toward the development of the floribunda rose.

FLOWERS   3–3½ in. wide. Even, medium pink. Double; 35 petals. Good midseason bloom followed by excellent repeat bloom. Little or no fragrance. Hybrid-tea-type form. Blooms singly and in clusters.

FOLIAGE   4–5 ft. tall. Upright, vigorous, slender habit. Disease resistant and winter hardy. Canes moderately thorny. Leaves medium green, semiglossy.

GRÜSS AN AACHEN, *p. 182*
(Geduldig, 1909)

Although the floribunda class was established some 30 years after this rose's introduction, Grüss an Aachen has been classed with the floribundas because many experts believe it expresses the qualities of this group. It was bred, however, from a Bengal (China) and a Bourbon, according to the introducer and hybridizer.

FLOWERS   3–3½ in. wide. Flesh pink fading to cream. Very double; perhaps 200 petals. Early to midseason bloom followed by good repeat bloom. Fragrant. Old rose form; when fully expanded, reflexes into a ball of tightly packed petals.

FOLIAGE   2–2½ ft. tall. Vigorous, bushy. Disease resistant and winter hardy. Canes very smooth, with few thorns. Leaves small, abundant, medium green, glossy.

H. C. ANDERSEN, *p. 179*
(Poulsen, 1986)

Hailed by some as an improved version of Europeana, this floribunda was named in Denmark for Hans Christian Andersen. It is also known as Touraine and America's Choice.

FLOWERS   2½–3 in. wide. Dark red. Semidouble; 15 petals. Excellent midseason bloom, good repeat bloom. Slight fragrance. Cupped form blooming in large clusters.

FOLIAGE   3–4 ft. tall. Upright, vigorous, bushy, spreading. Disease resistant and winter hardy. Canes moderately thorny, with dark green, glossy leaves.

HANNAH GORDON, *p. 187*
(Kordes, 1983)

A floribunda that can grow to shrub proportions, Hannah Gordon produces stunning pink-edged white blooms. Its bushy growth and thorny canes make it an excellent candidate for use as a rose barrier.

FLOWERS   4–4½ in. wide. White with cherry pink edge. Double; 35 petals. Abundant midseason bloom with a second crop of blooms in the fall. Slight fragrance. Slightly ruffled blooms open flat, in clusters.

FOLIAGE   4–6 ft. tall. Upright, vigorous, bushy. Disease resistant. Winter hardy. Thorny canes with large, medium green, semiglossy leaves.

ICEBERG, *p. 180*
(Kordes, 1958)

This pure white rose is known as Schneewittchen in Germany and Fée de Neiges in France. A Royal National Rose Society Gold Medal winner in 1958, it makes an excellent hedge.

FLOWERS   3 in. wide. Pure white. Double; 30 petals. Early to midseason bloom followed by reliable repeat bloom all season. Fragrant. Hybrid tea form, opening to cupped form, blooming in clusters.

FOLIAGE   4 ft. tall. Upright, bushy. Needs protection from black spot. Winter hardy. Leaves light green, semiglossy.

IMPATIENT, *p. 193*
(Warriner, 1984)

This All-America Rose Selection for 1984 is noted for its large sprays, which are very long-lasting when cut.

FLOWERS   3 in. wide. Orange with yellow base. Double; 20–30 petals. Good midseason bloom with fair repeat bloom. Slight fragrance. Hybrid tea form; blooms singly and in small clusters.

FOLIAGE   3–3½ ft. tall. Upright, vigorous, well branched. Disease resistant and winter hardy. Canes very thorny. Leaves dark green, semiglossy.

INTRIGUE, *p. 196*
(Warriner, 1984)

An All-America Rose Selection for 1984. There is another floribunda — a red one, by Kordes — that is also called Intrigue. Although Kordes's flower is sold mostly in Europe, there are some of them in the U.S., and the confusion is unfortunate.

FLOWERS   3 in. wide. Medium purple. Double; 20–30 petals. Good midseason bloom with good repeat bloom. Very fragrant. High-centered form, blooming singly and in clusters.

FOLIAGE   3 ft. tall. Upright, vigorous, well branched. Disease resistant, but not winter hardy without protection. Canes moderately thorny. Leaves dark green, glossy.

IVORY FASHION, *p. 179*
(Boerner, 1959)

The fragrant white floribunda was an All-America Rose Selection for 1959.

FLOWERS   3½ in. wide. Ivory white. Semidouble; 15–18 petals. Abundant midseason bloom with good repeat bloom. Fragrant. Open form, showing decorative yellow stamens. Blooms in clusters.

FOLIAGE   3½–4 ft. tall. Upright, vigorous, well branched. Disease resistant and winter hardy. Canes smooth, with few thorns. Leaves medium green, leathery, semiglossy.

LAVENDER PINOCCHIO, *p. 183*
(Boerner, 1948)

These flowers are an unusual shade of lavender, intense and somewhat grayed, making Lavender Pinocchio an unforgettable rose.

FLOWERS   3–3½ in. wide. Deep lavender. Double; 25–30 petals. Good midseason bloom with fair repeat bloom. Fragrant. Loose, open, ruffled form in clusters.

FOLIAGE   2½–3 ft. tall. Vigorous, bushy, compact. Disease resistant and winter hardy. Canes moderately thorny. Leaves medium green, leathery.

LITTLE DARLING, *p. 186*
(Duehrsen, 1956)

Winner of the Portland Gold Medal in 1958 and the American Rose Society David Fuerstenberg Prize in 1964, this fragrant floribunda could be used as a shrub rose. Some rosarians consider that it makes a good hedge.

FLOWERS   2½–3 in. wide. Yellow and salmon-pink blend. Double; 24–30 petals. Abundant early to midseason bloom, followed by good repeat bloom all season. Spicy fragrance. Open, cupped form, blooming in clusters.

FOLIAGE   2½–3½ ft. tall. Vigorous, bushy, spreading. Disease resistant and winter hardy. Leaves dark green, leathery, glossy.

MARGARET MERRIL, *p. 181*
(Harkness, 1977)

Often called the perfect floribunda, Margaret Merril won gold medals from Geneva, Monza, and Rome in 1978 and from New Zealand in 1982, and the Royal National Rose Society's Edland Fragrance Medal in 1978.

FLOWERS   ·4–4½ in. wide. Blush white. Double; 28 petals. Excellent all-season bloom. Powerful fragrance; citrus and spice scent. Hybrid-tea-type form, opening slightly ruffled. Blooms singly and in clusters.

FOLIAGE   3½–4½ ft. tall. Upright, vigorous, well branched, bushy. Disease resistant and winter hardy. Canes moderately thorny, with medium green, semiglossy leaves.

ORANGEADE, *p. 191*
(McGredy, 1959)

Orangeade, with its abundant bright orange blooms, claimed the Royal National Rose Society Gold Medal in 1959.

FLOWERS   3–3½ in. wide. Orange. Semidouble; 7–9 petals. Abundant midseason bloom, with good repeat. Slight fragrance. Open blooms in large clusters.

FOLIAGE 2½–3 ft. tall. Vigorous, bushy, spreading. Disease resistant, but needs protection from mildew in cool, wet climates. Not winter hardy without protection. Leaves dark green, round, rather sparse.

PLAYBOY, p. 190
(Cocker, 1976)

Winner of the Portland Gold Medal in 1989, Playboy exhibits dazzling orange, red, and gold blooms on a remarkably healthy plant.

FLOWERS 3½ in. wide. Scarlet-orange, gold eye. Single to semidouble; 7–10 petals. Good midseason bloom with good repeat bloom. Slight fragrance; sweet apple scent. Blossom form open, slightly cupped; blooms in clusters.

FOLIAGE 2½–3 ft. tall. Vigorous, compact, bushy. Disease resistant and winter hardy. Canes moderately thorny. Leaves dark green, extremely glossy.

PLAYGIRL, p. 190
(Moore, 1986)

One of the most spectacular single-petaled floribundas, Playgirl produces a stunning display of bright gold stamens against hot pink petals.

FLOWERS 3–3½ in. wide. Hot pink. Single; 5–7 petals. Excellent early to midseason bloom with good repeat bloom. Slight fragrance. Blooms have open, somewhat wavy form, and occur in large clusters.

FOLIAGE 3–3½ ft. tall. Upright, vigorous, bushy. Disease resistant and winter hardy. Canes have few thorns. Leaves medium green, semiglossy.

PLEASURE, p. 184
(Warriner, 1990)

The only All-America Rose Selection for 1990, Pleasure provides unusually rapid repeat bloom for a floribunda.

FLOWERS 4 in. wide. Coral-pink. Double; 33 petals. Profuse midseason bloom with excellent repeat bloom. Slight fragrance. Open, cupped form, with ruffled petals. Blooms in clusters.

FOLIAGE   3 ft. tall. Vigorous, compact, bushy. Disease resistant and winter hardy. Canes moderately thorny. Leaves dark green, semiglossy.

POULSEN'S PEARL, *p. 183*
(Poulsen, 1949)

A unique floribunda variety. Like all single roses, Poulsen's Pearl is very effective in garden display.

FLOWERS   3 in. wide. Light pink. Single; 5 petals. Midseason bloom with good repeat bloom. Fragrant. Bloom opens to become saucer-shaped; its showy pink stamens are an unusual feature.

FOLIAGE   2½–3 ft. tall. Upright, bushy. Disease resistant and winter hardy. Canes moderately thorny. Leaves light to medium green, semiglossy.

PRINCESS ALICE, *p. 178*
(Harkness, 1985)

Also known as Brite Lites and Zonta Rose, this exceptionally healthy variety has a narrow, upright growth habit that makes it easy to use in a variety of landscaping schemes. Princess Alice won a gold medal at Dublin in 1984.

FLOWERS   2½–3 in. wide. Medium yellow. Double; 28 petals. Good late-season bloom with repeat bloom in regular cycles. Slight fragrance. Open, cupped form with slightly ruffled petals. Blooms in very large clusters.

FOLIAGE   3½–5 ft. tall. Upright, vigorous, narrow. Disease resistant and winter hardy. Canes moderately thorny. Leaves medium green, semiglossy.

PRISCILLA BURTON, *p. 197*
(McGredy, 1978)

Perhaps the most dramatic of all the handpainted floribundas, Priscilla Burton received the President's International Trophy from Britain's Royal National Rose Society in 1976.

FLOWERS   2½ in. wide. Deep carmine-pink with lighter pink and white markings. Semidouble; 10 petals. Good all-season bloom. Fragrant. Open blossoms, in clusters.

FOLIAGE   3½–4 ft. tall. Upright, vigorous. Generally disease resistant, but may need protection from black spot. Winter hardy. Leaves dark green, glossy.

PURPLE TIGER, *p. 197*
(Christensen, 1992)

Also known as Impressionist, Purple Tiger provides a multitude of bizarrely striped blooms, no two of which are exactly alike.

FLOWERS   3–4 in. wide. Very deep purple with stripes and flecks of white and mauve-pink. Double; 26–40 petals. Good all-season bloom. Fragrant; damask scent. Blooms open flat, in small clusters.

FOLIAGE   1½–2 ft. tall. Compact, well branched. Disease resistant and winter hardy. Nearly thornless canes are very shiny. Leaves medium green, glossy.

REDGOLD, *p. 191*
(Dickson, 1971)

Redgold was an All-America Rose Selection for 1971. The red color of the petal tips does not develop unless the flowers are exposed to strong sunlight. The cut flowers have a long vase life.

FLOWERS   2½–3 in. wide. Yellow, edged with red. Double; 25–30 petals. Good midseason bloom, with fair repeat later in the season. Slight fruity fragrance. Hybrid tea form, opening to cup shape; blooms singly and in clusters.

FOLIAGE   3–3½ ft. tall. Upright, vigorous, well branched. Disease resistant and winter hardy. Canes very thorny. Leaves medium green, semiglossy, and rather sparse.

REGENSBERG, *p. 198*
(McGredy, 1979)

Here is a handpainted rose that maintains a pleasing compact habit, with none of the late-season spiky growth often associated with handpainteds. Also known as Buffalo Bill and Young

Mistress, Regensberg received a Baden-Baden Gold Medal in 1980.

FLOWERS　3½–4½ in. wide. Pink, edged and marked with white, with white eye and reverse. Double; 25 petals. Good all-season bloom. Fragrant; sweet apple scent. Cupped blooms open flat, in clusters.

FOLIAGE　1½–2 ft. tall. Compact, bushy, vigorous. Disease resistant and winter hardy. Canes have few thorns. Leaves medium green, semiglossy.

SARABANDE, p. 192
(Meilland, 1957)

An All-America Rose Selection for 1960, Sarabande captured the Bagatelle Gold Medal, the Geneva Gold Medal, and the Rome Gold Medal in 1957, as well as the Portland Gold Medal in 1958. Sarabande is a spectacular rose that grows best in cool climates.

FLOWERS　2½ in. wide. Orange-red. Semidouble; 10–15 petals. Profuse midseason bloom with excellent repeat bloom. Slightly spicy fragrance. Form cupped to flat, showing bright yellow stamens, blooming in large clusters.

FOLIAGE　2½ ft. tall. Vigorous, bushy. Disease resistant and winter hardy. Canes moderately thorny. Leaves medium green, semiglossy.

SEXY REXY, p. 199
(McGredy, 1984)

Sexy Rexy is a great floribunda, but it must be methodically deadheaded to ensure good repeat bloom. It is the recipient of two gold medals in New Zealand and a new name (Heckenzauber) in Germany.

FLOWERS　3½–4 in. wide. Medium to light pink. Double; 40-plus petals. Profuse late-season bloom, with good repeat bloom if deadheaded. Slight fragrance. Blooms cupped, approaching rosette shape, in very large clusters.

FOLIAGE　3–4 ft. tall. Upright, vigorous, bushy, well branched. Disease resistant and winter hardy. Canes are thorny, with small, dark green, glossy leaves.

SHOWBIZ, *p. 195*
(Tantau, 1981)

Showbiz was an All-America Rose Selection for 1985. It is also known as Ingrid Weibull and Bernhard Daneke Rose.

FLOWERS 2½–3 in. wide. Medium red. Double; 28–30 petals. Good all-season bloom. Slight fragrance. Open, cupped form, with ruffled petals. Blooms in clusters.

FOLIAGE 2½–3 ft. tall. Upright, vigorous, spreading. Disease resistant and winter hardy. Leaves dark green, glossy.

SIMPLICITY, *p. 186*
(Warriner, 1979)

A good hedge rose, Simplicity has been described as a pink version of Iceberg.

FLOWERS 3–4 in. wide. Medium pink. Semidouble; 18–20 petals. Abundant all-season bloom. Little or no fragrance. Flower form opens to become cupped. Blooms in clusters.

FOLIAGE 2½–3½ ft. tall. Upright, vigorous, bushy. Disease resistant and winter hardy. Leaves medium green, semiglossy.

SUNSPRITE, *p. 178*
(Kordes, 1977)

Sunsprite received a Baden-Baden Gold Medal in 1972, in part because of its remarkable fragrance. There is a climbing form.

FLOWERS 3 in. wide. Deep yellow. Double; 28 petals. Good midseason bloom with good repeat bloom. Very fragrant; sweet licorice scent. Cup-shaped blooms in clusters, opening to slightly ruffled form.

FOLIAGE 2½–3 ft. tall. Vigorous, bushy, upright. Disease resistant and winter hardy. Canes moderately thorny. Leaves medium green, semiglossy.

TRUMPETER, *p. 192*
(McGredy, 1977)

This hybrid-tea-type floribunda produces an abundance of brilliant orange-red blooms.

FLOWERS   3½ in. wide. Orange-red. Double; 35–40 petals. Excellent midseason bloom with excellent repeat bloom. Slight fragrance. High-centered, classic hybrid tea bloom form. Blooms singly and in clusters.

FOLIAGE   3½–4½ ft. tall. Upright, bushy, well branched. Disease resistant and winter hardy. Canes moderately thorny. Leaves dark green, glossy.

Grandifloras

The year 1954 witnessed the inauguration of a new class of roses: the grandifloras. Intended to combine the long stems and beautiful blossoms of the hybrid teas with the hardiness and the clustered flowers of the floribundas, the grandifloras are still a small group, and only a few varieties within the class have come close to realizing these goals. But it is early days yet, and rose growers hope to achieve a great deal in the coming years.

First and Finest

It is interesting that the very first grandiflora, the one for which the the new class was created, has also proven to be the finest. Queen Elizabeth, a variety introduced with much fanfare in the second year of that monarch's reign, has set the standard for all grandifloras. Queen Elizabeth was the progeny of Charlotte Armstrong (the seed parent and a hybrid tea) and Floradora (the pollen parent and a floribunda); the result of this union combined the best features of both classes. Queen Elizabeth has large, classic-shaped blossoms, usually occurring in small clusters. The robust, vigorous plant produces profuse blooms, with excellent repeat blooms throughout the growing season.

Permission from the Queen

Queen Elizabeth was hybridized by Dr. Walter E. Lammerts and introduced by Germain's, Inc. (Germain Seed and Plant Co.) of Los Angeles, California. Queen Elizabeth II granted Dr. Lammerts the right to use her name, and British lawmakers formalized this permission in an act of Parliament. Germain's presented the very first Queen Elizabeth rose to Her Majesty in 1954.

Since that date, many other cultivars have been placed in the grandiflora class, but no other rose has come up to the standard of Queen Elizabeth, and only a few, such as Comanche and Montezuma, have approached it.

A Difference of Opinion

Although the first rose in this class was named in honor of their queen, rose growers in Great Britain have never acknowledged the grandiflora class, classifying these cultivars instead as floribundas. In the United States, there are many varieties that cannot justifiably be placed in the grandiflora class; these roses are referred to as hybrid-tea-type floribundas.

A Blend of Traits

In most respects, grandifloras display characteristics intermediate to those of their parent classes. Generally more vigorous than both floribundas and hybrid teas, they are only a little hardier than the latter, and thus cannot survive harsh winters.

Like floribundas, grandifloras produce abundant blooms, but the flowers themselves have the form and size of the hybrid teas. Grandifloras exceed both parents, however, in height — most grow taller than members of these other two classes. Queen Elizabeth, for example, grows to a height of seven feet.

Making Use of Grandifloras

Because of their great height, grandifloras are well suited for use as hedges. They also make an excellent backdrop for other roses, or for all manner of different flowers in the garden. With their hybrid tea heritage, they produce wonderful long-stemmed blooms that are perfect for cutting and for use in a wide variety of arrangements.

Culture

You can grow your grandifloras much as you would hybrid teas, making allowances, of course, for their extra vigor and height. When pruning, be sure not to cut the canes back too far. Remember too that grandifloras are only a little hardier, on the whole, than hybrid teas, and certainly not as cold-tolerant as many floribunda varieties.

Future Considerations

As rose growers continue to perfect their techniques, the distinctions between certain classes of roses become smaller and smaller. This is what has happened with the floribundas, which have begun to resemble hybrid teas more and more; as grandiflora development becomes more advanced, the characteristics that set this class off may become less discernible. Until that time, modern rosarians will continue to produce better and better grandifloras.

AQUARIUS, p. 205
(Armstrong, 1971)

Aquarius was an All-America Rose Selection for 1971. Its blooms can be large for the grandiflora class, particularly when the plant is disbudded Flowers have a long vase life.

FLOWERS 3½–4½ in. wide. Medium pink blended with cream. Double; 35–40 petals. Good all-season bloom. Slight fragrance. High-centered, evenly petaled form.

FOLIAGE 4½–5 ft. tall. Upright, vigorous, bushy. Disease resistant and winter hardy. Leaves large, medium green, leathery.

CAMELOT, p. 206
(Swim & Weeks, 1964)

Camelot is particularly good for cutting, as its flowers have a long vase life. It was an All-America Rose Selection for 1965.

FLOWERS 3½–4 in. wide. Coral. Double; 40–55 petals. Good all-season bloom. Spicy fragrance. Cupped form.

FOLIAGE 5–5½ ft. tall. Upright, vigorous, well branched. Disease resistant and winter hardy. Leaves dark green, leathery, glossy.

GOLD MEDAL, p. 202
(Christensen, 1982)

Gold Medal has deep yellow blooms tipped with red; they hold their form and color well.

FLOWERS 3½ in. wide. Deep yellow, tipped red. Double; 35–40 petals. Good all-season bloom. Slight fruity, or tealike, fragrance. Classic high-centered form. Blooms singly and in clusters.

FOLIAGE 4½–5½ ft. tall. Upright, vigorous, bushy. Disease resistant, but needs protection from black spot. Tender. Leaves dark green, semiglossy.

LAGERFELD, *p. 203*
(Christensen, 1985)

True to the ideals of the grandiflora class, Lagerfeld has hybrid-tea-shaped blooms in large clusters on a bush that grows taller than the typical hybrid tea. It is also one of the most fragrant grandifloras.

FLOWERS   4½–5½ in. wide. Silvery lavender. Double; 30 petals. Good all-season bloom. Intense fragrance. Classic high-centered form. Blooms singly and in large clusters.

FOLIAGE   4½–5½ ft. tall. Upright, vigorous, bushy. Disease resistant and winter hardy. Canes moderately thorny. Leaves medium green, matte.

LOVE, *p. 207*
(Warriner, 1980)

This All-America Rose Selection for 1980 is a grandiflora that could just as easily be considered a hybrid tea, as its blooms have the classic, high-centered form.

FLOWERS   3½ in. wide. Red with white reverse. Double; 24–30 petals. Good continuous bloom throughout the season. Very slight fragrance. High-centered, hybrid-tea-type form holds well before developing a cupped form with confused center.

FOLIAGE   3–3½ ft. tall. Upright, moderately vigorous, sparsely branched. Disease resistant and winter hardy. Very thorny canes bear medium green, dull, rather sparse leaves.

MONTEZUMA, *p. 205*
(Swim, 1955)

Winner of the Geneva Gold Medal in 1955, the Royal National Rose Society Gold Medal in 1956, and the Portland Gold Medal in 1957. Montezuma comes very close to the grandiflora ideal.

FLOWERS   3½–4 in. wide. Deep coral. Double; 32–40 petals. Good all-season bloom. Slight fragrance. High-centered, classic form. Blooms singly and in small clusters.

FOLIAGE   4½–5 ft. tall. Upright, very vigorous, compact, and well branched. Disease resistant and winter hardy. Canes moderately thorny. Leaves medium green, leathery, semiglossy.

PINK PARFAIT, *p. 206*
(Swim, 1960)

An All-America Rose Selection for 1961, Pink Parfait also claimed the Portland Gold Medal in 1959 and the Royal National Rose Society Gold Medal in 1962.

FLOWERS 3½–4 in. wide. Light to medium pink. Double; 20–25 petals. Abundant midseason bloom followed by good repeat bloom. Slight fragrance. Bloom high-centered to cupped. Blooms singly and in particularly fine clusters.

FOLIAGE 3½–4½ ft. tall. Upright, vigorous, bushy. Disease resistant and winter hardy. Canes moderately thorny. Leaves medium green, leathery, semiglossy.

PROMINENT, *p. 202*
(Kordes, 1971)

Known as Korp in Europe, Prominent was an All-America Rose Selection for 1977 and the winner of the Portland Gold Medal that same year.

FLOWERS 3½ in. wide. Orange-red. Double; 30–35 petals. Excellent all-season bloom. Slight fragrance. Cupped form. Blooms singly and in clusters.

FOLIAGE 3½–4½ ft. tall. Upright, well branched. Moderately vigorous. Disease resistant and winter hardy. Canes thorny. Leaves dull, dark green, leathery.

QUEEN ELIZABETH, *p. 204*
(Lammerts, 1955)

The prototype of the grandiflora class, Queen Elizabeth has proved itself second in popularity only to Peace in this century. In addition to being an All-America Rose Selection for the year of its introduction, this magnificent rose has captured top honors over the course of many years. It was the Royal National Rose Society Gold Medal winner in 1955, winner of the American Rose Society Gertrude M. Hubbard Gold Medal in 1957, recipient of the American Rose Society National Gold Medal Certificate in 1960, and recipient of the Golden Rose of The Hague in 1968. There is a climbing form.

FLOWERS 3½–4 in. wide. Medium pink. Double; 37–40 petals. Abundant midseason bloom followed by excellent repeat bloom. Fragrant. Blossom high-centered to cupped. Blooms singly and in small clusters.

FOLIAGE   5–7 ft. tall. Upright, very vigorous, bushy. Disease resistant and winter hardy. Canes moderately thorny. Leaves dark green, leathery, glossy.

SHREVEPORT, p. 204
(Kordes, 1982)

An All-America Rose Selection for 1982, Shreveport is named for the Louisiana city that is the home of the American Rose Center. This rose's cut flowers have a long vase life.

FLOWERS   3½–4 in. wide. Orange blend. Double; 24–30 petals. Fair all-season bloom. Slight fragrance. Cupped form.

FOLIAGE   4½–5 ft. tall. Upright, vigorous, bushy. Disease resistant and winter hardy. Canes moderately thorny. Leaves dark green, glossy.

TOURNAMENT OF ROSES, p. 203
(Warriner, 1989)

An All-America Rose Selection in 1989, the coral-pink Tournament of Roses exhibits fascinating almond colorations in cool weather.

FLOWERS   3½–4 in. wide. Shades of coral-pink. Double; 35 petals. Good midseason bloom with excellent repeat bloom. No fragrance. High-centered, classic hybrid tea form. Blooms in clusters of 3–6.

FOLIAGE   3 ft. tall. Vigorous, bushy, compact. Disease resistant and winter hardy. Leaves dark green, semiglossy.

WHITE LIGHTNIN', p. 207
(Swim & Christensen, 1980)

This rose has rather small blossoms occurring in small clusters. Nonetheless, White Lightnin' is in many ways similar to the hybrid teas, and could easily be classed with them.

FLOWERS 3½–4 in. wide. White. Double; 26–32 petals. Good all-season bloom. Very fragrant. Cupped form. Blooms singly and in clusters.

FOLIAGE 4½–5 ft. tall. Upright, vigorous, bushy. Disease resistant and winter hardy. Canes moderately thorny. Leaves dark green, glossy.

Hybrid Teas

The year 1867 marks a watershed in the history of rose cultivation, for that year witnessed the introduction of La France, the variety generally recognized as the first hybrid tea of superlative distinction. In consequence, the American Rose Society has settled on this year as the dividing line between "old-fashioned" and "modern" roses. It is important to bear in mind, however, that this date is arbitrary, in one sense. It is simplistic to consider that hybrid teas did not exist before that time, because much development led up to the creation of La France. Indeed, in any class of roses, the true "firsts," by genetic standards, probably resemble their forebears much more than they do the typical members of that class.

Origins of the Class

The hybrid tea class was developed in the late 19th and early 20th centuries by crossing two kinds of old garden roses — hybrid perpetuals and teas. Until the development of the hybrid teas, the hybrid perpetuals had been the most popular roses worldwide. Unfortunately, they were not reliable repeat bloomers, which the teas (originating in China and other parts of Asia) were.

A melding of traits

Thus, experimentation in blending these two kinds of roses was begun. The resulting flowers were a little smaller than those of the hybrid perpetuals, but a good deal more shapely than those of the teas. And although these new roses produced a first bloom that was less profuse than that of their progenitors, their repeat flowering was much more reliable. The plants were not as strong, sturdy, and winter hardy as the hybrid perpetuals, but were much stronger, more upright, and hardier than the teas.

Early Adventures in Cross-Breeding

The first rose hybridizer known to have kept records of crosses was Henry Bennett, who introduced a series of "pedigreed roses" in the late 1800s. Before this time, the principles of cross-breeding were not well understood, and rose growers were apt simply to plant different roses next to each other; they could then wait and watch, hopeful that their plants would interbreed and that some useful mixing of characteristics would take place.

Doubtless, this process had proved somewhat fruitful over time, but it was not an efficient way to develop new varieties. But in the late part of the 19th century, as the principles of genetic inheritance came to be elucidated and understood, tremendous advances became possible.

Marvelous New Colors

Until the beginning of the 20th century, roses had been grown in shades of white, pink, red, and mauve, but there were very few yellow roses. Joseph Pernet-Dicher began experimenting in the late 1800s with Persian Yellow (*Rosa foetida persiana,* the double form of the Austrian Briar). In the early 1900s he succeeded in introducing the first hybrid tea roses of a rich, pure, deep yellow.

The addition of this new color to the rose grower's palette was of tremendous value, for it opened up a whole new world of color possibilities. At last breeders had the ability to create brilliant, vibrant colors: flame reds, burning coppers, and other brilliant shades that had for so long been out of reach.

These early yellow and yellow-blend hybrid teas were called "pernetianas" at the time, but through much interbreeding they soon became assimilated into the hybrid tea class. Unfortunately, this new group of roses also brought with them a susceptibility to black spot.

Tremendous Popularity

Today, the hybrid teas are the most popular of all roses. They also constitute a very large group, and new varieties are constantly being created. Grown in almost every part of the world, they bloom all season long, from spring to fall. With their elegant long-stemmed blooms, hybrid teas are well suited to formal rose gardens, but they also do nicely as shrubs in less formal settings.

AMERICAN PRIDE, p. 234
(Warriner, 1978)

Its bright color and profuse blossoms make this healthy red rose a garden asset.

FLOWERS   4½–5½ in. wide. Bright medium to dark red. Double; 45–50 petals. Blooms best in early summer and fall. Little or no fragrance. High-centered, becoming cupped with a confused center.

FOLIAGE   5–5½ ft. tall. Upright, well branched. Disease resistant and winter hardy. Leaves large, dark green, semiglossy.

BRANDY, *p. 237*
(Swim & Christensen, 1982)

This All-America Rose Selection for 1982 is popular for its outstanding color and fruity fragrance.

FLOWERS   4–4½ in. wide. Apricot blend. Double; 25–30 petals. Profuse all-season bloom. Moderately strong, fruity fragrance. Informal, loose form, opening quickly to show bright golden stamens.

FOLIAGE   4–5 ft. tall. Upright, vigorous. Disease resistant but needs protection from black spot. Winter hardy with some protection. Canes moderately thorny. Leaves large, abundant, medium green, glossy.

BRIDE'S DREAM, *p. 239*
(Kordes, 1985)

Originally known as Märchenkönigin, this pastel pink hybrid tea is noted for its perfect form, production of basal breaks, and exceptionally rapid repeat bloom.

FLOWERS   4½–5½ in. wide. Palest pink. Double; 32 petals. Good midseason bloom with excellent repeat bloom. Slight fragrance. High-centered, classic form.

FOLIAGE   4½–5½ ft. tall. Upright, vigorous. Disease resistant and winter hardy. Canes moderately thorny. Leaves large, deep green, glossy.

CENTURY TWO, *p. 221*
(Armstrong, 1971)

A result of crossing Charlotte Armstrong with Duet, Century Two is a proven performer in all climates.

FLOWERS 5 in. wide. Clear, rich pink. Double; 30–35 petals. Profuse all-season bloom. Fragrant. Blooms are high-centered, becoming cupped.

FOLIAGE 4–5 ft. tall. Upright, bushy, vigorous. Disease resistant and winter hardy. Leaves medium green, leathery.

CHARLOTTE ARMSTRONG, *p. 219*
(Lammerts, 1940)

An All-America Rose Selection for 1940, Charlotte Armstrong was the winner of the Portland Gold Medal in 1941. This rose is noted for its beautiful long slender buds, which open to an informal flower form, and for its brilliant deep pink color. A climbing form is available.

FLOWERS 3½–4½ in. wide. Deep cerise pink. Double; 35 petals. Good early-summer bloom with moderate repeat bloom. Good fragrance. Form rather loose and informal.

FOLIAGE 4–5 ft. tall. Upright, vigorous, compact. Disease resistant; winter hardy with some protection. Canes moderately thorny. Leaves large, dark green, leathery.

CHICAGO PEACE, *p. 215*
(Johnson, 1962)

This sport of Peace displays all of that famous rose's good qualities in a deeper color range.

FLOWERS 5–5½ in. wide. Deep pink with strong yellow at base; some streaks and patches of pink, yellow, and apricot. Double; 50–60 petals. Good all-season bloom. Some fragrance. Form even and full but not high-centered.

FOLIAGE 4½–5½ ft. tall. Upright, vigorous, well branched. Disease resistant and winter hardy. Canes moderately thorny. Leaves large, leathery, glossy, dark green.

CHRYSLER IMPERIAL, *p. 231*
(Lammerts, 1952)

An All-America Rose Selection in 1953, Chrysler Imperial won the Portland Gold Medal in 1951, the American Rose Society John Cook Medal in 1964, and the James Alexander Gamble

Rose Fragrance Medal in 1965. This classic hybrid tea has proven popularity. A climbing form is available.

FLOWERS   4½–5 in. wide. Deep red. Double; 40–50 petals. Profuse midseason bloom, with good repeat. Very fragrant; true-rose (damask) scent. High-centered form opening to a very full, evenly petaled bloom.

FOLIAGE   4–5 ft. tall. Upright, vigorous, compact. Disease resistant, but needs protection from mildew in cool, wet climates. Winter hardy. Canes moderately thorny; leaves dark green, semiglossy.

COLOR MAGIC, *p. 223*
(Warriner, 1978)

This All-America Rose Selection for 1978 is a "changing colors" variety; the deeper color spreads and intensifies as the petals are exposed to sunlight.

FLOWERS   5 in. wide. Ivory to deep pink. Double; 20–30 petals. Continuous all-season bloom. Slight fragrance. Very even, circular form, becoming cupped; blooms singly and in clusters.

FOLIAGE   3½–4 ft. tall. Upright, well branched. Disease resistant, but not winter hardy without protection. Canes moderately thorny. Leaves large, dark green, semiglossy.

CRIMSON GLORY, *p. 229*
(Kordes, 1935)

Crimson Glory claimed the Royal National Rose Society Gold Medal in 1936 and the James Alexander Gamble Rose Fragrance Medal in 1961. This classic hybrid tea is beloved for its fragrance, color, and petal texture. There is a very good climbing form.

FLOWERS   4–4½ in. wide. Deep, velvety crimson. Double; about 30 petals. Good all-season bloom. Very fragrant, with true damask rose scent. Classic form, but not extremely high-centered.

FOLIAGE   3½–4 ft. tall. Vigorous, spreading; needs judicious pruning to encourage a more upright habit. Disease resistant. Winter hardy. Moderately thorny. Leaves dark green, leathery, glossy.

CRYSTALLINE, *p. 237*
(Christensen & Carruth, 1987)

Originally bred for greenhouse production, Crystalline produces exquisitely formed flowers for cutting outdoors too. Especially popular in the South and Southwest, its blooms may spot in damp coastal climates.

FLOWERS 4½–5 in. wide. White. Double; 30–35 petals. Excellent all-season bloom. Fragrant; spicy scent. Classic, high-centered form.

FOLIAGE 4–5 ft. tall. Upright, vigorous, bushy. Disease resistant and winter hardy. Moderately thorny canes. Foliage is medium green and exceptionally rugose (crinkled) for a hybrid tea.

DAINTY BESS, *p. 219*
(Archer, 1925)

A Royal National Rose Society Gold Medal winner in 1925, this pink rose is the best-known and most widely grown of all the modern single roses. A climbing form is available.

FLOWERS 3½ in. wide. Medium to light pink. Single; 5 petals. Good all-season bloom. Fragrant. Petals open flat, revealing maroon stamens. Blooms singly and in clusters.

FOLIAGE 3½–4 ft. tall. Upright, well branched. Disease resistant and winter hardy. Canes very thorny. Leaves medium to dark green, leathery, semiglossy.

DOUBLE DELIGHT, *p. 224*
(Swim & Ellis, 1977)

This All-America Rose Selection for 1977 is a "changing colors" hybrid tea. It is popular for its color, form, and fragrance. Cut flowers have a long vase life.

FLOWERS 5½ in. wide. Creamy white with red edge, becoming red. Double; 35–45 petals. Excellent all-season bloom. Spicy fragrance. High-centered, classic form.

FOLIAGE 3½–4 ft. tall. Upright, spreading, very bushy. Disease resistant, but needs protection from mildew in cool, wet climates. Winter hardy. Leaves a dull medium green.

DUET, p. 216
(Swim, 1960)

This pink blend was an All-America Rose Selection for 1961. Its flowers — a light pink and deeper pink bicolor — have a long vase life.

FLOWERS   4 in. wide. Light pink with deeper pink reverse. Double; 25–35 petals. Good midseason bloom with excellent repeat. Fragrant. Classic high-centered hybrid tea form.

FOLIAGE   4½–5½ ft. tall. Upright, vigorous, well branched. Disease resistant and winter hardy. Leaves large, medium green, leathery.

ELECTRON, p. 228
(McGredy, 1970)

Called Mullard Jubilee in Europe, this All-America Rose Selection in 1973 is popular for its rich color and fragrance.

FLOWERS   5 in. wide. Deep pink. Double; 32 petals. Very fragrant. Abundant all-season bloom. Classic hybrid tea form.

FOLIAGE   2½–3½ ft. tall. Upright, vigorous, stocky. Disease resistant and winter hardy. Canes moderately thorny. Leaves medium green, leathery.

ELINA, p. 238
(Dickson, 1984)

Winner of Germany's ADR Award and New Zealand's Gold Star in 1987, Elina is equally attractive as a bud, a bloom, and fully open. Also known as Peaudouce, this is one of the most prolific of all hybrid teas.

FLOWERS   5½–6 in. wide. Primrose yellow. Double; 35 petals. Outstanding all-season bloom. Slight fragrance. High-centered, evenly petaled.

FOLIAGE   5 ft. tall. Bushy, vigorous. Disease resistant and winter hardy. Canes moderately thorny. Leaves dark green, semiglossy.

ELIZABETH TAYLOR, *p. 232*
(Weddle, 1985)

Bred by an amateur hybridizer in Indiana, this rose is popular with exhibitors and anyone who wants lots of perfectly formed, long-stemmed, deep pink cut flowers.

FLOWERS 4–5 in. wide. Deep pink with darker edges; an occasional petal may be striped lighter pink or white. Double; 35 petals. Good all-season bloom. Slight fragrance; spicy scent. Classic hybrid tea form.

FOLIAGE 4–5 ft. tall. Upright, vigorous, well branched. Disease resistant and winter hardy. Canes moderately thorny. Foliage large, dark green, semiglossy.

FIRST PRIZE, *p. 226*
(Boerner, 1970)

An All-America Rose Selection in 1970 and winner of the American Rose Society Gertrude M. Hubbard Gold Medal in 1971, this fragrant hybrid tea is a popular exhibition variety, and the cut flowers have a long vase life.

FLOWERS 5–5½ in. wide. Medium pink, center blended with ivory. Double; 30–35 petals. Good midseason bloom and good repeat bloom. Fragrant. Classic high-centered hybrid tea form.

FOLIAGE 5 ft. tall. Vigorous, spreading. Disease prone; requires protection from black spot and mildew. Very tender. Leaves dark green, leathery.

FOLKLORE, *p. 217*
(Kordes, 1977)

Folklore produces classically formed blooms on a semiclimbing, stalwart bush that is suitable for a tall hedge or barrier.

FLOWERS 4½–5 in. wide. Orange, reverse paler. Double; 44 petals. Blooms later than most hybrid teas, with good repeat in the fall. Fragrant. Classic high-centered hybrid tea form.

FOLIAGE 6–8 ft. tall. Very vigorous, upright, bushy. Disease resistant and winter hardy. Canes very thorny. Leaves medium green, glossy.

FRAGRANT CLOUD, p. 234
(Tantau, 1963)

Fragrant Cloud received the Royal National Rose Society Gold Medal in 1963, the Portland Gold Medal in 1967, and the James Alexander Gamble Rose Fragrance Medal in 1969. Called Duftwolke in West Germany, it is popular for its intense fragrance. Its coral-red color is somewhat grayed, but not unpleasing.

FLOWERS   5 in. wide. Coral-red. Double; 25–30 petals. Good all-season bloom. Intense fragrance; true rose (damask) scent. High-centered form opens to full, evenly petaled bloom.

FOLIAGE   4–5 ft. tall. Upright, vigorous, well branched. Disease resistant and winter hardy. Leaves dark green, glossy.

FRIENDSHIP, p. 224
(Lindquist, 1978)

All-America Rose Selection for 1979, this is a typical pink hybrid tea. There are a greater number of roses in the pink and pink-blend classes than in any other color; thus, those that appear on the market are more carefully monitored than roses in other color classes. Friendship has a long vase life.

FLOWERS   5½ in. wide. Medium to deep pink. Double; 25–30 petals. Good all-season bloom. Very fragrant. Classic high-centered hybrid tea form.

FOLIAGE   5–6 ft. tall. Upright, vigorous. Disease resistant and winter hardy. Leaves large, medium green, glossy.

GARDEN PARTY, p. 212
(Swim, 1959)

An All-America Rose Selection in 1960 and winner of the Bagatelle Gold Medal in 1959, Garden Party is a popular exhibition variety.

FLOWERS   5–5½ in. wide. White with light pink edge. Double; 25–30 petals. Profuse midseason bloom followed by good repeat. Fragrant. Classic high-centered form.

FOLIAGE   5–6 ft. tall. Upright, vigorous. Disease resistant but needs protection from mildew. Winter hardy. Leaves large, long, medium green, semiglossy.

GRANADA, *p. 214*
(Lindquist, 1963)

Winner of the James Alexander Gamble Rose Fragrance Medal in 1968, Granada presents a pleasing blend of colors and a spicy fragrance. It is a prolific bloomer.

FLOWERS 4–5 in. wide. Blend of pink, orange-red, and light yellow. Double; 18–25 petals. Excellent all-season bloom. Spicy fragrance. Classic high-centered form. Blooms singly and in clusters.

FOLIAGE 5–6 ft. tall. Upright, vigorous, bushy. Disease resistant, but needs protection from mildew. Not reliably winter hardy without protection in severe climates. Canes rather thorny. Leaves dark green, leathery.

HONOR, *p. 210*
(Warriner, 1980)

An All-America Rose Selection for 1980, Honor produces fragrant white blooms all season long. Cut flowers have a long vase life.

FLOWERS 4–5 in. wide. White. Double; 20–22 petals. Good all-season bloom. Slight fragrance. Form high-centered to open, loose. Blooms singly and in clusters.

FOLIAGE 5–5½ ft. tall. Upright, vigorous, well branched. Disease resistant. Not winter hardy without protection. Canes moderately thorny. Leaves large, dark green, leathery.

INGRID BERGMAN, *p. 229*
(Poulsen, 1985)

One of the most acclaimed roses of the 1980s, Ingrid Bergman received gold medals from Belfast in 1985 and Madrid in 1986 and the Golden Rose of The Hague in 1987. It has everything one wants in a red rose except strong fragrance.

FLOWERS 4–4½ in. wide. Bright crimson. Double; 35 petals. Good all-season bloom. Slight fragrance. High-centered form opens to full, evenly petaled bloom.

FOLIAGE 4 ft. tall. Upright, vigorous, well branched. Disease resistant and winter hardy. Canes moderately thorny. Leaves dark green, semiglossy.

JUST JOEY, p. 238
(Cants, 1972)

With a unique ruffled form, the deep apricot Just Joey always commands attention. This rose won the Royal National Rose Society's James Mason Gold Medal in 1986.

FLOWERS   4–5 in. wide. Rich apricot, fading to buff orange. Double; 30 petals. Good all-season bloom. Strong fragrance; fruity scent. Form high-centered with ruffled edges. Blooms singly and in clusters.

FOLIAGE   3–3½ ft. tall. Bushy. Moderately vigorous. Disease resistant. Winter hardy in all but the most severe climates. Leaves very large, dark green, glossy.

KAISERIN AUGUSTE VIKTORIA, p. 210
(Lambert, 1891)

Sometimes called K. A. Viktoria, this is one of the early hybrid teas and is still widely grown. A climbing form is available.

FLOWERS   4–4½ in. wide. Creamy white. Very double; 100 petals. Lavish early to midseason bloom, fair repeat bloom. Very fragrant. Flower form classic, very full, very evenly petaled.

FOLIAGE   5–7 ft. tall. Upright, vigorous, bushy. Disease resistant and winter hardy. Leaves dull, dark green.

KARDINAL, p. 233
(Kordes, 1986)

Officially known by its code name, KORlingo, to avoid confusion with a rose called Kardinal introduced in 1934, the 1986 Kardinal is a consistent producer of long-stemmed, medium-size, florist-type blooms. It is one of the most disease resistant of all hybrid teas.

FLOWERS   4–4½ in. wide. Bright red. Double; 30 petals. Good all-season bloom, in regular cycles. Slight fragrance. Classic high-centered hybrid tea form.

FOLIAGE   4–4½ ft. tall. Upright, vigorous, well branched. Disease resistant and winter hardy. Leaves medium green, semi-glossy.

KING'S RANSOM, *p. 239*
(Morey, 1961)

An All-America Rose Selection for 1962, King's Ransom has held its own over the years in spite of its faults. It is prone to mildew and somewhat tender, and its blooms do not quite achieve the classic hybrid tea form.

FLOWERS   5–6 in. wide. Deep yellow. Double; 35–40 petals. Profuse midseason bloom, good repeat bloom. Fragrant. Blossoms somewhat loose and cup-shaped. Blooms singly and in clusters.

FOLIAGE   4½–5 ft. tall. Upright, vigorous, well branched. Disease resistant, but needs protection from mildew. Somewhat tender in severe winter climates. Canes moderately thorny. Leaves light green, glossy.

KORDES' PERFECTA, *p. 214*
(Kordes, 1957)

This very fragrant hybrid tea was a Royal National Rose Society Gold Medal winner in 1957 and winner of the Portland Gold Medal in 1958.

FLOWERS   4½–5 in. wide. Cream, with red suffusing from petal edges. Very double; 65–70 petals. Good all-season bloom. Very fragrant. High-centered; rather loosely petaled, considering its high petal count. Blooms singly and in clusters.

FOLIAGE   4–5 ft. tall. Upright, vigorous, well branched. Disease resistant and winter hardy. Canes very thorny. Leaves dark green, leathery, glossy.

LADY X, *p. 220*
(Meilland, 1966)

The very tall and stately Lady X produces blooms that tend toward the pink side of mauve.

FLOWERS   4½–5 in. wide. Mauve. Double; perhaps 30–35 petals. Good all-season bloom. Fragrant. Classic high-centered form. Blooms mostly singly, few clusters.

FOLIAGE   5–7 ft. tall. Upright, well branched, vigorous. Disease resistant and winter hardy. Very thorny canes bear sparse, medium green, leathery, semiglossy leaves.

LA FRANCE, p. 213
(Guillot Fils, 1867)

One of the early hybrid teas, La France is considered by many to be the prototype of the class. A climbing form is available.

FLOWERS   4–4½ in. wide. Silvery pink with bright pink reverse. Very double; 60 petals. Profuse early to midseason bloom; good repeat, particularly in the fall. Very fragrant. High-centered, evenly petaled.

FOLIAGE   4–5 ft. tall. Upright, well branched. Moderately vigorous. Disease resistant and winter hardy. Leaves medium size, medium green, semiglossy.

MARIJKE KOOPMAN, p. 222
(Fryer, 1979)

Winner of a gold medal at The Hague in 1978, Marijke Koopman combines superior bloom production for a hybrid tea with a high degree of resistance to weather-spotting.

FLOWERS   4–5 in. wide. Medium pink. Double; 25 petals. Outstanding all-season bloom. Fragrant. Classic high-centered form. Blooms singly and in clusters of 3–5.

FOLIAGE   4½–5½ ft. tall. Upright, vigorous, bushy. Disease resistant. Winter hardy. Canes have red thorns. Leaves dark green, leathery.

MEDALLION, p. 216
(Warriner, 1973)

An All-America Rose Selection for 1973, Medallion is a variable hybrid tea rose, changing with climatic conditions. It grows best in mild, cool weather. Cut flowers have a long vase life.

FLOWERS   5–5½ in. wide. Light apricot. Double; 25–35 petals. Profuse midseason bloom followed by good repeat bloom. Fruity fragrance. Bloom form loose, tuliplike.

FOLIAGE   4½–5½ ft. tall. Upright, vigorous, well branched. Disease resistant, but not reliably winter hardy without protection. Leaves medium green, large, leathery.

MIKADO, p. 232
(Suzuki, 1988)

An All-America Rose Selection for 1988, this intensely colored rose is called Koh-Sai in its native Japan. Mikado is rarely without bloom.

FLOWERS 4½–5 in. wide. Luminous scarlet, suffused with yellow. Double; 25 petals. Good all-season bloom. Light fragrance; spicy scent. Classic hybrid tea form.

FOLIAGE 4–5 ft. tall. Upright, bushy, vigorous. Disease resistant and winter hardy. Canes well armed with purple-tinged thorns. Leaves medium green, glossy.

MILESTONE, p. 240
(Warriner, 1985)

This colorful hybrid tea received the 5000th plant patent issued by the U.S. Patent Office, thus the name Milestone.

FLOWERS 5–5½ in. wide. Red with silvery red reverse, changing to coral-pink. Double; 40-plus petals. Good all-season bloom. Slight fragrance. High-centered bloom, becoming cup-shaped.

FOLIAGE 4–5 ft. tall. Upright, vigorous. Disease resistant and winter hardy. Leaves medium green, semiglossy.

MIRANDY, p. 230
(Lammerts, 1945)

This classic hybrid tea was an All-America Rose Selection for 1945. Its velvety dark red petals tend to hold their color instead of developing purple tones.

FLOWERS 4½–5 in. wide. Very dark red. Double; 40–50 petals. Good all-season bloom. Very strong true-rose (damask) fragrance. Classic hybrid tea form; high-centered, very full.

FOLIAGE 4–5 ft. tall. Upright, vigorous, well branched. Disease resistant and winter hardy. Canes moderately thorny. Leaves medium green, leathery, semiglossy.

MISS ALL-AMERICAN BEAUTY, p. 235
(Meilland, 1965)

An All-America Rose Selection for 1968, this rose is called Maria Callas in Europe.

FLOWERS   5 in. wide. Deep pink. Very double; 50–60 petals. Abundant midseason bloom with good repeat bloom. Very fragrant. Classic high-centered form. Blooms singly and in clusters.

FOLIAGE   4–5 ft. tall. Upright, vigorous, bushy. Disease resistant. Winter hardy. Canes moderately thorny. Leaves medium green, leathery.

MISTER LINCOLN, p. 231
(Swim & Weeks, 1964)

Perhaps the most popular hybrid tea in its color range. Mister Lincoln was an All-America Rose Selection for 1965.

FLOWERS   5–5½ in. wide. Dark red. Double; 30–40 petals. Good all-season bloom. Very fragrant. Classic high-centered bloom becomes somewhat cupped, well filled with petals.

FOLIAGE   4½–5½ ft. tall. Upright, vigorous, well branched. Disease resistant and winter hardy. Leaves dark green, leathery, semiglossy.

MON CHERI, p. 225
(Christensen, 1982)

An All-America Rose Selection for 1982. A "changing colors" variety, Mon Cheri has bright pink blossoms that slowly deepen to red with exposure to sunlight. Its fragrance may not be detected in the garden, but a vase of cut flowers will perfume a room.

FLOWERS   4½ in. wide. Pink-edged red, becoming red. Double; 30–35 petals. Good all-season bloom. Moderate fragrance. Classic hybrid tea form, but not particularly high-centered.

FOLIAGE   2½–3 ft. tall. Upright, compact. Disease resistant and winter hardy. Canes moderately thorny. Leaves dark green, glossy.

OKLAHOMA, p. 228
(Swim & Weeks, 1964)

This is the deepest hybrid tea in color; it remains a pure, deep maroon-red in most climates, without developing violet or purple shadings. A climbing form is available.

FLOWERS   4–5½ in. wide. Maroon. Double; 40–55 petals. Abundant all-season bloom. Very fragrant. Classic high-centered hybrid tea form.

FOLIAGE   5–6 ft. tall. Upright, vigorous, well branched. Disease resistant and winter hardy. Canes moderately thorny. Leaves dull green, leathery.

OLYMPIAD, p. 233
(McGredy, 1984)

This All-America Rose Selection for 1984 has particularly velvety petals. Olympiad's bright color holds extremely well, and cut flowers have a long vase life.

FLOWERS   4–4½ in. wide. Brilliant medium red. Double; 24–30 petals. Good all-season bloom. Slight fragrance. Classic high-centered hybrid tea form. Blooms mostly singly, few clusters.

FOLIAGE   4–5 ft. tall. Upright, vigorous, compact. Disease resistant and winter hardy. Canes very thorny. Leaves medium green, semiglossy.

PARADISE, p. 226
(Weeks, 1978)

This hybrid tea, with its classically formed, red-edged blooms, was an All-America Rose Selection for 1979. Cut flowers have a long vase life.

FLOWERS   3½–4½ in. wide. Mauve, edged with red. Double; 26–30 petals. Good all-season bloom. Fragrant. Classic high-centered hybrid tea form, with petals unfurling evenly.

FOLIAGE   4–4½ ft. tall. Upright, vigorous, well branched. Disease resistant, but needs protection from mildew in cool, wet climates. Winter hardy. Canes moderately thorny. Leaves dark green, glossy.

PASCALI, *p. 211*
(Lens, 1963)

An All-America Rose Selection for 1969, Pascali won The Hague Gold Medal in 1963 and the Portland Gold Medal in 1967. This medium-size hybrid tea may be the most popular variety in its color class.

FLOWERS   4–4½ in. wide. Creamy white. Double; 30 petals. Very slight fragrance. Excellent all-season bloom. Classic hybrid tea form.

FOLIAGE   3½–4 ft. tall. Upright, vigorous, well branched. Disease resistant. Winter hardy. Canes moderately thorny. Leaves dark green, semiglossy.

PAUL SHIRVILLE, *p. 221*
(Harkness, 1981)

Winner of the Royal National Rose Society's Edland Fragrance Medal in 1982, Paul Shirville displays elegantly formed blooms on a spreading, robust, shrublike bush. It was originally classified as a shrub, and could just as easily be considered a grandiflora.

FLOWERS   4 in. wide. Light salmon pink. Double; 30 petals. Excellent all-season bloom. Very fragrant. Classic hybrid tea form. Blooms singly and in clusters of 3.

FOLIAGE   3–4 ft. tall, and as wide. Vigorous, bushy, spreading. Disease resistant and winter hardy. Large reddish thorns. Leaves large, dark green, semiglossy.

PEACE, *p. 213*
(Meilland, 1945)

Peace is the rose of the century, without doubt the most popular hybrid tea of all: All-America Rose Selection for 1946 and winner of the Portland Gold Medal in 1944, the American Rose Society National Gold Medal Certificate in 1947, the Royal National Rose Society Gold Medal in 1947, and the Golden Rose of The Hague in 1965. The climbing form is one of the finest and most beautiful of hybrid tea climbers, although it requires a few years to become well established and blooms somewhat sparsely until then. The variety is known as Madame Antoine Meilland in France, Gloria Dei in Germany, and Gioia in Italy.

FLOWERS 5½–6 in. wide. Yellow, edged pink. Double; 40–45 petals. Good all-season bloom. Slight fragrance. Classic high-centered hybrid tea blossoms often open to confused or divided centers.

FOLIAGE 5–6 ft. tall. Upright, vigorous, branching. Disease resistant and winter hardy. Canes moderately thorny. Leaves large, dark green, leathery, glossy.

PETER FRANKENFELD, *p. 222*
(Kordes, 1966)

One of the most productive of all hybrid teas, Peter Frankenfeld is offered by more nurseries each year, despite its uncommercial name. There is a climbing version.

FLOWERS 4–5 in. wide. Rose pink. Double; 30 petals. Profuse early-season bloom, with excellent repeat through the season. Slight fragrance. Classic high-centered hybrid tea form.

FOLIAGE 4–5 ft. tall. Upright, vigorous, well branched. Disease resistant and winter hardy. Canes moderately thorny. Leaves medium green, semiglossy.

PINK FAVORITE, *p. 227*
(Van Abrams, 1956)

Winner of the Portland Gold Medal in 1957, Pink Favorite has bright, glossy leaves.

FLOWERS 3½–4 in. wide. Medium pink. Double; 21–28 petals. Profuse midseason bloom and good repeat. Slight fragrance. Loose, cupped form, singly and in clusters.

FOLIAGE 4–4½ ft. tall. Upright, bushy, vigorous. Disease resistant; hardy. Canes moderately thorny. Leaves green, very glossy.

PINK PEACE, *p. 223*
(Meilland, 1959)

Pink Peace claimed the Geneva Gold Medal and the Rome Gold Medal in 1959.

FLOWERS 4½–6 in. wide. Medium to deep pink. Very double; 50–65 petals. Good all-season bloom. Very fragrant. Classic form, very full, very evenly petaled.

FOLIAGE   4½–5½ ft. tall. Upright, vigorous, bushy. Disease resistant and winter hardy. Canes moderately thorny. Leaves medium green, leathery, glossy.

POLARSTERN, p. 236
(Tantau, 1982)

Winner of Britain's Rose of the Year Award in 1985, this is a variety that excels in all but the warmest climates. The name is sometimes anglicized to Polar Star.

FLOWERS   4–5½ in. wide; smaller in heat. Palest yellow opening to white. Double; 35 petals. Profuse midseason bloom with excellent repeat. Very slight fragrance. Classic high-centered hybrid tea form.

FOLIAGE   4½–5½ ft. tall. Upright, vigorous, bushy. Disease resistant and winter hardy. Canes moderately thorny. Leaves medium green, matte.

PRECIOUS PLATINUM, p. 230
(Dickson, 1974)

Precious Platinum is an extremely prolific bloomer. Its cut flowers have a long vase life.

FLOWERS   3½ in. wide. Medium red. Double; 35–40 petals. Abundant all-season bloom. Slight fragrance. Typical hybrid tea form, but not very high-centered. Blooms singly and in clusters.

FOLIAGE   4 ft. tall. Upright, vigorous, well branched. Disease resistant and winter hardy. Canes moderately thorny. Leaves dark green, leathery, glossy.

PRISTINE, p. 212
(Warriner, 1978)

In a fully expanded bloom, one or more of Pristine's outer petals drop down below the others.

FLOWERS   4½–6 in. wide. White with pink edge. Double; 30–35 petals. Good all-season bloom. Slight fragrance. Classic hybrid tea form. Blooms mostly singly.

FOLIAGE   4–4½ ft. tall. Upright, moderately vigorous, slender habit. Disease resistant. Winter hardy. Canes smooth with few thorns. Leaves very large, dark green, glossy.

ROYAL HIGHNESS, p. 218
(Swim & Weeks, 1962)

This All-America Rose Selection for 1963 won the Portland Gold Medal in 1960, the Madrid Gold Medal in 1962, and the American Rose Society David Fuerstenberg Prize in 1964.

FLOWERS   5–5½ in. wide. Light pink. Double; 40–45 petals. Good all-season bloom. Very fragrant. Classic high-centered hybrid tea form.

FOLIAGE   4½–5 ft. tall. Upright, vigorous, bushy. Disease resistant. Not winter hardy. Canes moderately thorny. Leaves light green, leathery, glossy.

SEASHELL, p. 227
(Kordes, 1976)

An All-America Rose Selection for 1976. Seashell's color is much deeper than its name might suggest.

FLOWERS   4–5 in. wide. Coral to apricot blend. Double; 35–40 petals. Fair all-season bloom. Fragrant. Classic hybrid tea form. Blooms singly and in clusters.

FOLIAGE   3½–4 ft. tall. Upright, moderately vigorous, well branched. Disease resistant and winter hardy. Canes moderately thorny. Leaves dark green, glossy.

SHEER ELEGANCE, p. 240
(Twomey, 1991)

This All-America Rose Selection for 1991 offers excellent health and long-lasting cut flowers.

FLOWERS   4½–6 in. wide. Coral pink blended with cream; edges are darker pink. Double; 35 petals. Good all-season bloom. Light fragrance; musk scent. Classic hybrid tea form. Blooms singly, but may cluster in the fall.

FOLIAGE   4–5 ft. tall. Upright, vigorous, well branched. Disease resistant. Winter hardy. Canes moderately thorny. Foliage very large, dark green, glossy.

STERLING SILVER, p. 220
(Fisher, 1957)

The first of the lavender or mauve hybrid teas, this is still one of the best for bloom form and color. There is a climbing form.

FLOWERS   3½ in. wide. Mauve. Double; 30 petals. Fair all-season bloom. Very fragrant; lemon scent. Classic hybrid tea form. Blooms mostly singly, some clusters.

FOLIAGE   2½–3 ft. tall. Upright, well branched. Very little vigor. Disease resistant, but needs protection from black spot and mildew. Winter hardy. Canes quite smooth. Leaves medium green, leathery, semiglossy.

SUMMER DREAM, p. 217
(Warriner, 1986)

In addition to being one of the healthiest and hardiest hybrid teas in the apricot color range, Summer Dream produces outstanding repeat bloom.

FLOWERS   4–5 in. wide. Apricot-pink. Double; 30 petals. Excellent midseason bloom with outstanding repeat bloom. Slight fragrance; fruity scent. Classic hybrid tea form.

FOLIAGE   4–5 ft. tall. Upright, vigorous, well branched. Disease resistant and winter hardy. Canes moderately thorny. Leaves dull, medium green.

SUTTER'S GOLD, p. 236
(Swim, 1950)

An All-America Rose Selection for 1950, Sutter's Gold claimed the Portland Gold Medal in 1946, the Bagatelle Gold Medal in 1948, the Geneva Gold Medal in 1949, and the James Alexander Gamble Rose Fragrance Medal in 1966. It is the most strongly fragrant of the fruit-scented hybrid teas.

FLOWERS   4–5 in. wide. Yellow, overlaid and veined with orange-gold and tipped red. Double; 30–35 petals. Good all-season bloom. Very fragrant; fruity scent. Classic hybrid tea form.

FOLIAGE   4–4½ ft. tall. Upright, vigorous, well branched. Disease resistant. Fairly winter hardy. Canes moderately thorny. Leaves dark green, leathery, semiglossy.

SWARTHMORE, p. 241
(Meilland, 1963)

Introduced to mark the centenary of Swarthmore College, this classic hybrid tea requires full sun to develop its optimum coloration. There is a climbing form.

FLOWERS   4–5 in. wide. Rich rose pink with charcoal edges. Double; 50 petals. Good all-season bloom. Slight fragrance; spicy scent. Classic high-centered hybrid tea form.

FOLIAGE   4–5 ft. tall. Vigorous, upright, bushy. Generally disease resistant, but may require protection from mildew. Winter hardy. Leaves dark green, leathery.

SWEET SURRENDER, p. 223
(Weeks, 1983)

This fragrant pink hybrid tea was an All-America Rose Selection for 1983.

FLOWERS   3½–4½ in. wide. Medium pink. Double; 40–44 petals. Fair all-season bloom. Very fragrant. Very evenly petaled form opens rather flat.

FOLIAGE   3½–5 ft. tall. Upright, compact. Not reliably winter hardy. Leaves large, dull, medium green.

THE TEMPTATIONS, p. 241
(Winchel, 1993)

Winner in 1989 of the second-ever gold certificate from the American Rose Center trial grounds in Shreveport, Louisiana, this "changing colors" variety is usually at its best in hot weather.

FLOWERS   4–5 in. wide. Shades of pink, coral, and cream. Double; 35 petals. Good midseason bloom, with good repeat bloom. Light fragrance. Classic high-centered hybrid tea form.

FOLIAGE   3½–4½ ft. tall. Upright, bushy, vigorous. Disease resistant. May need winter protection in severe climates. Canes moderately thorny. Leaves dark green, semiglossy.

TIFFANY, *p. 218*
(Lindquist, 1954)

One of the most popular hybrid teas, Tiffany was an All-America Rose Selection for 1955. It also captured the David Fuerstenberg Prize in 1957 and the James Alexander Gamble Rose Fragrance Medal in 1962. There is a climbing form.

FLOWERS 4–5 in. wide. Medium pink to deep pink blend. Double; 25–30 petals. Good all-season bloom. Very fragrant. Classic high-centered form. Blooms singly and in clusters.

FOLIAGE 4–4½ ft. tall. Upright, very vigorous, bushy. Disease resistant and winter hardy. Canes moderately thorny. Leaves dark green, glossy.

TOUCH OF CLASS, *p. 215*
(Kriloff, 1984)

An All-America Rose Selection for 1986 and winner of the Portland Gold Medal in 1988, Touch of Class is a top exhibition hybrid tea that is also a very dependable garden performer.

FLOWERS 5–5½ in. wide. Medium pink, shaded coral-orange and cream. Double; 33 petals. Excellent all-season bloom. Slight fragrance; tea scent. High-centered form has set a new standard for hybrid tea perfection.

FOLIAGE 4–5 ft. tall. Upright, vigorous, bushy. Disease resistant. Winter hardy. Canes moderately thorny. Leaves dark green, semiglossy.

TROPICANA, *p. 235*
(Tantau, 1960)

Called Super Star in Europe, Tropicana was an All-America Rose Selection for 1963. It was the first pure fluorescent orange rose and is still the best in its color range, as evidenced by the 7 gold medals it has captured. Tropicana is the third-biggest-selling rose in this century. A climbing form is available.

FLOWERS 5 in. wide. Orange. Double; 30–35 petals. Excellent all-season bloom. Very fragrant; fruity scent. High-centered form, becoming cup-shaped.

FOLIAGE 4–5 ft. tall. Upright, vigorous, well branched. Disease resistant and winter hardy. Canes moderately thorny. Leaves dark green, leathery, glossy.

WHITE MASTERPIECE, *p. 211*
(Boerner, 1969)

This exhibition hybrid tea has large white blossoms that are unfortunately rather sparse.

FLOWERS 5–5½ in. wide. White. Very double; 50–60 petals. Sparse all-season bloom. Slight fragrance. Classic high-centered form.

FOLIAGE 3 ft. tall. Upright, moderate vigor, compact. Disease resistant. Needs winter protection. Leaves medium green, semiglossy.

Miniatures

Present-day rose growers display a tremendous amount of enthusiasm for miniature roses. These little plants are at the forefront of interest, and new varieties are constantly being created. This was not always the case, however. In times past, rose growers were apt to discard weak varieties; thus many true miniatures have probably turned up, only to be roughly excluded from the nursery bed. Miniatures were considered a curiosity until recent times, when rose breeders began to find an eager market for them.

In the second quarter of this century, there were only a handful of well-known miniature varieties. However, the promise of these little plants was apparent, and some breeders — among them, Jan de Vink and Ralph Moore — set about creating new cultivars. There are now many more rose breeders who are busy creating all manner of miniature varieties.

Miniatures have been crossed with nearly every other class of roses, yielding still more miniature varieties. Drawing on the traits of many of the larger roses in cultivation, breeders have developed compact little bushes and sprawling miniatures that make excellent ground covers — all in a rainbow of colors. There are even climbing miniatures, a few of which may grow as high as five feet, although they retain other class characteristics.

What Makes a Mini?

Miniature roses range in height from about 3 inches to 18 inches, with the average being about a foot. Their stature alone does not entirely justify their classification, as they have other determining characteristics: the well-formed buds and closely spaced foliage are extremely small, the canes are thin, and the plants are very free-flowering and comparatively hardy.

Miniature roses are extremely adaptable. They can be grown in rock gardens, in containers, and along borders; they also hold their own when grown indoors in pots during the winter. Miniatures are a big favorite of city dwellers, who brighten their window ledges with these colorful little plants. These roses are also perfect for small yards; the small size and compact habit of many varieties enable the ambitious rose grower who has limited space to fill the garden with a wonderful bounty of blossoms.

Uncertain Origins

The miniature rose class is probably derived from *Rosa roulettii* (which is generally believed to be identical to *Rosa chinensis minima,* an ancient Chinese dwarf rose). Cultivated perhaps as far back as 1815, *Rosa roulettii* was first brought to public attention by a Colonel Roulet, who discovered the plant in a Swiss village at about the turn of the century and was quick to recognize its potential. Pompon de Paris, another ancient miniature rose, has been cultivated since about 1839; it was sold in the markets of 19th-century Paris as a pot plant. Some authorities hold that these varieties are identical, but the descriptions that exist from the early 19th century do not support this view. (Such uncertainty illustrates one problem common to all very old varieties, namely, knowing whether a plant has always been properly labeled. Some varieties have been known by different names at different times in history, contributing to the confusion.)

Culture

You should be sure to plant your miniatures where they will receive plenty of sunlight — although small, they need as much sunshine as their larger relatives.

Considering their size, these plants are surprisingly hardy — a little more so than the hybrid teas. In areas with very mild winters, they will survive with little or no protection; in colder regions, mulching should provide the shelter they require.

Miniature roses are very easy to hybridize and work with. They root readily from cuttings, and this is the accepted method of propagation, since these roses lose their miniature status when budded onto a vigorous understock.

Pruning

Like the larger roses, miniatures will lose the energy they need to produce flowers if they are not pruned carefully. Be sure to clear away deadwood and any canes that are weak and spindly. Pruning will help to keep pests and diseases at bay and allow the plant to concentrate on producing vibrant blooms.

Growing Miniatures Indoors

Although miniature roses will grow indoors, they nonetheless need plenty of sunlight — a commodity that is in short supply in most houses or apartments. A southern exposure, unobscured by buildings or trees, will be your best bet.

You can also make use of supplemental artificial light, in the form of fluorescent bulbs, to help your minis grow indoors. In recent years, growing miniatures indoors under lights has become very popular.

ANGEL DARLING, *p. 254*
(Moore, 1976)

Excellent for bedding and borders, this mauve miniature is good for container planting. It is important when planting miniature roses in containers always to keep them well watered.

FLOWERS   1½ in. wide. Mauve. Nearly single; 10 petals. Midseason bloom with good repeat bloom. Slight fragrance. Bloom form open, cup-shaped, with bright yellow stamens.

FOLIAGE   12–18 in. tall. Vigorous, upright, well branched. Disease resistant, but may need protection from black spot and mildew. Winter hardy. Leaves dark green, glossy, leathery.

BEAUTY SECRET, *p. 257*
(Moore, 1965)

Winner of the American Rose Society Award of Excellence in 1975, this fragrant miniature is good for garden beds and borders, edgings, and containers. It also grows well in pots indoors over the winter.

FLOWERS   1½ in. wide. Medium red. Double; 24–30 petals. Excellent midseason bloom with excellent repeat bloom. Very fragrant. Bloom form classic hybrid tea type in miniature.

FOLIAGE   10–18 in. tall. Upright, vigorous, well branched. Disease resistant and winter hardy. Leaves medium green, semiglossy.

BLACK JADE, *p. 247*
(Benardella, 1985)

This deep red miniature comes nearest to being black of any modern rose. It received the American Rose Society's Award of Excellence in 1985.

FLOWERS ¾ in. wide. Deepest red. Double; 35 petals. Midseason bloom with good repeat bloom. No fragrance. Classic hybrid tea bloom form.

FOLIAGE 14–18 in. tall. Upright, bushy. Disease resistant and winter hardy. Leaves dark green, semiglossy.

CINDERELLA, *p. 250*
(de Vink, 1953)

This classic miniature rose is one of the most popular varieties of all time. One of the very petite "micro-minis," Cinderella is especially good for growing in miniature rose beds and rock gardens and indoors over winter. Its creator, Jan de Vink, was the first breeder of modern miniatures.

FLOWERS ¾ in. wide. Light pink, fading to white. Very double; 45 petals. Excellent midseason bloom and excellent repeat bloom. Very spicy fragrance. Bloom cupped, tightly filled with even rows of petals.

FOLIAGE 8–10 in. tall. Upright, vigorous, compact. Disease resistant and winter hardy. Leaves medium green, semiglossy.

DREAMGLO, *p. 256*
(E. D. Williams, 1978)

Excellent for bedding and borders, Dreamglo is a popular exhibition miniature as well.

FLOWERS 1 in. wide. Red, blended with white at base. Very double; 50 petals. Excellent midseason bloom with good repeat bloom. Slight fragrance. Very full, classic hybrid tea type, with petals unfurling evenly from a high center.

FOLIAGE 18–24 in. tall. Vigorous, upright, well branched. Disease resistant and winter hardy. Leaves medium to dark green, semiglossy.

GIGGLES/KINgig, *p. 215*
(King, 1987)

An excellent garden performer with perfectly formed hybrid-tea-shaped blooms that make this variety popular for exhibition as well. The code name KINgig is necessary to distinguish this variety from another pink miniature rose called Giggles, introduced in 1982.

FLOWERS   1½ in. wide. Medium pink, reverse creamy pink. Double; 22 petals. Profuse midseason bloom with excellent repeat bloom. Little or no fragrance. Classic hybrid-tea-type form, with petals unfurling evenly from a high center.

FOLIAGE   15–18 in. tall. Vigorous, upright, bushy. Disease resistant and winter hardy. Canes have white thorns. Foliage light to medium green, matte.

GREEN ICE, *p. 246*
(Moore, 1971)

A miniature rose with extra-long, lax canes, Green Ice can be trained as a climber but is just perfect for a hanging basket. The pink buds open to whitish pink blooms, becoming light green as they age, with a very pleasing effect.

FLOWERS   1¼ in. wide. White changing to green. Double; 30 petals. Midseason bloom with good repeat bloom. Slight fragrance. Bloom form classic hybrid tea type, with petals unfurling evenly from a high center.

FOLIAGE   8 in. tall and 16 in. wide. Vigorous, dwarf, bushy, spreading. Disease resistant and winter hardy. Leaves medium green, leathery, glossy.

JEAN KENNEALLY, *p. 247*
(Bennett, 1984)

This apricot-colored rose is excellent for garden display in beds, borders, edgings, and container plantings. A popular exhibition variety, it is good for growing in pots indoors over the winter.

FLOWERS   1½ in. wide. Apricot blend. Double; 24–30 petals. Midseason bloom with excellent repeat bloom. Slight fragrance. Classic hybrid-tea-type form.

FOLIAGE   10–14 in. tall. Upright, well branched, bushy. Disease resistant and winter hardy. Leaves medium green, semi-glossy.

JEANNE LAJOIE, *p. 253*
(Sima, 1975)

One of the few climbing miniatures that has resulted from hybridization rather than mutation, Jeanne Lajoie received the American Rose Society's Award of Excellence in 1977. For sheer production of miniature blooms, it has not yet been matched.

FLOWERS 1 in. wide. Medium pink, reverse darker. Double; 40 petals. Profuse midseason bloom with excellent repeat bloom. Slight fragrance. Bloom form high-centered; blooms singly and in clusters.

FOLIAGE 4–8 ft. tall. Vigorous, bushy, upright. Disease resistant and winter hardy. Leaves small, dark green, glossy.

LITTLE JACKIE, *p. 253*
(Saville, 1982)

Winner of the American Rose Society Award of Excellence in 1984, this fragrant miniature rose is suitable for bedding and borders. It is a popular show variety.

FLOWERS 1½ in. wide. Orange blended with pink and yellow. Double; 24–30 petals. Very fragrant. Classic hybrid tea-type form.

FOLIAGE 14–18 in. tall. Upright, vigorous, bushy, well branched. Disease resistant and winter hardy. Leaves medium green, semiglossy.

MAGIC CARROUSEL, *p. 255*
(Moore, 1972)

Winner of the American Rose Society Award of Excellence in 1975. Suitable for bedding and borders, it is an eye-catcher in the garden, and a popular show variety.

FLOWERS 1¾–2 in. wide. White with red edges. Semidouble; 12–20 petals. Midseason bloom with good repeat bloom. Little or no fragrance. Open blossoms, cup-shaped to flat.

FOLIAGE 15–18 in. tall; sometimes reported up to 30 in. tall. Very vigorous, spreading. Disease resistant and winter hardy. Leaves medium green, semiglossy.

MARY MARSHALL, *p. 254*
(Moore, 1970)

Mary Marshall received the American Rose Society Award of Excellence in 1975. It is excellent for garden display and popular in exhibitions. A climbing form is available.

FLOWERS   1½ in. wide. Deep coral; yellow-orange tones quite pronounced at certain seasons. Double; 24–30 petals. Midseason bloom followed by good repeat bloom. Slight fragrance. Classic hybrid-tea-type bloom form.

FOLIAGE   10–14 in. tall; climbing form reported to reach 5 ft. Upright, bushy, well branched. Disease resistant and winter hardy. Leaves medium green, semiglossy.

MINNIE PEARL, *p. 251*
(Saville, 1982)

Minnie Pearl is deservedly popular for its perfect hybrid-tea-type form and delicate pink coloration. Unfortunately, its blooms are easily spoiled by rain.

FLOWERS   1½ in. wide. Porcelain pink, reverse slightly darker. Double; 35 petals. Midseason bloom with good repeat bloom. Slight fragrance. Classic hybrid-tea-type bloom, with petals unfurling evenly from a high center.

FOLIAGE   10–14 in. tall. Upright, vigorous, bushy. Disease resistant and winter hardy. Leaves small, medium green, semiglossy.

OLYMPIC GOLD, *p. 245*
(Jolly, 1983)

This maxi-miniature is an argument for a new class of roses to accommodate varieties much larger than traditional miniatures but too small to be floribundas or hybrid teas.

FLOWERS   2–2½ in. wide. Butter yellow, sometimes tinged pink in cool weather. Double; 31 petals. Midseason bloom with steady repeat bloom. Slight fragrance. Classic hybrid-tea-type bloom form.

FOLIAGE   18–24 in. tall. Vigorous, upright, bushy. Disease resistant and winter hardy. Leaves large, medium green, semiglossy, widely spaced.

PARTY GIRL, *p. 248*
(Saville, 1979)

Winner of the American Rose Society Award of Excellence in 1981, Party Girl is suitable for beds, borders, edgings, and rock gardens as well as containers and indoor pots in winter. It is a popular exhibition variety.

FLOWERS   1¼ in. wide. Apricot-yellow blended with salmon-pink. Double; 25 petals. Midseason bloom with good repeat bloom. Sweet, spicy fragrance. Classic hybrid-tea-type bloom form.

FOLIAGE   12–14 in. tall. Bushy, compact. Disease resistant and winter hardy. Leaves medium to dark green, semiglossy.

PIERRINE, *p. 250*
(M. C. Williams, 1988)

One of an increasing number of miniatures bred from Party Girl, the salmon-pink Pierrine performs dependably in all climates.

FLOWERS   1½ in. wide. Salmon-pink, reverse slightly lighter. Double; 40 petals. Good midseason bloom with good repeat bloom. Slight fragrance; damask scent. Classic hybrid-tea-type blooms.

FOLIAGE   12–16 in. tall. Upright, vigorous, dense, bushy. Disease resistant and winter hardy. Leaves medium green, semiglossy.

POMPON DE PARIS, *p. 252*
(1839)

Some authorities believe this is the same as *Rosa roulettii,* although the descriptions do vary slightly. The problem is compounded when plants are sent out under the wrong name, as can happen with any variety.

FLOWERS   ¾ in. wide. Deep pink. Double; 65 petals. Midseason bloom with good repeat. Little or no fragrance. Bloom full, cupped.

FOLIAGE   8–10 in. tall. Very bushy. Disease resistant and winter hardy. Leaves medium green, glossy.

POPCORN, *p. 245*
(Morey, 1973)

Excellent for beds, borders, edgings, rock gardens, and container plantings, this honey-scented variety is one of the most popular in its color class. The clusters of little white flowers look like popcorn; hence the name.

FLOWERS   ¾ in. wide. White. Single; 5 petals, with yellow stamens showing. Midseason bloom with excellent repeat bloom. Honey fragrance. Blossom cupped; blooms in clusters.

FOLIAGE   12–14 in. tall. Vigorous, compact. Disease resistant and winter hardy. Leaves medium green, glossy.

RAINBOW'S END, *p. 249*
(Saville, 1984)

Excellent in beds, borders, and edgings and suitable for container plantings, this yellow-blend miniature rose is good for growing in pots indoors over winter.

FLOWERS   1½ in. wide. Yellow blend. Double; 24–30 petals. Midseason bloom with good repeat bloom. Little or no fragrance. Classic hybrid-tea-type bloom form.

FOLIAGE   10–14 in. tall. Upright, bushy, well branched. Disease resistant and winter hardy. Leaves dark green, glossy.

RED BEAUTY, *p. 257*
(E. D. Williams, 1981)

Red Beauty adds color to beds, borders, edgings, rock gardens, and container plantings; this dark red rose is also suited to indoor pots in winter. It is a popular exhibition variety.

FLOWERS   1½ in. wide. Dark red. Double; 35 petals. Midseason bloom with good repeat bloom. Slight fragrance. Classic hybrid tea form, with petals unfurling evenly from a high center.

FOLIAGE   10–12 in. tall. Bushy, compact. Disease resistant and winter hardy. Leaves dark green, glossy.

RISE 'N' SHINE, *p. 249*
(Moore, 1977)

Winner of the American Rose Society Award of Excellence in 1978, this yellow miniature is outstanding in its color class. It is well suited to beds, borders, edgings, and container plantings, and it is a popular show variety.

FLOWERS   1½–1¾ in. wide. Medium yellow. Double; 35 petals. Midseason bloom with good repeat bloom. Slight fragrance. Classic hybrid tea bloom form.

FOLIAGE   10–14 in. tall. Upright, bushy, rounded. Disease resistant and winter hardy. Leaves dull, medium green.

ROSA ROULETTII, *p. 252*
(1815)

Also known as *Rosa chinensis minima,* this pink miniature is thought by some authorities to be the same as Pompon de Paris, which is reported to be a more double rose. Some experts favor classifying this rose with the Chinas rather than with the miniatures.

FLOWERS   ¾–1 in. wide. Deep pink. Double; 20–30 petals. Midseason bloom with good repeat bloom. Little or no fragrance. Bloom form cupped.

FOLIAGE   15–18 in. tall. Upright, bushy, well branched. Disease resistant and winter hardy. Leaves medium green, glossy.

SCARLET MOSS, *p. 248*
(Moore, 1988)

The brightest red of any moss rose, this miniature also displays especially attractive yellow stamens when open. Young plants may require winter protection in colder climates.

FLOWERS   1 in. wide. Intense scarlet. Semidouble; 10–12 petals. Midseason bloom with good repeat bloom. No fragrance. Blooms are cupped to open, in clusters of 3–10.

FOLIAGE   10–14 in. tall. Upright, bushy. Disease resistant. Winter hardiness improves as plant matures. Leaves medium green, glossy.

SIMPLEX, *p. 244*
(Moore, 1961)

Perhaps the most popular of the single rose varieties, Simplex is good for beds and borders. Under glass and in cool, cloudy weather, this white rose produces pink blossoms.

FLOWERS   1¼ in. wide. White; occasionally pink. Single; 5 petals. Bloom opens flat with showy yellow stamens.

FOLIAGE   15–18 in. tall. Very vigorous, upright, well branched. Disease resistant and winter hardy. Leaves light to medium green, semiglossy.

SNOW BRIDE, *p. 244*
(Jolly, 1982)

Acclaimed as the best white miniature with hybrid tea form, Snow Bride is usually a good performer but can sulk if neglected. Winner of the American Rose Society's Award of Excellence in 1983.

FLOWERS   1½ in. wide. White. Double; 20–22 petals. Midseason bloom with good repeat bloom. Slight fragrance. Blooms display classic high-centered hybrid tea form.

FOLIAGE   10–14 in. wide. Bushy. Disease resistant and winter hardy. Leaves medium green, semiglossy.

STARINA, *p. 256*
(Meilland, 1965)

Once the most popular exhibition miniature, Starina remains the most widely sold of any variety. It is the standard against which other miniature rose varieties in its color class are judged in the public mind.

FLOWERS   1½ in. wide. Orange-red. Double; 35 petals. Midseason bloom with excellent repeat bloom. Little or no fragrance. Classic hybrid-tea-type bloom form.

FOLIAGE   12–16 in. tall. Upright, bushy, dense, compact. Disease resistant and winter hardy. Leaves dark green, semiglossy.

STARS 'N' STRIPES, *p. 255*
(Moore, 1975)

One of the first of the Ralph Moore striped miniatures, and still perhaps the most popular, Stars 'n' Stripes performs well in the garden, in a hanging basket, and in shows.

FLOWERS   1¾ in. wide. Red and white stripes. Semidouble; 14 petals. Midseason bloom with good repeat bloom. Little or no fragrance. Bloom form cupped, open.

FOLIAGE   10–14 in. tall. Upright, spreading; canes can attain 36 in. in length. Disease resistant and winter hardy. Leaves medium to dark green, semiglossy.

SWEET CHARIOT, *p. 246*
(Moore, 1984)

Although officially a miniature, the result of a cross between a miniature and a rambler, Sweet Chariot exhibits many of the characteristics of a polyantha. No matter how it is classified, this rose is notable for its exceptional winter hardiness and extraordinarily rich fragrance.

FLOWERS   1½ in. wide. Lavender to purple blend. Very double; 40-plus petals. Heavy midseason and autumn bloom. Very fragrant. Blossoms cup-shaped, in large clusters.

FOLIAGE   18 in. tall, and as wide. Vigorous, bushy, well branched. Disease resistant. Very winter hardy. Leaves medium green, matte.

Appendices

Pests & Diseases

Plant diseases and insects and other pests are a fact of life for a gardener. No matter what you grow or how large your garden, it is helpful to become familiar with the common problems in your area and to learn how to control them. Since the general symptoms of plant problems — yellowing of leaves, death or disappearance of plant parts, stunting, poor growth, and wilting — can be caused by a multitude of diseases or pests, some experience is needed to determine which culprit is attacking your roses.

Diseases

Fungi and bacteria cause a variety of diseases, ranging from leaf spots and wilts to root rot, but bacterial diseases usually make the affected plant tissues appear wetter than fungi do. Viruses and mycoplasma are microorganisms too small to be seen with an ordinary microscope. They are usually transmitted in the propagation process, through the use of infected budding eyes or understocks, and cause mottled yellow leaves and stunted growth. Nematodes are microscopic roundworms that usually live in association with plant roots; they cause stunting and poor growth, and sometimes produce galls on leaves. The way a particular disease organism has spread to your roses influences the control measures you may need to take.

Insects and Other Pests

Roses attract many different kinds of insects. Sap-sucking insects — including aphids, leafhoppers, and scale insects — suck plant juices, leaving the victim yellow, stunted, and misshapen. They also produce honeydew, a sticky substance that attracts ants and sooty mold fungus. Thrips and spider mites scrape plant tissue and suck the juices that well up in the injured areas. Beetles and caterpillars consume leaves, whole or in part. Borers tunnel into shoots and stems, where they deposit their eggs; the larvae that hatch feed on plant tissue. Some insects, such as grubs and maggots, are rarely seen above ground. They are destructive nonetheless, because they feed on roots, weakening or killing the plant.

Environmental Stresses

Some plant injuries are caused by severe weather conditions, salt toxicity, rodents, nutritional deficiencies or excesses, pesticides, or damage from lawnmowers. You can avoid many of these injuries by being aware of potential dangers and taking proper precautions.

Methods of Control

Controlling plant pests and diseases is not as overwhelming a task as it may seem. Many of the measures, performed on a day-to-day basis, are preventive, so that you don't have to rely on pesticides, which may not be very effective once a culprit has attacked your roses. Observe plants each week for signs of trouble. That way you can prevent or limit a disease or infestation in the early stages.

Your normal gardening routine should include preventive measures. By cultivating the soil regularly, you expose insect and disease-causing organisms to the sun and thus lessen their chances of survival. In the fall, destroy infested and diseased canes, remove dead leaves and flowers, and clean up plant debris. Do not add diseased or infested material to the compost pile. Spray plants with water to dislodge insects and remove suffocating dust. Pick off larger insects by hand. To discourage fungal leaf spots and blights, water plants in the morning and allow leaves to dry off before nightfall. For the same reason, provide adequate air circulation around leaves and stems by giving plants sufficient space. Weeds provide a home for insects and diseases, so pull them up.

Always buy healthy, certified, virus-free plants. Check leaves and canes for dead areas and for off-color and stunted tissue. Make sure that your roses are properly cared for.

To protect plant tissue from damage done by insects and diseases, you may choose among many available insecticides and fungicides. While diseases that result from bacteria, viruses, and mycoplasma can often be controlled under laboratory conditions, there is usually no practical remedy for the home garden.

Organic-based pesticides are "protectorant" in nature. Protectorants ward off insects or disease organisms from uninfected foliage. Botanical insecticides such as pyrethrum and rotenone have a shorter residual effect on pests than many chemical-based products but are considered generally safer for the user and the environment than inorganic chemical insecticides. The multipurpose pesticides based on neem extract provide great promise to the rosarian seeking to avoid the use of chemical sprays.

Biological control through the use of organisms such as *Bacillus thuringiensis* (a bacterium toxic to moth and butterfly larvae) is effective and safe. Even when using a nonsynthetic pesticide, it is important to read the product label thoroughly and follow recommendations regarding safety precautions, dosage, and frequency of application. Learn about the life cycle of the pest so you know when to begin — and stop — spraying.

Learning to recognize the most common insects and diseases that can plague roses is a first step toward controlling them. The following chart describes the most common pests and diseases that attack roses, the damage they cause, and measures you can take to control them.

Pest or Disease

Aphids

Black Spot

Borers

Bristly Roseslugs

Cankers

Description	Damage	Controls
Tiny green, brown, or reddish, pear-shaped, soft-bodied insects in clusters on buds, shoots, and undersides of leaves.	Suck plant juices, causing stunted or deformed blooms and leaves. Some transmit plant viruses. Secretions attract ants.	Spray with strong stream of water, insecticidal soap, sabadilla, neem extract, or rotenone/pyrethrin. Encourage beneficial insects, such as lacewings and parasitic wasps.
Round, fringed, black spots on leaves. Usually detected during humid or wet weather.	Leaves may turn yellow near spots and drop off prematurely.	Increase air circulation. Water at soil-line or early in day. Remove and destroy infected canes and leaves. Discard fallen debris. Spray sulfur or copper.
Several kinds of wormlike, legless, cream-colored larvae tunneling in canes.	Swollen bands on canes indicate presence within. Girdling causes dieback of canes and shoots.	Remove and destroy infested branches, pruning several inches below swelling. Fertilize and water deeply to increase vigor. Inject with beneficial nematodes.
Hairy, greenish-white, ½-inch-long sawfly larvae; present on undersides of leaves.	Make holes in leaves by feeding from underside.	Handpick — wear gloves to avoid getting bristles in fingers. Rid garden debris of cocoons in fall.
Fungal disease causing spots and dead areas on canes. Black dots of fungal spores in dead areas.	Red to purple spots on canes. Spots enlarge, becoming light or dark and dry. Shoots wilt and canes die back.	Prune and destroy infected canes. Avoid wounding healthy canes in wet weather.

Pest or Disease

Crown Gall

Leaf-feeding Beetles

Leaf-feeding Caterpillars

Nematodes

Powdery Mildew

Description	Damage	Controls
Soil-borne bacterial disease, forming cancerlike growths on plant stems and roots.	Rounded growths on stem near soil-line. May also be present on roots and occasionally on canes.	Remove and destroy infected plants. Buy only healthy, certified disease-free bushes. Plant in uninfested soil.
Hard-shelled, oval to oblong insects on leaves, stems, and flowers. Common species including Japanese, Fuller, rose chafer, and curculio.	Chew plant parts, leaving holes. Larvae of some species feed on roots.	Handpick and destroy. Spray with sabadilla, rotenone, or rotenone/ pyrethrin mix.
Soft-bodied, wormlike crawling insects with several pairs of legs. May be smooth, hairy, or spiny. Adults are moths or butterflies.	Consume part or all of leaves. Flowers and shoots may also be eaten.	Handpick and destroy. Spray with *Bacillus thuringiensis,* neem extract or rotenone/ pyrethrin.
Microscopic roundworms, usually associated with roots that cause various diseases.	Stunted, off-color plants that do not respond to water or fertilizer. Minute galls may be present on roots.	Remove and destroy badly infested plants. Plant nematode-resistant stock. Treat soil with plenty of organic matter, CLANDOSAN, beneficial nematodes, or neem extract.
Powdery, white fungal disease on aerial plant parts.	Powdery fungal growth. Leaves may become distorted and drop off. Stems, buds, and flowers also affected.	Discard fallen debris. Remove and destroy infected canes and leaves. Wash weekly with heavy stream of water. Spray with sulfur or Bordeaux mixture.

Pests & Diseases

Rust

Scale

Spider Mites

Thrips

Viruses

Description	Damage	Controls
Fungus causing powdery orange spots on lower sides of leaves.	Leaves, stems, and sepals may be attacked. Infected leaves may drop.	Increase air circulation. Water at soil-line or early in day. Discard fallen debris. Remove and destroy infected canes and leaves. Spray with sulfur.
Small, waxy, soft or hard-bodied stationary insects on shoots and leaves. May be red, white, brown, black, or gray.	Suck plant juices, causing stunted, off-color plants. May cover large portion of cane.	Prune off badly infested plant parts. Spray with insecticidal soap, horticultural oil, or lime-sulfur. Release lacewings.
Tiny golden, red, or brown arachnids on undersides of leaves. Profuse, fine webs seen, with heavy infestations.	Scrape leaves and suck plant juices. Leaves become pale and dry. Plant may be stunted.	Spray with strong jet of water, insecticidal soap, horticultural oil, or sulfur. Release predatory mites.
Small, brown, elongated insects with feathery wings. Black frass or droppings on affected plant tissue.	Scrape plant tissue and suck juices. Leaves and blossoms are tannish and dry.	Remove infested flowers and buds. Spray with insecticidal soap, horticultural oil, neem, or rote-none/pyrethrin.
Various diseases, including mosaics, that cause off-color, stunted plants. May be transmitted by aphids or by using infected grafting tools.	Crinkled, mottled, deformed leaves, stunted plants, and poor growth.	Remove and destroy infected plants. Control the insect vector (aphids), if present, and use a clean grafting knife. Buy only healthy, certified virus-free plants.

Nurseries

The Antique Rose Emporium
Route 5, Box 143
Brenham, TX 77833

The Roseraie at Bayfields
P.O. Box R
Waldoboro, ME 04572

Blossoms & Bloomers
East 11415 Krueger Lane
Spokane, WA 99207

Bridges Roses
2734 Toney Road
Lawndale, NC 28090

Butner's Old Mill Nursery
806 South Belt Highway
St. Joseph, MO 64507

Carlton Rose Nurseries, Inc.
P.O. Box 366
Carlton, OR 97111

Carroll Gardens
444 East Main Street
P.O. Box 310
Westminster, MD 21157

Country Bloomers Nursery
Route 2, Box 33-B
Udall, KS 67146

Donovan's Roses
P.O. Box 37800
Shreveport, LA 71133-7800

Edmunds' Roses
6235 S.W. Kahle Road
Wilsonville, OR 97070

Henry Field's Seed & Nursery Co.
415 North Burnett
Shenandoah, IA 51602

Flowers 'n Friends Miniature Roses
9590 100th Street S.E.
Alto, MI 49302

Forestfarm
990 Tetherow Road
Williams, OR 97544-9599

Forevergreen Farm
70 New Gloucester Road
North Yarmouth, ME 04097

Garden Valley Nursery
P.O. Box 750953
Petaluma, CA 94975

Giles Ramblin' Roses
2966 State Road 710
Okeechobee, FL 34974

Gloria Dei Nursery
36 East Road
High Falls Park
High Falls, NY 12440

Greenmantle Nursery
3010 Ettersburg Road
Garberville, CA 95542

Gurney's Seed & Nursery Co.
110 Capital Street
Yankton, SD 57079

Heirloom Old Garden Roses
24062 N.E. Riverside Drive
St. Paul, OR 97137

Heritage Rosarium
211 Haviland Mill Road
Brookeville, MD 20833

Heritage Rose Gardens
Tanglewood Farms
16831 Mitchell Creek Drive
Fort Bragg, CA 95437

Historical Roses
1657 West Jackson Street
Painesville, OH 44077

Howerton Rose Nursery
1656 Weaversville Road
Allen Township
Northampton, PA 18067

Ingraham's Cottage Garden
370 C Street
Box 126
Scotts Mills, OR 97375

Inter-State Nurseries
P.O. Box 10
Louisiana, MO 63353

Jackson & Perkins Co.
One Rose Lane
Medford, OR 97501-0702

J. W. Jung Seed Co.
335 South High Street
Randolph, WI 53957-0001

Justice Miniature Roses
5947 S.W. Kahle Road
Wilsonville, OR 97070

Kimbrew-Walter Roses
Route 2, Box 172
Grand Saline, TX 75140

Lowe's Own Root Roses
6 Sheffield Road
Nashua, NH 03062

Magic Moment Miniatures
P.O. Box 499
Rockville Centre, NY 11571

Mendocino Heirloom Roses
P.O. Box 670
Mendocino, CA 95460

Michigan Miniature Roses
45951 Hull Road
Belleville, MI 48111

Milaeger's Gardens
4838 Douglas Avenue
Racine, WI 53402-2498

The Mini-Rose Garden
P.O. Box 203
Cross Hill, SC 29332

Mini Roses of Texas
P.O. Box 267
Denton, TX 76202

Nor'East Miniature Roses, Inc.
P.O. Box 307
Rowley, MA 01969

Oregon Miniature Roses, Inc.
8285 S.W. 185th Avenue
Beaverton, OR 97007-5742

Richard Owen Nursery
2300 East Lincoln Street
Bloomington, IL 61701

Pixie Treasures
4121 Prospect Avenue
Yorba Linda, CA 92686

The Rose Ranch
P.O. Box 10087
Salinas, CA 93912

Rosehaven Nursery
8617 Tobacco Lane S.E.
Olympia, WA 98503

Rosehill Farm
Gregg Neck Road
Galena, MD 21635

Roses & Wine
6260 Fernwood Drive
Shingle Springs, CA 95682

Roses of Yesterday & Today
802 Brown's Valley Road
Watsonville, CA 95076

Roses Unlimited
Route 1, Box 587
Laurens, SC 29360

Sequoia Nursery (Moore Miniature Roses)
2519 East Noble Avenue
Visalia, CA 93277

Stanek's Garden Center
East 2929 27th Avenue
Spokane, WA 99223

Stark Bro's
Box 10
Louisiana, MO 63353-0010

Tate Nursery
10306 Fm Rd 2767
Tyler, TX 75708-9239

Taylor's Roses
P.O. Box 11272
Chickasaw, AL 36671-0272

Thomasville Nurseries, Inc.
1842 Smith Avenue
P.O. Box 7
Thomasville, GA 31799

Tiny Petals Nursery
489 Minot Avenue
Chula Vista, CA 91910

Trophy Roses
1308 N. Kennicott
Arlington Heights, IL 60004

Vintage Gardens
3003 Pleasant Hill Road
Sebastopol, CA 95472

Wayside Gardens
1 Garden Lane
Hodges, SC 29695-0001

White Flower Farm
Litchfield, CT 06759-0050

A World of Roses
P.O. Box 90332
Gainesville, FL 32607

York Hill Farm
271 N. Haverhill Road
Kensington, NH 03833

Resources

The American Rose Society
P.O. Box 30,000
Shreveport, LA 71130
An organization for amateur rose enthusiasts; there is an emphasis on rose exhibiting. Members receive *The American Rose* magazine, issued 11 times a year, and a colorful magazine-format *Annual.* The ARS can refer you to a consulting rosarian with cultural advice for your locality, and to the nearest local rose society.

The Heritage Rose Group
An informal organization devoted to the preservation and study of old garden roses. Publishes *The Rose Letter,* an acclaimed and very readable quarterly journal. For information, send a stamped, self-addressed envelope to the regional coordinator nearest you.
NORTHEAST: Lily Shohan, RD 1, Box 299, Clinton Corners, NY 12514
NORTH CENTRAL: Henry Najat, M.D., W. 6365 Wald Road, Monroe, WI 53566
NORTHWEST: Judi Dexter, 23665 41st Avenue S., Kent, WA 98032
SOUTHWEST (Last names A–G): Betty L. Cooper, 925 King Drive, El Cerrito, CA 94530
SOUTHWEST (Last names H–O): Marlea Graham, 100 Bear Oaks Drive, Martinez, CA 94553
SOUTHWEST (Last names P–Z): Frances Grate, 472 Gibson Avenue, Pacific Grove, CA 93950
SOUTH CENTRAL: Conrad Tips, 1007 Highland Avenue, Houston, TX 77009
SOUTHEAST: Jan Wilson, 1700 South Lafayette Street, Shelby, NC 28152

The Heritage Rose Foundation
1512 Gorman Street
Raleigh, NC 27606
Promotes the study of old garden roses; publishes a quarterly newsletter.

Rose Hybridizers Association
3245 Wheaton Road
Horseheads, NY 14845
For people interested in creating their own cultivars.

Autumn Checklist of Horizon Roses
Box 8237
College Heights
Bowling Green, KY 42101
Published each September; provides evaluations of the newest
rose varieties and will be of special interest to rose exhibitors.

Bev Dobson's Rose Letter
215 Harriman Road
Irvington, NY 10533
An independent voice in the rose world, containing information
not found elsewhere.

Combined Rose List
P.O. Box 677
Mantua, OH 44255
A 175-plus-page booklet containing up-to-date mail-order
nursery sources for over 8000 roses, including all of the roses
described in this book. Published annually; edited by Beverly R.
Dobson and Peter Schneider.

Glossary

Anchor root: A large root serving mainly to hold a plant in place in the soil.

Anther: The terminal part of a stamen, containing one or more pollen sacs.

Basal cane: One of the main canes of a rose bush, originating from the bud union.

Bud eye: A dormant bud in the axil of a leaf, used for propagation in bud-grafting. Also called an eye.

Bud union: The junction, usually swollen, between the understock and the top variety grafted to it, at or near soil level.

Budded: Propagated from a bud eye.

Button center: A round center in a rose blossom, formed by unexpanded petaloids in the very double roses.

Calyx: Collectively, the sepals of a flower.

Calyx tube: A tube formed partly by the united bases of the sepals and partly by the receptacle.

Confused center: A flower center whose petals are disorganized, not forming a pattern.

Corolla: Collectively, the petals of a flower.

Crown: The region of the bud union, the point near soil level where the top variety and the understock are joined.

Cultivar: An unvarying plant variety, maintained by vegetative propagation or by inbred seed.

Cupped form: In a rose bloom, having an open center, with the stamens visible.

Deadheading: Removing old flowers during the growing season to encourage the development of new flowers.

Disbudded: Having the side buds removed to encourage the growth of the flower at the tip of the stem.

Double: Having 24 to 50 petals.

Eye: *See* Bud eye.

Feeder root: One of the numerous small roots of a plant, through which moisture and nutrients are absorbed from the soil.

Filament: The threadlike lower portion of a stamen, bearing the anther.

Floriferous: Blooming profusely.

Guard petals: The outer petals of a rose, especially when these are larger than the inner petals and enclose them.

High-centered: Having the central petals longest; the classic hybrid tea rose form.

Hip: The closed and ripened receptacle of a rose, containing the seeds, and often brightly colored.

Lateral cane: A branch of a basal cane.

Leaf axil: The angle between a petiole and the stem to which it is attached.

Leaflet: One of the leaflike parts of a compound leaf.

Main shoot: A basal cane or a strong lateral cane.

Muddled center: A flower center whose petals are disorganized, not forming a pattern. A term applied to old garden roses.

Ovary: The swollen base of a pistil, in which one or more seeds develop.

Peduncle: The stalk of an individual flower.

Petal: One of a series of flower parts lying within the sepals and outside the stamens and pistils; in roses, the petals are large and brightly colored. Collectively termed the corolla.

Petaloids: Small, very short petals located near the center of a flower.

Petiole: The stalk of a leaf.

Pistil: The female reproductive organ of a flower, consisting of an ovary, a style, and a stigma.

Quartered: Having the petals arranged in three, four, or five radial segments.

Receptacle: The terminal part of a peduncle, bearing the flower parts, and in roses enfolding the developing ovaries to form a hip.

Retentive sepals: Sepals that remain attached to the apex of the receptacle after it has ripened into a hip.

Rhachis: The central axis of a compound leaf, to which the leaflets are attached.

Root stock: *See* Understock.

Rugose: Having the leaf veins deeply etched into the upper surface of the leaf.

Semidouble: Having 12 to 24 petals.

Single: Of flowers, having 5 to 12 petals. Of varieties, having only one bloom per stem.

Sport: An abrupt, naturally occurring genetic change resulting in a branch that differs in appearance from the rest of the plant, or, a plant derived by propagation from such a genetically changed branch. Also called a mutation.

Stamen: The male reproductive organ of a flower, consisting of a filament and a pollen-bearing anther.

Stem: A branch of a cane, emerging from a bud eye and bearing leaves and at least one flower.

Stigma: The terminal portion of a pistil, consisting of a sticky surface to which pollen grains adhere during pollination.

Stipule: A small, leaflike appendage at the base of the petiole of a leaf.

Style: The columnar portion of a pistil, extending between the ovary and the stigma.

Sucker: A young cane emerging below the bud union and therefore representing the variety of the understock rather than the top variety.

Top variety: The variety bud-grafted to the understock, and thus the variety that will be represented by the flowers.

Understock: The plant providing the root system to which the top variety is attached in bud-grafting. Also called a root stock.

Very double: Having more than 50 petals.

Photo Credits

All America Rose Selections: 89A, 97A, 111A, 181A, 184B, 199B, 240A.

Rich Baer: 71B, 104B, 105B, 115B, 119B.

Gillian Beckett: 60A, 70A, 91A, 100B, 101B, 128B, 130A, 130B, 131A, 131B, 133A, 135B, 137B, 138B, 140B, 141B, 145B, 146A, 155B, 158A, 162B, 164A, 170B, 173B.

Kitty Belendez: 239B.

Charles Beutel: 76B, 113B, 115A, 117A, 118A, 121B, 122A, 124B, 178B, 187B, 232A, 238A.

Bullaty/Lomeo: 50B, 52B, 95A, 98A, 102B, 126–27, 158A, 223A, 223B.

Al Bussewitz, PHOTO/NATS: 55B.

Tom Carruth: 122B, 123A

Stuart C. Dobson: 49B, 50A, 52A, 62B, 68B, 83A, 136B, 140A, 142A, 147B, 150A, 151A, 154A, 156B, 159A, 160A, 161A, 161B, 167B, 171A, 172B, 174A, 174B, 175A, 175B.

John E. Elsley: 76A, 110B, 112B, 113A.

Derek Fell: 70B, 90A, 155A, 163B, 189A, 214B, 239A.

Judy Goldman: 205A.

P. A. Haring: 51A, 60B, 61A, 62A, 63B, 65B, 66B, 72B, 73B, 77B, 81A, 86B, 91B, 95B, 97B, 99A, 99B, 101A, 103A, 107A, 107B, 108A, 109A, 109B, 110A, 112A, 114A, 114B, 116A, 116B, 117B, 118B, 120A, 120B, 121A, 123B, 124A, 125A, 129B, 132B, 133B, 138A, 141A, 143A, 144B, 146B, 147A, 148A, 148B, 157A, 157B, 163A, 164B, 165A, 165B, 166A, 166B, 168B, 172A, 173A, 178A, 179A, 180B, 181B, 184A, 186B, 202A, 202B, 212B, 217B, 220B, 224B, 226B, 227A, 229A, 229B, 230B, 231B, 233A, 233B, 236B, 241B, 245B, 246B, 247A, 248A, 249A, 250A, 251B, 255A, 256A, 256B, 257A, 257B.

Pamela J. Harper: 44-45, 46A, 46B, 47A, 47B, 48A, 48B, 49A, 53A, 53B, 54A, 54B, 55A, 56A, 56B, 57A, 57B, 58-59, 61B, 63A, 64A, 65A, 66A, 67A, 67B, 68A, 71A, 74A, 74B, 75B, 78–79, 80A, 80B, 81B, 82A, 82B, 83B, 84A, 84B, 85A, 85B, 86A, 87A, 87B, 88B, 89B, 90B, 92A, 92B, 93A, 93B, 94A, 94B, 96A, 96B,

98B, 100A, 102A, 103B, 129A, 132A, 134B, 135A, 136A, 139A, 139B, 142B, 143B, 144A, 145A, 149A, 149B, 150B, 151B, 153A, 154B, 156A, 158B, 159B, 160B, 169A, 170A, 171B, 182B, 183A, 183B, 185A, 185B, 188A, 191A, 194A, 195A, 196A, 196B, 198A, 200-201, 204B, 206B, 207B, 210A, 211A, 213A, 219A, 224A, 225A, 226A, 228B, 230A, 234B, 242–43, 245A, 246A, 252A, 254A, 255B.

Walter H. Hodge: 176-77, 191B, 192A, 192B, 193A, 194B, 195B, 208–9, 212A, 216B, 218B.

Jackson Perkins: 88A.

Paul E. Jerabek: 77A, 104A, 105A, 106A, 106B, 108B, 111B, 199A, 125B, 187A, 190A, 190B, 193B, 197A, 197B, 198B, 199A, 203A, 203B, 215A, 217A, 221A, 221B 222A, 222B, 232B, 236A, 237A, 238B, 240B, 241A, 244A, 247B, 248B, 250B, 251A, 253A.

John A. Lynch: 75A.

Al Medino: 180A, 220A, 234A.

Ann Reilly: 51B, 72A, 167A, 254A.

Joy Spurr: 64B, 69A, 69B, 134A, 162A, 169B, 179B, 182A, 186A, 188B, 189B, 204A, 206A, 207A, 210B, 211B, 214A, 216A, 219B, 225B, 227B, 228A, 231A, 244B, 249B, 252B, 253B.

Doug Wechsler: 73A, 205B, 213B, 215B, 218A, 235A, 235B, 237B.

Peggy Wingood/Bermuda Rose Society: 128A, 137A, 152B, 153B, 168A.

Index

Titles available in the Taylor's Guide series:

At your bookstore or by calling 1-800-225-3362

Prices subject to change without notice